Regulating Transnational Heritage

There is a vast body of international and national law that regulates cultural heritage. However, the current regulation remains quite blind to the so-called "transnational heritage". This is heritage where there is no community recognised in law that it can be directly attributed to and that can be responsible for its safekeeping and preservation. It can also be items of heritage where the claim of ownership is disputed between two or more peoples or communities. Transnational heritage challenges the idea of monolithic, mono-cultural, ethno-national states. There are a number of examples of such cultural heritage, for instance the Buddhist Bamiyan statutes in Afghanistan, Palmyra in Syria, the Jewish heritage of Iraq, or various items that are currently housed in large, often Western, museums, as a result of colonial practices. This book explores the regulation of transnational heritage. By discussing many cases of transnational heritage and the problems that arise owing to the lack of regulation, the book analyses the manifestations of memories and constructions of communities through heritage. It focuses particularly on the concept of community. How are communities constructed in cultural heritage law and what falls outside the definitions of community? The book underlines that the issues surrounding transnational heritage involve more than a communal right to culture. It is argued that transnational heritage also directly affects wider matters of law such as citizenship, human rights, sovereignty, as well as the movement of people and cultural goods.

Merima Bruncevic is senior lecturer and director of Center for Intellectual Property at the Department of Law, School of Business, Economics and Law, University of Gothenburg.

Routledge Studies in Cultural Heritage and International Law

Regulating Transnational Cultural Heritage
Diversity, Memory and Identity
Merima Bruncevic

Regulating Transnational Heritage

Memory, Identity and Diversity

Merima Bruncevic

Routledge
Taylor & Francis Group
LONDON AND NEW YORK

First published 2022
by Routledge
2 Park Square, Milton Park, Abingdon, Oxon OX14 4RN

and by Routledge
605 Third Avenue, New York, NY 10158

Routledge is an imprint of the Taylor & Francis Group, an informa business

Library of Congress Cataloging-in-Publication Data
A catalog record for this title has been requested

ISBN: 978-1-032-06735-3 (hbk)
ISBN: 978-1-032-08059-8 (pbk)
ISBN: 978-1-003-21268-3 (ebk)

DOI: 10.4324/9781003212683

Typeset in Bembo
by Taylor & Francis Books

To everybody who might be experiencing that their narrative, heritage or history runs the risk of being silenced

Contents

Prologue

As this book is being finalised, events that go to the very heart of the research project that initiated it are still unfolding. What you will read here are sometimes comments on ongoing situations, and sometimes stories concerning matters of cultural heritage that go back thousands of years. I have, more often than not, chosen to include the developing global events and integrate them in my larger and wider analyses and discussions throughout the book, even though they were more difficult to capture, as they were, as they still *are*, taking place before my eyes. What we as a world witnessed while this book was being written, it seemed to me, is the culmination of activities, emotions and efforts that have bubbled under the surface for a long time. As such, the ongoing current events have, in many ways, historical ties which are as deeply rooted as the examples and cases that deal more directly with ancient matters of cultural heritage. All of a sudden, an unprecedented momentum opened up new ways of discussing heritage when several redefining moments that were happening in the art world converged with wider global political movements taking place simultaneously: the anti-racist movements, the feminist movements, the environmental movements, the decolonise movements. All of these were naturally further fuelled by the state of exception in which the world found itself during the lock-downs brought on by the Covid-19 pandemic. This unprecedented moment in history has allowed me to interrogate my material for the book in an unexpected way and comment on what was happening globally in a much more immediate manner. It also made my study more concrete, and in many ways even more urgent. The events of 2019 and 2020 thus became inscribed here in this book, which deals with the regulation of transnational heritage – because, as it became quite evident, they truly come together in manners that, prior to this point in history, were not equally apparent.

And here we are, still in some sort of state of exception, locked in, distanced, yet the matters of transnational heritage remain more vital than ever.

At home.

Merima Bruncevic

New Year's Eve, 2020.

Acknowledgements

The research for this book was enabled thanks to the very generous grant that I received from the Swedish Research Council (*Vetenskapsrådet*) for the project, initially entitled *Heritage without Borders: The legal administration and ownership of transnational and borderless cultural heritage (No. 2016–01768)*. The grant facilitated the writing of this book including the research stints at Università Degli Studi, Roma Tre in Rome as well as at UNESCO in Paris, between 2016 and 2018.

My access to UNESCO and the navigation through its regulatory system and other institutional and spatial structures and labyrinths, not to mention learning how to get around the building itself, were made much easier by the kind assistance that I received from the Swedish UNESCO Delegation and the then Swedish ambassador to UNESCO, Annika Markovic.

The commissioning editor Siobhan Poole at Routledge and the series editor Professor Valentina Vadi saw the importance of including in the series *Cultural Heritage and International Law* a book that deals with the complicated, emotionally laden and politically charged matter of transnational heritage. For this, I am of course extremely grateful. The entire Routledge team involved in the production of the book are also owed a huge thank you.

The work on my cases was made much easier by so many people that generously granted me access to various archives and works-in-progress, particularly Nora Al-Badri and Jan Nicholai Nelles, as well as The Architectural Center, Architektūros Centras, in Vilnius.

The members of the Tangible/Intangible reading group, convened by Danilo Mandic at the University of Westminster and Henrique Carvalho at Birkbeck College in London, provided the academic comradeship as well as the intellectual environment where parts of this book could be tested. It is a group that fosters and encourages critical thinking in the broad field of Law and Aesthetics, and I have been inspired by their creativity and wit. The same is true of my colleagues at the Center for Intellectual Property at the Department of Law at Gothenburg University, where the team has continuously supported, challenged and encouraged my work.

Thank you to students, friends, family, loved ones, of course, as always, for being patient with me and for listening to me the many times I was frustrated, lost, when I could not find solutions to some of the problems I encountered along the way, or when I was quite simply overwhelmed by the sheer gravity of the subject matter at hand. Rest assured, you were never taken for granted.

This research started with a question concerning how to prevent the loss, neglect and peril of transnational cultural heritage. It ended up being a book written during a global pandemic, now dedicated to anybody *who might be experiencing that their narrative, heritage or history runs the risk of being silenced.* I know that we are living in unpreceded times of exception, but in coming together to prevent cultural losses, the exclusion of voices, and in the persistent work towards building ever more diverse and inclusive societies, friends, regardless of the global or political circumstances, we are a legion.

1 Introduction

Memories in transit

Memories make us who we are. Our identity, belonging and sense of self are derived from our past, from the remembrance of how the people we once were became the people who we are today. The past is at once behind us, something that we inherit, a *fait accompli*, but at the same time it is also omnipresent, parallel, continuously constructed and reconstructed, told and retold. The past tends to manifest itself in objects, places, sites and rituals that have followed us through history. It is our heritage. Heritage records and documents the legacy of the people that came before us, but it also legitimises our existence here and now as it ties us to our families, communities, cities and nations. Ultimately heritage provides a historical explanation and justification, a genealogy, of how the societies we inherited were created through a cross-generational dialogue, of how the people we were then became the people who we are today.

But these stories are often also state sponsored, constructed, invoking a nostalgic history that perhaps never was. These are the so-called *authorised heritage discourses*,[1] hidden in the grand narratives of heritage, where the historical power relations play out. The stronger groups of people tend to write history while the less privileged ones and their memories tend to be forgotten or neglected, remain invisible to history, and to law.

Remembrance and memory is materialised in heritage, emanating from a multitude of voices. Because of historical power asymmetries, some voices have been silenced, systematically toned down or left unheard. Theirs are the stories that contest or nuance the official grand narratives and authorised heritage discourses. They tend to resist the unquestioned originary myths of how events are generally, or officially, remembered and recounted. Most of these stories remain untold, and because of that many communities and their heritage are yet to be acknowledged and defined. Can such heritage be acknowledged through law? And would further regulation ensure that it can be protected from destruction, neglect and peril?

1 Smith, 2006.

DOI: 10.4324/9781003212683-1

This book explores the regulation of *transnational heritage*. "Transnational heritage" is a subcategory of cultural heritage. Most commonly, the term refers to heritage that physically exists over several national borders, or to heritage that is for some reason moved from one place to another. The term can also refer to cultural expressions created by people in exile and diaspora, or to heritage that emanates from migrant communities. Therefore, the concept of transnational heritage will have to be developed here to show how it gains meaning through its various uses and applications. It can have different meanings in different contexts, and we will explore that here, what that means, how it can be regulated and why it is problematic. I will discuss how to legally conceptualise the regulation of such multicultural and diverse heritage.

I employ the term "transnational heritage" in its widest sense in this book as I study monuments, sites, buildings, practices, expressions, knowledges, yes quite simply heritage, that is diverse, multicultural, multi-national and heterogeneous in nature. Such heritage does not fit neatly in any category of cultural heritage law. It tends to sit in between communities, or, conversely, belong to communities that are not recognised in regulation. It will be argued that some transnational heritage is systematically silenced, neglected, and its communities potentially dispossessed by not being seen, acknowledged or protected in law and through regulation. If heritage is memory, and if transnational heritage is the unacknowledged memory of multicultural and diverse communities, and if it is not adequately recognised and protected in law, it may fall into oblivion or, worse yet, be completely destroyed.

It is startling how easy it is for heritage to be sidelined or neglected, even forgotten and destroyed. Transnational heritage is exposed to an intensified risk as it is not recognised in law. That it is systematically exposed to genuine risks is something we will see throughout this book. This means that some items of cultural heritage that can serve as historical proofs of peoples and cultures, that directly legitimise the existence of communities and their heritage, seem to be at risk of neglect and peril.

People care profoundly about cultural heritage. It is a marker of a deep-seated sense of belonging, an integral part of history, traditions, common practices, what people identify as their own. It also identifies individuals that together form a "we": a community. Heritage is family, home, safety. It is *homeland*, and how it is defined is unquestionably a political, as well as an emotional, matter, as it ultimately justifies self-determination.[2] The strong bond between community, self-determination and cultural heritage is undeniable.

All cultural heritage comprises of sedimentations of time. People come and go. Borders are drawn and redrawn. Political alliances shift. The questions that remain and that have to be asked over and over again are: What has happened, on a territory, in a given period of time, where the heritage originates from/ where it was made/where it was found? Who was the dominant power? Who is the dominant power today? And even more importantly: Which are the

2 See e.g. Crawford, 2001.

silenced voices? Who are the systematically oppressed people whose stories remain untold, their heritage unacknowledged?

Transnational cultural heritage is prone to greater risk given that it remains largely unregulated. This book sets to explore whether the safekeeping of such heritage could be ensured through developing further regulation and legal strategies that ensure its protection. The purpose of the book is somewhat twofold. First, to *demonstrate* that current cultural heritage law often leaves out transnational heritage, and therefore it and its communities remain unrecognised and unprotected. And two, to *develop* conceptual arguments towards a regulatory framework that can handle the safekeeping of such multicultural, diverse, heterogeneous, polyphonic, heritage. This heritage defies the notions of mono-cultural, ethno-national societies. It often goes against the state and the national authorised heritage discourses. This is the reason why transnational heritage is of the utmost importance to study further, particularly as we are committing to fostering more inclusive and diverse societies. Recognising transnational heritage in regulation could potentially mean recognising and strengthening multicultural, diverse and heterogeneous communities. As such, transnational heritage directly affects more than a communal right to shared cultural heritage, it also bears on the matters that concern inclusion and exclusion, and in extension also citizenship, human rights, sovereignty, as well as fundamental rights such as the right to live, speak, believe, *exist*.

How the notion of diverse, multicultural communities and the heritage that emanates from such communities can be reconciled with the overwhelmingly nationalist, mono-ethnic cultural heritage law and its doctrines frames the discussion here. It has to do with how to legally deal with shared memories that stem from heterogeneous co-existences. I do not intend to focus on contested heritage, even though many of the examples of heritage that I will analyse throughout this book have been fiercely contested. Instead, I want to focus on the shared experiences that give rise to multicultural and diverse practices, collective as well as disputed memories that in the end become transnational heritage. How groups of people are envisioned as a community and how their communal identity is constructed in and through cultural heritage law will also become one of the interests of this book.

Ultimately, safeguarding the manifestations of shared memories as materialised in heritage is what this book will address. It has to do with more than advocating for a widened right to culture. It also has to do with more than protecting the symbolic nature that shrouds heritage. Laurajane Smith[3] stresses for instance the importance of the immateriality of heritage – for were it not for the immaterial symbolic notions and social practices that are embedded in heritage, she claims, it would just be a question of artefacts like any other everyday artefact, and not heritage.[4] According to Smith, it is the symbolic that makes the everyday objects into heritage. On the contrary, I am interested here

3 Smith, 2006:44.
4 See also Macmillan, 2021.

in the very everydayness of objects, the materiality and tangibility of heritage, how it is exhibited, used, framed, and how it acts as a constituent of community. Perhaps "contrary" is not right. I do of course accept and agree with Smith's argument, but I want to inflate it to its full potential and then continue to build on it and explore the various materialisations of transnational heritage. Transnational heritage becomes in that vein the embodiment of shared memories that belong to diverse communities. So it is an oscillation between the tangible and material on the one hand and the intangible and symbolic on the other that I explore here, and argue that the two must be seen as inseparable. The transnational memory, and the materiality of such memory that is explored here, is therefore not merely an individual memory. It is foremost the expression of shared communal remembrances that are allowed to shine through the materiality of heritage.

By engaging in a critique of how heritage is portrayed and envisioned in law, the many taken-for-granted assumptions that are reproduced in and through authorised heritage discourses will often become the focus of my discussion. Thus, the doctrinal legal definitions of "heritage" and "community" will be studied, questioned, as well as deconstructed. I will also search for the unexplored potential in current law. We will see how the existing regulation can be problematic, stifling, *suffocating*, as it is based on homogenic, mono-ethnic societies. But we will also see how it can be flexible and the many possible routes that have already been opened for envisioning the regulation of more inclusive heritage. More often than not, current legal tools fail to take into account the multicultural, the diverse and/or the multi-ethnic in heritage, but there are nonetheless regulatory possibilities that emerge here and there. The cultural heritage that can somehow be described as "transnational" thus becomes the empirical point, as the term itself challenges most of the doctrinal concepts of heritage that almost always require heritage to structurally be somehow attributed to, or at least acknowledged by, a clearly defined, monolithic, mono-cultural, ethno-national, state.

Transnational heritage is not sufficiently regulated and, even though it is in danger, it still exists and in one way or another is often legally tied to at least one nation state, if not several. It will be argued here that this reliance on the attribution to states can be problematic. The nation state-based approach has so far been legitimised by the post-WWII logic that recognised the newly independent or decolonised states that were formed after the war. Heritage thus became connected to a sovereign territory, self-determination, national jurisdictions and to independent peoples.[5] Within this tradition, heritage remains tied to nation states legally, but also politically and morally. This is an argument that is favoured and advanced in many authorised heritage discourses. Legal, political and moral ownership of heritage is, and must be, tied to a state territory or at least to a group of people that a state recognises as a community.

5 This logic can be traced even further back, and it can be argued that it was established as early as in 1815 at the so-called Congress of Vienna. However, I place it after WWII, in order to directly tie it to the decolonisation that took place after the war.

Such territorial assumption functions as a doctrinal starting point. It advances an argument that where something is, or was once created or found – it must *ipso facto* belong to that territory. In extension, that means that it is strongly argued in legislation that heritage must always be kept *in situ*, that is, on site, where it is found, and that any dislocation, decontextualisation or transfer must be avoided. This is important in many ways, particularly when it comes to decolonisation and the return and repatriation[6] of looted heritage taken by former colonisers. Repatriation, derived of course from the Latin word *patria*, homeland, means to return an item to its homeland. As such, it is indirectly assumed that the *patria* of all heritage must be connected to a state's soil. However, such arguments can be difficult to uphold for transnational heritage as we will see here. Where something is today, or where something was once found, must not be taken as an undisputed indication as to where that something should be kept, or to whom it morally and legally belongs. This argument is relevant to stay with when it comes to transnational heritage. The obvious example of transnational heritage that runs the risk of destruction if it is kept *in situ* is the heritage that belongs to oppressed people, or people who are expelled, in diaspora, or who for other reasons are dispossessed or forced to flee to another territory in order to seek refuge. The question is whether the understanding of *patria* can be given more than a territorial meaning in law. These are the matters of transnational heritage, and we will here discuss ways to frame the regulation of such heritage that enable it to be legitimised and recognised, without necessarily requiring it to be tied to one particular territory.

Transnational cultural heritage: some possible approaches

There are several, in many ways disparate, meanings of "transnational" and "transnational heritage" as employed in legal and cultural heritage scholarship. I have taken a keen interest in these variations, to understand why they differ, and what implications such differences may have for regulation. The initial insight is that the term "transnational heritage" oscillates, that its meaning tends to change over time or depending on its context. This provides us with a first clue as to why, perhaps, this is such a problematic area to regulate.

6 A lot can be said about the different meanings, yet similar-sounding words return, repatriation and restitution. Within the context here, restitution will be used to refer to the process by which cultural heritage items are returned to an individual or a community, e.g. the restitution of Nazi looted art. I will not discuss restitution in detail in this book. However, I will focus on the issues that have to do with repatriation and return. Repatriation and return are here used more or less synonymously, even though they can have different technical meanings legally. When used here, they refer to the processes by which cultural heritage items are returned to a nation or state at the request made by a government. See e.g. Herscher, 1998; Palmer, 1998; Greenfield, 2007; Stamatoudi, 2011. Please also note that UNESCO has set up an Intergovernmental Committee for Promoting the Return of Cultural Property to its Countries of Origin.

It is necessary to account for this and to begin with the variations in meaning. The definitions I am about to list here do not of course constitute in any way an exhaustive list of ways in which the term can be understood and defined. Rather, I would like to propose that the various meanings exist simultaneously side by side, and that they can serve as general representatives of a much broader umbrella category, of how the concept of transnational heritage can normally be captured and how it tends to be understood. The variations range from the many legal approaches that can be found mainly in cultural heritage law, to a range of other approaches that exist outside of legal scholarship.

The term "transnational heritage" in cultural heritage law is most commonly employed to denote heritage that exists across national borders, e.g. the Silk Road. The term "transnational" connected to culture can also be found in "transnational law". In that context it can refer to cultural items that cross national borders for some reason, such as matters that concern international trade in art, antiquities and cultural artefacts. The term is also used within the context of "transitional justice"[7] in the aftermath of armed conflicts and wars, often when abuses of human rights might have occurred, e.g. armed destruction of cultural property. Finally, there are the broader uses of the term "transnational" or "transnational heritage" that are much more explicitly sociological, ethnographic or anthropological in nature. I will try to present some of these variations briefly below and then develop the regulatory frameworks in the forthcoming chapters.

International public law and UNESCO

One of the most common uses of the term "transnational heritage" in law can be found in international public law, often within the context of the UNESCO legal regime. It is here we find the most common approach, where the term is used to denote heritage that sits across national borders geographically. That is, within this context the term refers to large heritage sites that quite physically cross state territories. Examples of transnational heritage in this sense are the natural, cultural or mixed sites, e.g. the Qhapaq Ñan Main Andean Road (also known as the Inca Trail). It can also refer to a collection of heritage sites that exist in several countries, e.g., the collective architectural work of Le Corbusier that comprises 17 sites of serial individual properties spread across different countries and continents, meaning that it is also transcontinental, like the Silk Road.

Within the UNESCO regulatory framework there are also a number of internal variations of the term. Sometimes the terms "transborder" or "transboundary" are employed synonymously, such as "Transborder Rainforest Heritage of Borneo, Indonesia and Malaysia", or when referring to transboundary cooperation between the UNESCO member states, for example. The vast majority of legal and heritage scholarship still employs the term "transnational heritage" in this geographical, physical, sense.

7 Lixinski, 2015, 2019 and 2021.

However, within the context of the UNESCO regulatory framework the term can have a wider meaning too. It is also applied to refer to transnational intangible heritage. Intangible heritage is not physically constrained to a territory and can move more freely across borders, such as coffee culture.[8] With time, the geographical and physical meaning of "transnational heritage" in international public law has grown to include shared intangible heritage that exists in many different territories.

Additionally, transnational heritage in international public law might also refer to heritage that is so outstanding that it is somehow important for "humanity as a whole" without necessarily being attributed to one community. This is not an obvious meaning of the word "transnational", but heritage that stems from nomadic communities for instance, from people in the diaspora, dead civilisations, or quite simply from people that are somehow oppressed in their own countries, can still be identified as transnational. Some of the more famous examples of such heritage are the Buddhist Bamiyan statues in Afghanistan, or the Jewish heritage of Iraq. There are also a number of other, lesser known, in many ways much more complicated, examples. In this book I have chosen to focus on the lesser known heritage, for instance the Brutalist Soviet building in Vilnius, Lithuania that I will discuss in Chapter 4, because these not-so-sensationalist yet complicated cases tend to be easily missed or dismissed as transnational heritage.

The term "transnational heritage" in international public law thus still continues to evolve, becoming broader as a concept over time. It is important to bear in mind that, other than as a territorial description of physical heritage, the term "transnational heritage" now also applies for certain shared intangible heritage, as well as potentially heritage that belongs to oppressed and unacknowledged communities. This last instance is more complicated to show, and I will continue to discuss it in the last two chapters of this book.

Transnational law and UNIDROIT

The second most common context and another significant category where the reference to transnational culture or transnational cultural heritage can be found is "transnational law".[9] For a reader that does not come from a legal background, it can be pointed out that transnational law is not the same as international public law. Whereas international public law can be described as the law of states, or that body of law that regulates the relationship between sovereign nation states, transnational law on the other hand involves *any and all* national, international or mixed relations that take place across national borders. Transnational law thus applies both to states and to persons, corporations, non-governmental organisations, essentially any legal subject that in any capacity performs or acts across state lines. Generally, it can be said that international law deals with public matters,

8 See Chapter 4, section Intangible Heritage.
9 See e.g. Zumbansen, 2012.

while transnational law regulates mostly private ones. Transnational law encompasses for instance international trade law, *lex mercatoria*. If international public law administers the regulatory framework for cultural heritage by the UNESCO legal regime, the private aspects of transnational regulatory systems often fall under the auspices of The International Institute for the Unification of Private Law (UNIDROIT) and its regimes. For the regulation of cultural objects, the 1995 UNIDROIT Convention on Stolen or Illegally Exported Cultural Objects (1995 UNIDROIT Convention) is particularly relevant to look at.

Other than the private matters of law, such as trade, import and export, there are also criminal law aspects that are regulated in transnational law. Criminal law in this context has to do with, e.g., stolen and illegally exported art objects. Import, export and (il)legal handling and transfer of cultural artefacts and antiquities are thus some of the other matters that are regulated under transnational legal regimes. The roles, responsibilities and accountabilities of criminal networks, traffickers, as well as curators, *bona fide* purchasers, etc. are frequently discussed within this regulatory context. Issues of restitution and criminal sanctions can be relevant for this category of law too.

I will return to the UNIDROIT framework and how it functions together with the UNESCO regime in more detail in the next chapter, but for now, suffice it to say that transnational aspects of culture that are regulated in and through transnational law have to do with culture that in some way, legally or illegally, simply crosses national borders.[10] Worth noting here is also the use of terminology: within the context of transnational law and the UNIDROIT regulation, the preferred term is "cultural objects" and not "cultural heritage" or "cultural property" as within the UNESCO regime, as we will see in the next section. I will discuss this further in Chapter 2.

Transitional justice and the Hague Convention

A third field of interest where transnational culture is regulated is within the contexts of "transitional justice".[11] Transitional justice deals with the aftermath of wars and regulates war crimes and violations of human rights in transitional periods after times of war. A relevant legal instrument that deals with culture and that is of interest for us here is the 1954 Hague Convention for the Protection of Cultural Property in the Event of Armed Conflict and its two (1954 and 1999) Protocols (The Hague Convention).

This convention regulates the damage and destruction of "cultural property" in, as its name reveals, the event of armed conflict. It makes an explicit distinction between "cultural property" and "cultural heritage". Already in its preamble it is stated that there is a regulatory and a *de facto* difference between the two, cultural property and cultural heritage, and that the Hague

10 See e.g. Prott, 1996. See also Vrdoljak, 2008.
11 Lixinsky, 2015.

Convention regulates the former.[12] The Hague Convention also includes in its scope the properties moved or removed in times of war and during armed conflicts, both as loot or in order to be saved. Looted cultural property forms the backbone of the legal and moral arguments for return and repatriation. The transnational matters of return and repatriation of cultural items displaced after armed conflicts fall under the 1954 Hague Convention, but some cultural items that were once moved in order to be saved can also become tied to more than one territory over time. These are the issues that we will return to many times in this book.

The Hague Convention also covers cultural property that has not been moved *per se*, but where, as a result of wars or armed conflicts, national borders may have been shifted or redrawn. In such cases the cultural property that has technically stayed in one place can still formally change national belonging without having been moved.[13] Therefore it is important to bear in mind that these types of heritage that are static and remain in one place can also theoretically fall under the regulatory spheres of transitional justice, international humanitarian law and the Hague Convention.

Non-legal definitions

Fourthly, there are the broader sociological variations of "transnational" and "transnational heritage". These approaches can be found outside of the regulatory sphere, legal doctrines and legal scholarship. The term in those contexts often refers to migrant cultures, or culture produced by migrants in diaspora, where "transnational heritage" more directly has to do with the conception and constitution of identity and belonging in multicultural communities. For instance, the term "transnational heritage" has been used in order to denote how national identities are formed and influenced by the diasporic communities that start to participate in shaping and transforming the societies in which they have settled.[14] Sherri Grasmuck and Annika Marlen Hinze have an even more narrow approach and define transnational heritage as "'heritage migration', namely, the independent movement of immigrant offsprings as adults to their parents' homeland".[15] The notions of transnational heritage used in this context are tied to Pierre Nora's theory on "realms of memory" or *lieux de mémoire*.[16] Such sociological definitions of transnational heritage are therefore frequently also linked to the broader notion of "transnationalism" as developed and elaborated on by Steven Vertovec.[17] Vertovec describes the concept of transnationalism as:

12 Merryman, 1986.
13 See e.g. Bruncevic, 2011.
14 See e.g. Beschea-Fache, 2012.
15 Grasmuck and Hinze, 2016:1959.
16 Nora, 1992.
17 Vertovec, 2009.

> a condition in which, despite great distances and notwithstanding the presence of international borders (and all the laws, regulations and national narratives they represent), certain kinds of relationships have globally intensified and now take place paradoxically in a planet-spanning yet common – however virtual – arena of activity.[18]

Finally, there are the more theoretical approaches that do not necessarily use the term "transnational heritage" but that are nonetheless closely connected to its understanding. One such theoretical approach comes from memory studies and the scholarship on *entangled memories.*[19] Gerard Delanty, for instance, sets the term "transnational heritage" in motion and gives it a significant meaning in connection with entangled memories. In arguing that, rather than seeing cultural heritage as predominantly expressed and embedded within national contexts, it should instead be seen as transnational and as such always in a way plural, Delanty develops the concept of entangled memory as a driver for acknowledging the multiple and shared memory in and as transnational heritage. Using the common European heritage as an example of the entangled mosaic of histories and memories, he rejects both nationalist and universalistic approaches to heritage. In this sense the entangled memories become both the *raison d'être* for the promotion of transnational heritage as well as a potential way of bridging the tension between the hegemonic views that place nationalistic and universalistic approaches as each other's opposites. It is through the idea of entanglement that the transnational unfolds, according to Delanty. He writes:

> Rather than see cultures as primarily clashing, they should be seen as interacting in multiple ways, leading to complex outcomes that include entanglement and hybridity.[20]

Which leads to an understanding, at least in Delanty's work, of European transnational heritage as one that emanates from an "entangled history" that highlights the overlapping nature of European societies and a conception of Europe as "an inter-civilisational constellation". On this view, the European past can be seen in terms of a rainbow of cultures shaped from cultural encounters and translations that have emerged from the logic of transnationalism.[21]

Delanty is not the only one who has applied the term "entangled memories" in direct connection with transnational heritage. In the volume *Entangled Memories: Remembering the Holocaust in a Global Age*, edited by Julia Lange and Marius Henderson,[22] a strong link between entangled memories and transnational heritage is

18 Vertovec, 2009:3.
19 Delanty, 2017a and Delanty, 2017b.
20 Delanty, 2017a:133.
21 Delanty, 2017a:134.
22 Lange and Henderson, 2017.

also established. The objective of Lange and Henderson's study is described as "transnational entangled memories of the Holocaust in North America, Western and Eastern Europe, and Israel".[23] One of the thematic aspects that is particularly highlighted is the

> interplay between national, local, and global perspectives in the medial construction of the historical event. How have interdependencies between and cultural appropriations of specific national memories contributed toward the emergence of transnational patterns of Holocaust commemoration?[24]

Their approach underlines the importance of understanding entangled memories as potentially having a legal bearing on the conception of heritage and, as such, being extremely relevant when it comes to the regulation of transnational heritage.

Finally, historical scholarship on transnational heritage can also be mentioned. Joan Beaumont, for instance, studies transnational heritage from a historical point of view. She provides a definition of the term that is very flexible in nature and that in many ways comes close to the approach to transnational heritage adopted within the context of this book. She describes transnational cultural heritage as:

> [h]eritage that is shared or contested between two or more nations [and that] sits awkwardly between the pillars of sovereign control of national heritage and world heritage, the latter of which envisages a world polity rather than a bilateral or multilateral relationship.[25]

Like many scholars before me, I will have reason to return to the distinction between these two approaches: the universalist (legitimised as "World Heritage") and statist (legitimised through "national sovereignty"). I particularly appreciate that Beaumont stresses not just the contested but also the shared heritage. Overall, hers is a helpful and straightforward definition that comes close to how the term "transnational cultural heritage" is employed here. I will give it more meaning as I go along.

However, unlike Beaumont I have chosen to use the term "community" here instead of "nation". Community, I believe, as will become apparent quite soon, is a far more interesting and pertinent term able to designate and indicate the diversity of voices, the heterogeneity of groups and the panoply of players that will be revealed through the discussions and cases analysed throughout this book. The focus on diversity is particularly important when it comes to transnational heritage as it inherently challenges the idea of monolithic, mono-

23 Lange and Henderson, 2017.
24 Lange and Henderson, 2017:5.
25 Beaumont, 2009:300.

cultural, ethno-national states. That is also the other reason why community, in my view, is a term far better suited than nation here.

These are some of the approaches to transnational heritage that exist simultaneously that will be studied and analysed in this book. There are more approaches that I will have omitted to mention, of course. But these are in my view the most common ones. I will criticise some of them, look for the hidden potential in many of them, as well as discuss the sustainable and ethical future regulation of transnational heritage.

Community and other relevant matters for the regulation of heritage

Matters concerning moral and legal ownership of heritage are deeply at issue when it comes to regulating transnational heritage. One of the most common questions posed in the field of cultural heritage law is precisely "Who owns the past?"[26] When it comes to transnational heritage, this question morphs into another even more complicated one: "Who owns the past that cannot be attributed to any of the categories of people recognised in law?" These questions can in many ways be non-starters too, or at least unsatisfactory as starting points. First of all, what are unrecognised communities? Second, why refer to it as a past at all? Is it truly a past or is it in fact the core of the present and the foundation for the future that is being regulated? "Who owns the parallel simultaneity of time and memory?" might perhaps not trip off the tongue, but it is exactly what might be at stake. And third, why "owns"? Why place these important matters that concern memories, identity, belonging, the sense of self and home, in a proprietary framework? Must we resort to a commodifying rationality in order to save something from being lost?

To be able to "own" heritage, or at least have heritage attributed to its people, a community must be recognised as falling under one of the three categories of communities that exist in cultural heritage law. These are:

- *the nation state* as a sovereign community and a legal subject;
- *the Indigenous community* as a nation but not a nation state; and
- *the recognised minority* as another type of identifiable minoritarian community that is recognised by the state.

Which brings us to transnational heritage. Transnational heritage does not fit neatly in any of these existing communities that are articulated in one way or another in cultural heritage law. Nowhere in law is a transnational community or its heritage envisioned, directly defined or necessarily even mentioned. What

26 To name but a few that pose the question directly (in chronological order): Kenety, 1990; Selkirk, 1997; Petersen, 2001; Gulliford, 2002; Carpenter and Sandford, 2003; Fitz Gibbon, 2005; Smith, 2006:52; Bandyopadhyay, 2016; Wallinder-Pierini, 2018. Or variations thereof, e.g. Who owns history? by Foner, 2003.

a "transnational" community is or could be, as opposed to the three recognised communities listed above, is a matter for case-by-case negotiation. What we do know is that transnational heritage does not fit in any one of the acknowledged community categories that can be identified in and through current law. The existing community categories find their justification in national sovereignty or in identifiable, and recognised, shared commonalities in terms of, e.g., identity, religion, culture or language. When it comes to the transnational communities and their heritage on the other hand, such constitutive commonality is not necessarily present, at least not in this way. It means that group formations that do not fall within the three recognised community types are either not yet conceived of in regulation, politically difficult to deal with or simply not recognised at all in international cultural heritage law as communities.

To become recognised as a community, and in the end a sovereign nation state, seems to be what all communities, acknowledged or unacknowledged, strive to become eventually. Becoming a state, the legal subject with the highest dignity in international law, the one that has sovereignty, self-determination and agency, is the ultimate goal. A community as state is able to act on behalf of itself, its people and its heritage. When a community is recognised as a state by the international community, it thus also becomes recognised as a sovereign legal subject in international law.

Naturally, becoming a recognised community can be the first step in the process of becoming a state. In order to become a state, i.e. to be recognised as a member of the international community, both an external and an internal communal identity must be ascertained and shown. External identity means being acknowledged by all other states as a state – in practice this means becoming a member of the UN. There are many peoples that are communities but not nation states. These peoples are recognised in law as communities, as, e.g., minorities or Indigenous people, but they are not (yet) nation states. Being recognised as a state by the international community is directly tied to the geopolitical climate in which the global political and military powers play key roles.

To achieve recognition in international law and to show an external identity, a community must also be able to show a discernible internal identity. This means that the community within itself must recognise a togetherness through, e.g., a common identity. In practice that could mean having a definable common language, religion, cohesive traditions, a common history, culture, etc. The internal identity of a community is ultimately the formation around which the external identity of a state can eventually be built. A demonstrable common culture and cultural heritage are vital for the internal identity.

It therefore becomes obvious how significant cultural heritage is. It is experienced at a profound level, as a memory or as a home, but also as a first building block towards self-determination. As such, much more is at stake than protecting beautiful items or nostalgic traditional cultural practices. That this is something that has a much broader impact on human rights and political rights thus emerges as evident. This is why regulation of heritage is difficult. And further still, to make it even more complicated, regulating *transnational* heritage, heritage that does not sit neatly within any recognised community, or any authorised heritage discourse, becomes even more intricate. When it comes to transnational cultural heritage, diversity, heterogeneity and sensitivity become added, and the law has to deal with that too, in an already fraught regulatory context.

Who is seen a member of a group that is not formally recognised in law, and who is not, therefore becomes a matter that is at issue here as it can lead to exclusions, disputes, of constructing and reconstructing narratives, or conversely, of dissenting, refusing and reclaiming the existing narratives, dominant discourses and hegemonic structures. It is undoubtedly a question of power distribution. The problems with transnational heritage culminate when groups of people and their heritage are completely left out as unacknowledged or where people experience themselves, in the best case scenario, as excluded or undefined, and in the worst case as forced out, expelled, dispossessed, extinguished or destroyed, as a group. I study the regulation of *that* heritage in this book. These are the multicultural, multi-ethnic matters where nothing is easily placed within any one of the existing taxonomies in cultural heritage law and its concepts, yet these are the matters that are important because ultimately, if left unacknowledged, unprecedented historical, cultural and human losses might occur. That understanding forms the backbone of this study. If transnational heritage is not acknowledged in law, it will be exposed to the risk of being neglected, destroyed, and it might eventually perish.

The questions of memory, identity, history, ethics, belonging and politics are always present when it comes to cultural heritage. How the people of a community imagine their past through their heritage is directly tied to their sense of self, who they are, who they consider themselves to be. When it comes to transnational heritage all of these questions become intensified, yet they remain completely unregulated and generally unexplored legally.[27] This is not innocuous. The lack of regulation puts many an item of transnational heritage at grave risk, as we will see throughout this book.

The work has taken more than four years to compile. During that time I have been overwhelmed by how much people care about matters of heritage, and surprised by the intense emotions conjured up, mine and other people's, when matters of cultural heritage are brought up and discussed. I hope to be able to respectfully account for all of this in the course of this book. And with that in mind, I now invite you to join me as we explore the regulation of transnational heritage.

27 Willems, 2014.

2 Matter: current regulation and transnational heritage

There is a vast body of international and national law that regulates what we call cultural heritage. Here, my aim is to first introduce and discuss the cultural heritage legal instruments and regulatory frameworks that do exist and how they relate to transnational heritage. I will leave the minutiae and details for other legal and heritage scholars to provide further.[1] The main argument that is advanced in this chapter is broad and in many ways philosophical in nature, namely that even though there may be a large number of laws and instruments regulating the field of cultural heritage, there still seems to be an unsettling silence when it comes to the regulation of transnational cultural heritage. This lack of specific legal attention to transnational matters may put transnational cultural heritage in danger.

In this chapter I will map out the core legal instruments pertaining to cultural heritage.[2] In that sense, for a reader acquainted with cultural heritage law, most of it will indeed be familiar. But I aim to do more than provide a cursory introduction to the legal instruments. The main purpose in this chapter is to point out what is missing from current cultural heritage law in terms of transnational heritage or where there are possibilities that can be developed further. Therefore, I have chosen to focus on, and begin with, the core regulation that is generally applied, and indicate where it is lacking or to show where and how it has potential. This will then be developed further and in more detail throughout the forthcoming chapters.

First, a note on the choice of terminology here. As I have already remarked on in the previous chapter, the cultural expressions that are regulated in cultural heritage law are referred to by many names, as we will see to a greater extent in this chapter. The earlier conventions such as the 1954 Convention for the Protection of Cultural Property in the Event of Armed Conflict (The 1954

1 See e.g. Merryman, 1999; Vrdoljak, 2008; Lixinsky, 2013; Blake, 2015; Lixinsky, 2019.

2 I am very grateful to Professor Fiona Macmillan and her support and inspiration while I was researching the legal instruments and studying cultural heritage law for the purposes of this book. My stint as visiting researcher at Università Degli Studi, Roma Tre in Rome greatly contributed to this chapter, as well as Chapter 3. Many of the analyses that I present here were inspired by my work and conversations with Professor Macmillan conducted during my stay in Rome. See also Macmillan, 2021.

DOI: 10.4324/9781003212683-2

Hague Convention) and the 1970 Convention on the Means of Prohibiting and Preventing the Illicit, Import, Export and Transfer of Ownership of Cultural Property (the 1970 Convention) both utilise the term "cultural property". The more recent UNESCO conventions employ the wider, more encompassing term "cultural heritage".[3] Whether it should be referred to as cultural heritage or as cultural property is something that is discussed in legal scholarship.[4] For instance, Fiona Macmillan writes:

> [N]ow [it] seems clear that understanding what cultural property is, or could be, depends on understanding its relationship to the concept of cultural heritage, which replaced that of cultural property and with which the UNESCO regime now concerns itself.[5]

Macmillan implies that UNESCO has moved away from the term "property" and instead leans toward the broader term "heritage". A number of scholars have also, if not moved away from using the concept of property in these contexts, at least acknowledged and commented on this very difference between heritage and property in law and cultural heritage scholarship.[6] Very broadly, it could be stated that when something is referred to as cultural property it is in a sense tied to the institution of "property" and "ownership rights".[7] Private rights. The property concept is assumed to be narrower than the broader, more flexible term "heritage", which is often defined as a transgenerational or an international public good.[8]

Here, I have chosen to stay with the term "cultural heritage" as far as possible in order to indicate the broadness and inclusivity of my approach.[9] However, and as a side remark that is also something that Macmillan points out, the question whether the concept of property also has or could have wider, more radical, implications is nonetheless interesting in general. Maybe there is a way to employ a critical approach to property in order to empower weaker groups and provide them with a stronger proprietary tool with which to claim rights, sanction misappropriation as well as providing them with a clear instrument that can be used strategically in dispute resolution and mitigation. The term "heritage" seems in no doubt to be elusive and cumbersome in that sense as it is difficult to capture in regulation, and also to

3 Convention Concerning the Protection of the World Cultural and Natural Heritage (1972), Convention for the Safeguarding of the Intangible Cultural Heritage (2003), Convention on the Protection of the Underwater Cultural Heritage (2001).

4 There are only a handful of articles that have treated the subject so far: Blake, 2000; Flessas, 2003; Prott and O'Keefe, 2007; Macmillan, 2013; Macmillan, 2015.

5 Macmillan, 2015.

6 Macmillan, 2015. See also e.g. Blake, 2000 and Prott and O'Keefe, 2007.

7 Some have even suggested that cultural property ought to become a so-called "fourth" estate together with *real property, personal property* and *intellectual property*, see e.g. Crewdson, 1984. Please note that the UNIDROIT 1995 Convention refers to it as "cultural objects".

8 Nafzinger, 2012.

9 Cf. Mastalir, 1992.

enforce. I will return to this question regarding the perils and potentials of the instrument of property, and alternatives to it, towards the end of the book. Still, for now and for the general discussion, I have chosen to stay with the term "cultural heritage" because I think it provides clarity, whereas "property" would have needed to be pried open theoretically in a more systematic manner in order to show its radical potential and indicate how it perhaps could function as a critical and emancipatory tool, something that Macmillan does admirably in her work, but that I will leave without further comment here so as not to create an unnecessary digression.[10]

Whether it should be referred to as "cultural heritage" or just "heritage" is an additional and very much ongoing discussion particularly among critical heritage scholars. I have also chosen to keep the prefix "cultural" as far as possible even though I agree with the critique of its use, namely that we now know that *nature* and *culture* should not be neatly separated, nor can they ever be. I do agree. Yet, most of the examples I provide here are so clearly matters of culture and art, that I think it warrants my choice, if not for the sake of clarity. But I am committed to using the term "culture" responsibly, to not reinforcing the nature–culture dichotomy and to engaging in a profoundly theoretical understanding of cultural heritage.

With that in mind we can continue. Transnational cultural heritage can and does go unregulated even within this vast existing body of regulation. Cultural heritage law quite simply does not have a clear provision in place through which transnational heritage can be satisfactorily defined, safeguarded, preserved, *envisioned*. As will become apparent, most of the existing regulatory instruments occlude in one way or another transnational heritage. That being the case, cultural heritage that is transnational in nature is in many ways denied, put in danger and, in the worst cases, destroyed and lost for ever, and with it memories, and eventually, people to whom it once belonged.

That transnational heritage remains as a comparatively unregulated sphere in cultural heritage law is perhaps not that surprising given the politically perilous and sensitive nature of the matter, and the fact that it is almost impossible to reach a consensus concerning its definition, as we saw above. By mapping out current and existing regulation of heritage in general, I hope to show where current regulation fails in safeguarding transnational heritage, thus leaving it open for further regulation.

The core cultural heritage regulation that does exist, is also difficult to describe fully. There are several reasons for this. The main one that many scholars have pointed out and that I agree with seems to be the issue of the multiple regulatory layers. Cultural heritage is not regulated in any one legal field alone, but rather through a number of different legal orders that operate on various levels, ranging from international,[11] national,[12] regional,[13] as well as penetrating other broader norm systems such as museum regulations and guidelines. It is regulated in both

10 See also Katyal and Riley, 2009.

11 Mainly the UNESCO legal regime.

12 Francioni, 2013:9.

13 EU directive 93/7/EEC from 15 March 1993 on the return of cultural objects unlawfully removed from the territory of a Member State; Regulation (EC) no. 116/2009 from 18 December 2008 on the export of cultural goods.

public law and private law.[14] The private sphere tends to be concerned with its ownership, whereas the public sphere deals with the public interest connected to it as well as the fundamental rights and the issues of citizenship, inclusion and democracy. Most of these will need to be accounted for somehow here.[15]

Another aspect is that cultural heritage regulation is framed by political and diplomatic agreements which add a further bi- or multi-lateral level. The regulation of cultural heritage can thus appear to be as unendingly multi-layered and difficult to describe and capture sufficiently. Something is always left out, and it seems to be almost impossible to present the regulation in a cohesive manner or in its entirety.

Therefore I have chosen to focus on ten legal instruments that I have identified as the core ones in the current regulatory framework. These are, in chronological order:

1. 1948 Universal Declaration of Human Rights (UDHR)
2. 1954 Hague Convention for the Protection of Cultural Property in the Event of Armed Conflict and its two Protocols (1954 Hague Convention)
3. 1970 Convention on the Means of Prohibiting and Preventing the Illicit Import, Export and Transfer of Ownership of Cultural Property (1970 Convention)
4. 1972 Convention Concerning the Protection of the World Cultural and Natural Heritage (1972 Convention)
5. 1995 UNIDROIT Convention on Stolen or Illegally Exported Cultural Objects (1995 UNIDROIT Convention)
6. 2001 Convention on the Protection of the Underwater Cultural Heritage (2001 Convention)
7. 2003 Convention for the Safeguarding of the Intangible Cultural Heritage (2003 Convention)
8. 2005 Convention on the Protection and Promotion of the Diversity of Cultural Expressions (2005 Convention)
9. 2007 Declaration on the Rights of Indigenous Peoples (DRIPS), and
10. 2015 Recommendation concerning the Protection and Promotion of Museums and Collections (2015 Recommendation)

There are other regulatory instruments that also govern the field of cultural heritage. Some I have explicitly left out, often when I have deemed them to be too specific or not relevant for the discussion concerning the regulation of transnational heritage. Others will be mentioned later in the forthcoming chapters, or in conjunction with specific cases, such as the convention on Social, Economic and Cultural Rights.[16] It does not mean that if an instrument

14 Francioni, 2013:9.
15 E.g. sociolegal norms.
16 United Nations International Covenant on Economic, Social and Cultural Rights (1976).

has been omitted here and if it is not discussed among the ten core instruments, it is not important. On the contrary, omission can also indicate that instruments such as the convention on Social, Economic and Cultural Rights are enormously important, in fact too significant to only mention in a cursory manner or in passing here. And it can also mean that even though they are significant in general they are not specifically relevant for the regulation of transnational heritage. One such legal instrument that has been omitted but that could have been mentioned in much more detail and perhaps even been included in this chapter is the EU Directive 93/7 On the return of cultural objects unlawfully removed from the territory of a Member State. I have, however, chosen not to discuss that, or any other EU directive for that matter, partly because their broad principles will already be covered under some of the other core conventions or regulatory instruments that I present here, and partly because they are region specific. Because I am focusing on the transnational nature of heritage, I have tried to avoid national and region-specific regulation. Furthermore, there are a number of UNESCO recommendations that could also have been relevant to mention here that have been left out.

The ten instruments that I will present and use as the general international regulatory framework that governs the field, are those that I think are the guiding, thematic, tone-giving ones, always in one way or another being referenced or relied on, applied and discussed by lawyers, diplomats, and heritage and museum practitioners. Because of their dignity they in turn influence most other international, national and regional regulations, customary law, discourses and practices, through various "trickle-down" effects. When matters of heritage, as well as obliquely transnational heritage, are discussed, most stakeholders tend to begin, and stay, with these instruments. They fall predominantly within the framework of international public law, but some stem from private law too, notably the 1995 UNIDROIT Convention.

A short note on referencing. I have chosen to use the abbreviations for the legal instruments as per the UNESCO practice. There are other ways to abbreviate and refer to the instruments that often have long titles, but I think for the sake of clarity and cohesion the UNESCO abbreviation system is the most convenient to use here. With this way of referencing, the main conventions are referred to by their year so for instance the 1972 Convention Concerning the Protection of the World Cultural and Natural Heritage is simply referred to as the 1972 Convention. I am aware of the fact that only referencing the year of the convention can be confusing for a reader who is not very familiar with UNESCO legal instruments. To facilitate for readers of all levels, where the context does not directly indicate which convention is discussed, I will also strive to point out more specifically what instrument I am rereferring to; for instance I will use longer abbreviations such as "the 1972 World Heritage Convention".

I will not present the instruments in a purely chronological manner. Instead, and for pedagogical reasons, I have chosen to group them in three thematic categories in this chapter: *General regulatory instruments, Criminal law* and

Declarations & Recommendations. I have done so in an attempt to present the field more succinctly and indicate how it tends to be structured. The ten instruments placed in one of the three groups should in no way be read as the only way to approach or categorise this regulation, or as in any way exhaustive. This is my way to approach this multi-layered and broad regulatory framework, and I think it is helpful, at least within the context of this chapter. There are, as I have already stressed, other regulatory instruments that could have been mentioned, as well as other taxonomic groups in which the ten instruments could have been presented, or in a much more detailed manner.

In international public law, cultural heritage is regulated as both *lex generalis* and *lex specialis*. These are categories of general international law that I do not think need to be defined in detail here. Suffice it to say, as a guideline to readers not familiar with the structure of international law, and as the names indicate, *lex generalis* governs general matters of international law, while *lex specialis* governs specific matters of international law. In a conflict of laws, *lex specialis* overrides *lex generalis*. *Lex generalis* can follow the so-called *erga omnes* principle, which means that any obligations undertaken by a contracting party are also owed to the international community as a whole. The *lex specialis* doctrine on the other hand refers to the regulation that governs specific situations and binds specific parties to undertake specific obligations in particular instances. This is significant as it affects how far-reaching and tone-setting a regulatory instrument will be.

I have therefore chosen to go through the ten instruments in a manner that approximately follows the *lex generalis* and *lex specialis* divide. The first group of legal instruments that I will present more or less consists of instruments of the *lex generalis* kind, which is why I call it *General regulatory instruments*. The second group, the *Criminal law* instruments, however, consists of both *lex generalis* and *lex specialis*, but the common denominator for the instruments in that group is precisely that they all focus on the criminal aspects connected to cultural heritage. The last group of instruments comprise what can be called "softer" regulation, namely *Declarations & Recommendations*, which means that those instruments generally have a lower legal stature and are more difficult to enforce.

Furthermore, the first group that will be described presents what I have deemed to be the overarching legal instruments. These tend to be broad, global and general in tone. They often address the humanity as a whole and encompass wide-ranging fields of law. They are in many ways overwhelmingly universalist in nature, i.e. they often adopt a universalist, "humanity as a whole", language. Some of the instruments that will be mentioned within this regulatory group are the UDHR, the 1972 World Heritage Convention, the 2003 Intangible Cultural Heritage Convention, the 2005 Cultural Diversity Convention and the 2001 Underwater Heritage Convention.

The second group, the *Criminal law* instruments, generally comprise the regulation concerning illegal activities and crimes, such as the 1954 Hague Convention on destruction that occurs in the events of armed conflict, the 1970 Convention on illicit import and export, and the 1995 UNIDROIT Convention on stolen and illegally exported cultural objects.

The last group of instruments that will be presented comprises one declaration and one recommendation, namely the 2007 Declaration on the Rights of Indigenous Peoples (DRIPS) and the 2015 Recommendation on museum collections, which are both extremely significant in this context, even though neither have resulted in a convention, at least not yet.

By mapping out the multi-layered international legal field of cultural heritage law in this way, I hope to set the stage for the argument that will eventually be developed in detail throughout the book, that is, that the ten instruments in many ways fail to cover transnational heritage (adequately). However, they also open up various potential avenues for new discussions and possibly even for further regulation.

Universalist: the general regulatory instruments

In the introduction of their influential book *Cultural Heritage and Human Rights*, Silverman and Fairchild Ruggles outline that cultural heritage has "an uneasy place in the United Nations' call for universal human rights and it merits examination as an urgent contemporary problem".[17] What this uneasy place means will be discussed throughout the book, but we have already seen some of the political tensions that cultural heritage regulations can give rise to. The uneasy place can also be referring to the fact that cultural heritage can be used in the process of state building and in order to constitute communities within a state. Conversely, there are instances where cultural heritage can equally be used in destructive ways, as a direct political tool for oppression, where entire groups of people and their heritage are disposed, excluded, or where heritage is misappropriated or misused in a condescending, colonial or racist manner, perpetuating caricatural or demeaning representations of a community. Therefore the first legal instrument we must begin with and recognise as significant here has to be the iconic 1948 Universal Declaration of Human Rights (UDHR).

UDHR lays out the human rights that fall under the administration of the UN, and which are regulated in detail through a number of other binding conventions and national and international regulatory instruments. UDHR lists the human rights that are generally considered to be of the utmost fundamental nature for humanity, such as the right to life (art 1), freedom of thought (art 18), freedom of expression (art 19), freedom of movement (art 13), freedom from slavery (art 4), freedom from torture (art 5), as well as many other social, economic and cultural rights. Among these is the right to cultural life as expressed in art 27 UDHR, which states that everyone has the right to freely participate in the cultural life of their community, as well as that everyone has the right to the protection of the artistic production of which they are the author. It is generally stated that the first paragraph in art 27 UDHR is the legal ground for the 1972 World Heritage Convention and the 2003 Convention on the Intangible Cultural Heritage. The second paragraph legitimises and provides the legal ground

17 Silverman and Fairchild Ruggles, 2007:3.

for intellectual property laws including authors' moral rights that are administrated by the World Intellectual Property Organization (WIPO) within the UN context.

The UDHR is iconic precisely because it is tone-setting for other conventions in this way, and, as it is extremely well known, it is much studied and tremendously influential. It inaugurates the entire discourse of human rights as we know it today. Article 27 thus plays a pivotal role for the regulation of cultural heritage; it renders visible the importance of culture and cultural heritage for human rights and its vital significance for the constitution of people's communities, identities and belonging. Cultural rights thus function as one of the core human rights.

Janet Blake argues that recognising human rights as a starting point for the regulation of heritage serves as the justification for taking the protection of cultural heritage very seriously.[18] A consequence of her argument is that culture becomes key in the human rights discourse and that "cultural heritage can be understood as a resource that enables individuals and communities in developing [the] capacities which they, implicitly or explicitly, wish to transmit to future generations".[19] As such, the dignity and importance of cultural heritage cannot be underplayed. It is strengthened by the human rights regimes, beginning with the UDHR. This founding declaration articulates a right to culture as a human right, as well as connects this right to the constitution of community and belonging. It also acts as a platform for two UNESCO conventions (1972 and 2003), as well as for intellectual property rights (as administrated by WIPO).

The second instrument that can be mentioned here is the founding instrument for cultural heritage law and one of the two instruments that emerged directly from the UDHR, namely the 1972 World Heritage Convention. This is perhaps the main legal instrument in international public law that directly regulates the protection of cultural heritage in connection with the human rights regime. More specifically, the 1972 Convention regulates the protection of world cultural and natural heritage resources. These are the resources that are considered to be important, of fundamental significance for the whole of humankind, because they are *outstanding*. It is articulated that such resources must be safeguarded for the sake of humanity as a whole and be protected and transmitted to future generations. What cultural heritage means within the context of this convention is defined in the first article of the convention as monuments, groups of buildings or sites of "outstanding universal value".[20]

The 1972 Convention has been signed by over 190 state parties at the time of writing, which means effectively every member state of the UN. It protects three types of heritage: natural, cultural and mixed sites. It operates and administrates two heritage lists: the list of heritage deemed to be of outstanding

18 Blake, 2015:271.
19 Blake, 2015:273.
20 Art 1.

universal value (the World Heritage List) and heritage deemed to be in danger (the Heritage in Danger List). It is interesting to point out that there are currently around thirty listings on the World Heritage List that are deemed to be "trans-boundary". This is thus the first legal instrument that recognises that cultural heritage can have a transnational side.

The 1972 Convention is concerned with tangible heritage, and more often than not it is actually a question of immovable tangible heritage, such as landscapes and buildings. These are sites, monuments and buildings that elsewhere in law would be categorised as *immovables* or *immovable property*. Famous examples of sites (both cultural and natural) that are protected under the convention and placed on the World Heritage List are the Everglades National Park in Florida, USA, Machu Picchu in Peru, the Sydney Opera House in Australia, Angkor Wat in Cambodia, the cities of Rome, Paris and Vienna, etc.[21]

I will focus extensively on this legal instrument in chapters 3 and 4 as it is so significant. Therefore I will not discuss it in too much detail here. What is important to highlight is the following: the convention is connected to the human rights regime, it is universalist in tone as it refers to global humanity as a whole, and it recognises the transnational aspects of heritage. However, and as we will study in chapters 3 and 4, even though it acknowledges a universalist logic and the transnational in heritage, it is still constructed around the notion of the sovereign nation state. For instance, only a nation state can nominate heritage to be placed on the two lists, and this can be detrimental for unacknowledged transnational heritage if it is not selected by the nation state. As such, this convention is also shrouded in authorised heritage discourse, and it is often criticised for failing to safeguard that which is not selected by states. Another problem with the convention is that it can be criticised for invisible Western bias. When something is selected as "outstanding", the nomination and selection processes seem to adhere mostly to Western conceptions of beauty, art and monumentality, which can be problematic, unjust and indirectly perpetuate colonising practices.[22]

Intangible heritage is not included in the 1972 Convention. It is governed by a more recent convention, the 2003 Convention on the Intangible Cultural Heritage.[23] The 2003 Convention is the second instrument that builds on and draws its legal justification from the UDHR. Already in the preamble, the 2003 Convention is placed in the context of the broader human rights regimes as established by the UDHR, for example, as well as other binding conventions such as the International Covenant on Economic, Social and Cultural Rights of 1976, and the International Covenant on Civil and Political Rights of 1976. The preamble of the 2003 Convention further states that the heritage that can be listed as intangible cultural heritage must be "compatible with existing

21 See further, Forrest, 2010; see also Baslar, 1998.

22 See Chapter 5.

23 See further Brown, 2004; Hilty, 2009; Lixinski, 2013; Kapchan, 2014.

international human rights instruments, as well as with the requirements of mutual respect among communities, groups and individuals, and of sustainable development".[24] The link with the human rights regimes is thus explicit.

The 2003 Convention highlights the interdependence of intangible cultural heritage and tangible heritage, something that we will explore further in Chapter 4. It mentions globalisation and social transformation and the conditions they create for the renewed dialogues among communities. It is also a broadly signed convention. However, even though it has around 170 signatories, it is worth noting here that there are some states that one might have perhaps expected to be parties to the convention, that are absent from it. Those are the USA, Canada, Australia and New Zealand. Why this is the case will be discussed in more detail in some of the forthcoming chapters such as chapters 3 and 5, but it can be pointed out here that these are states with large Indigenous communities. How the 2003 Convention corresponds with, for example, the Declaration on the Rights of Indigenous Peoples (DRIPS) will also be discussed further in Chapter 3.

In the 2003 Convention "intangible heritage" is defined in art 2 as practices, representations, expressions, knowledge, skills – as well as the instruments, objects, artefacts and cultural spaces associated with intangible heritage – that communities, groups and, in some cases, individuals recognise as part of their cultural heritage. Intangible heritage is also described as intergenerational, as being transmitted from generation to generation, constantly recreated by communities and individuals in response to their environment, their interaction with nature and their history. As such, it provides the community with a sense of identity and continuity, as well as promoting respect for global cultural diversity and human creativity, which is an important point for the regulation of transnational heritage.

What is interesting to note is that the 2003 Convention does not focus so much on nation states as subjects to whom intangible heritage can be attributed, but rather it highlights the *communities*. This is also a very important distinction particularly when it comes to the recognition of transnational heritage. Furthermore, as for the matters concerning the regulation of transnational heritage, the 2003 Convention can be understood as promoting multicultural practices and as such recognising the importance of the cultural creation that takes place in diverse communities within states, as opposed to assuming a mono-cultural output. In that way, it is not as tied to a nation state discourse, and it opens up a potential path towards conceiving of transnational heritage.

The fact that communities, not states, are explicitly highlighted as subjects to whom heritage is attributed and that such communities are held up as necessary for global cultural diversity opens up arguments for inferring that transnational heritage falls under the scope of the 2003 Convention. However, and as we will see in chapters 4 and 5, on closer scrutiny the communities that the 2003 Convention addresses seem to be the other two recognised communities in law

24 Preamble, 2003 Intangible Heritage Convention.

(i.e. Indigenous and minority) and not transnational communities. Still, it is an important convention for transnational heritage because it stresses the significance of diversity for cultural heritage as well as opens up non-nation state-based understandings of communities.

Which brings us to the next general instrument and the newest convention in this category, namely the 2005 Cultural Diversity Convention. The 2005 Convention builds on, as well as vastly differs from, the 1972 and 2003 Conventions. It builds on the previous two because it continues to promote human rights and fundamental freedoms through cultural expressions. It differs from the previous two in that the 2005 Convention is more modern in tone and approach. For instance, the 2005 Convention deals with the cultural industry, cultural diversity in media and the digital environment.[25] It was once even pointed out to me as a side remark by someone who works at the UNESCO Secretariat for the 2005 Convention that the convention does not in fact deal with "heritage" at all, but rather focuses on what they described as "intellectual property". I think that this was, if not a heavy-handed statement, probably a statement where the individual in question had perhaps a very narrow definition of heritage in mind. Their statement divulged something about how "heritage" is generally defined and approached within UNESCO, namely as that which is expressly named as heritage in the legal instruments. The member of the Secretariat for the 2005 Convention seemed to be referring to "heritage" as that which falls under the regulatory systems of the 1972 and 2003 Conventions. In my view, I think that the 2005 Convention very much deals with heritage, albeit with the "living" or "contemporary" aspects of heritage, something that I will discuss in detail in Chapter 5.

As is apparent even in the preamble, the 2005 Convention is also inscribed within the human rights regime. The convention can also be connected to art 27 UDHR, and the right to participate in one's own culture. It expressly aims to promote global cultural diversity, where all people take part in a diverse cultural output and where culture acts as an expression of human rights.

Currently the 2005 Convention has around 140 signatories, most notably excluding the USA. Strictly legally speaking, the convention is probably not a very strong instrument – it is broadly understood that it is difficult to enforce. Nonetheless, it is still considered as carrying important political weight. Due to the fact that it strongly champions cultural diversity and recognises heterogeneous communities as important for human rights, this is a regulatory instrument that is significant to bear in mind when discussing recognition and regulation of transnational heritage. However, this convention recognises and promotes global cultural diversity in what can be described a universalist manner, like the previous conventions mentioned so far. The 2005 Convention still indirectly relies on the nation state as being the primary driver for the protection of "internal" or "national" culture. The protection of "global diversity" within the context of this convention must be understood as referring

25 See further Graber, 2006; Hahn, 2006; Macmillan, 2008; Hanania, 2014.

to the national, less commercial, cultural outputs and not the cultural outputs from the global entertainment industries that are in many ways multinational, but that are also commercial, standardised and corporate. The entertainment industry has a tendency to standardise culture on a global level, and the 2005 Convention aims to strengthen the weaker, less commercial, cultural, yet national expressions. It does not recognise transnational heritage. As mentioned, some argue that it does not even regulate cultural heritage, which is in my view wrong, at least within the understanding of heritage presented here.

The last relevant convention to be presented in this section is also a universalist, general regulatory instrument, namely the 2001 Convention on Underwater Cultural Heritage. The 2001 Convention is very specific and is often discussed primarily in connection with maritime law and laws of the seas. It deals with heritage that exists under water, be it movable (like ships) or immovable (like sunken cities or buildings). This is defined in art 1 of the convention, which describes "Underwater cultural heritage" as

> all traces of human existence having a cultural, historical or archaeological character which have been partially or totally under water, periodically or continuously, for at least 100 years.

Apart from the unusual terminology applied in the convention that defines heritage as a "trace of human existence", as opposed to the other definitions presented so far, the 2001 Convention is quite precise in its definition. The convention for instance has a hundred-year timeframe, meaning that only heritage that has been underwater for at least a hundred years falls under its scope. As such, it is not applicable to recently sunk heritage.

Perhaps unsurprisingly, the convention has comparatively few signatories. At the time of writing it has fewer than sixty state parties. Notable states that are not party to the convention but that do have vast coastlines, and probably a lot of heritage in their national waters, are the USA, the UK, Greece, Ireland, Sweden and Malta. This is significant to point out as it seems to indicate that states with large coastlines might be reluctant to accept the provisions of the convention. Therefore, we can assume that the convention is somehow understood to be controversial, at least for many of the European states with coastlines, and the USA. It could perhaps also have something to with the fact that these states have a tradition of seafaring, and therefore they might be interested in bringing up the heritage that has been lost at sea and that still sits on the sea bed that is within their territories.

The notions of "own territory", "foreign territory" and "sovereignty" are not necessarily approached in this convention as they would have been for the conventions that apply to heritage on land. For instance, there is the notion of sailing under a state's flag, that is, a movable territory. When a ship carries a state flag it places itself under that flag's jurisdiction regardless of where in the world the ship is. This means that at sea, a territory is always something movable, floating, unfixed. The 2001 Convention therefore takes as its main point of reference this navigating understanding of territory. As mentioned, it is inscribed within the context of the United Nations Convention on the Law of the Sea (UNCLOS). UNCLOS is a regime that governs the overall sovereignty at sea. It focuses on territorial waters as regulated by UNCLOS and the five zones defined therein.

UNCLOS begins by outlining the so-called "baseline" as a marker for a land's territory and its sovereign jurisdiction. The baseline is defined as the coastline, i.e. the low watermark where the tide is at its lowest, then:

Zone 1: Territorial Sea (TS) – 12 nautical miles (nm) from the baseline;
Z2 – Contiguous Zone (CZ) – up to 24 nm from TS;
Z3 – Exclusive Economic Zone (EEZ) – 200 nm from CZ;
Z4 – Continental Shelf (CS) – 200–350 nm (measured from TS);
Z5 – High Seas – Everything else.[26]

The regulation looks differently depending on where in the five zones heritage is found. The sovereignty is diluted the further one gets from the baseline. In Z1 we are still within the sovereign jurisdiction where the state has an exclusive right over the regulation. In Z2 the state can regulate and authorise regulation, but it must comply with the rules of the Annex of the UNCLOS. For Z3–Z4 the state has the *responsibility to protect*[27] the resources that are under water, including underwater heritage. Z5, the High Seas, depends on how one sees it, is either without sovereignty, or under a universal sovereignty. Thus, the responsibility to protect underwater resources and heritage in accordance with the 2001 Convention is *erga omnes*,[28] owed to the entire international community. As cited in the 5th recital, the states must protect underwater heritage in all five zones, alone or together.

Underwater heritage must also be protected *in situ*, that is, without moving it or raising it onto land, while ensuring public access to it, as well as preventing commercialisation or privatisation of it.[29] This is regulated in the 8th recital, which states that the international community is: "*[d]eeply* concerned by the increasing commercial exploitation of underwater cultural heritage, and in particular by certain activities aimed at the sale, acquisition or barter of underwater cultural heritage".[30] This is the whole reason for keeping sunken heritage on the seabed,[31] *in situ*, in order to ensure that access to it is non-commercial and open for all, and for the heritage to be enjoyed in common, or perhaps *as* a global commons.

26 The vessels bearing a flag of a state are considered to be under the jurisdiction of that state. Ships with no state flag are considered to be pirates, outlaws, and not entitled to the protection of the law.
27 See Chapter 6.
28 I will return to this when I discuss the 1954 Hague Convention below.
29 See e.g. arts 17 and 18 that grant the sanction to stop private enterprises that seek to commercialise or to remove heritage from the sea.
30 [original emphasis].
31 Strati, 1991.

This indicates that the 2001 Convention differs from many other *lex generalis* instruments. Namely, it is not concerned with the proprietary "ownership" logic to the same extent, one that understands cultural heritage as directly belonging to a state or a community. Rather it focuses, according to its 5th recital, on

> the public's right to enjoy the educational and recreational benefits of responsible non-intrusive *access* to *in situ* underwater cultural heritage, and of the value of public education to contribute to awareness, appreciation and protection of that heritage.[32]

The focus on public, *in situ*, access and education rather than ownership is important for our discussion here. In legal philosophy, the sea is not generally framed as "property" but as a commons. The 2001 Convention adapts this logic in a truly fascinating way, as it highlights access over ownership. The moving sovereignty, the responsibility to protect and the focus on commons rather than ownership are some of the potentially interesting openings that this convention creates.

This is the only UNESCO convention that seems to be establishing a transnational cultural commons for heritage. But of course, while this is very interesting to highlight, this type of regulation only applies to underwater heritage. The idea that a global commons is created only applies to heritage that is underwater, far from the baseline, and which is usually very difficult if not impossible to raise or to visit. Nonetheless, the 2001 Convention opens up a clear interesting avenue for further discussing cultural commons solutions for transnational heritage that I will discuss in detail in Chapter 6.

Before we leave the *lex generalis* instruments, let me summarise the main themes that emerge from this regulatory category. UDHR defines cultural heritage as an individual as well as a communal right. The 1972 World Heritage Convention is universalist in tone but in practice very state based in application, and it directly connects heritage to a nation state. The 2003 Intangible Heritage Convention opens up for communal heritage that is not state based and recognises diversity of culture within a nation state, yet it also operates under a strong state-based logic, for example when it comes to the nomination and selection of heritage. The 2005 Cultural Diversity Convention and the 2001 Underwater Heritage Convention both seem to be based on a different logic that is not dependent on nation states. While these two instruments open up regulatory possibilities in terms of "commons" or transnational heritage as commons, they still have a comparatively weak legal standing and few signatories. Taken together, the *lex generalis* conventions that in many ways make up the core of the cultural heritage law favour and pursue the logic emanating from the authorised heritage discourse, that is, one that is based and legitimised by the nation state as the legal subject, and as the only community

32 [my emphases].

category that can bear rights and responsibilities under international law. The only alternative to such state-based logic is the "universalist" approach that sees the entire human kind as a community. A third alternative, i.e. a transnational logic, is simply not directly envisioned within this regulatory category, even if there are some promising potential openings for further regulation.

Statist: the criminal law instruments

Leaving aside the broad and all-encompassing *lex generalis* instruments for a while, we can now look more closely at the legal instruments that deal with the criminal acts committed against cultural heritage. When it comes to crimes and the wrongful treatment of cultural heritage, there are three main legal instruments to consider: two UNESCO conventions and one UNIDROIT convention. The first and the oldest one is the already mentioned 1954 Hague Convention for the Protection of Cultural Property in the Event of Armed Conflict and its two Protocols (the Hague Convention). The second one is the 1970 Convention on the Means of Prohibiting and Preventing the Illicit Import, Export and Transfer of Ownership of Cultural Property (1970 Convention) and the third is the 1995 UNIDROIT Convention on Stolen or Illegally Exported Cultural Objects (1995 UNIDROIT Convention). One is a *lex generalis* instrument (the 1970 Convention), and two are *lex specialis* (1954 Hague Convention and the 1995 UNIDROIT Convention). These three conventions are often presented together as a package,[33] or as a regulatory category that generally deals with illegal acts committed against cultural heritage. Whereas the previous group of conventions, which were more general in tone, were mainly concerned with ownership, belonging and access to heritage, this second category of instruments deals with the protection, return, restitution and repatriation of heritage. The legal instruments here are in a much more explicit way formulated around a clear state-based logic, and the universalist logic does not figure as prominently. Let me briefly introduce the three conventions before making some overarching remarks about the meaning they could carry for the future regulation of transnational heritage.

The 1954 Hague Convention is the only convention in cultural heritage law that falls under international humanitarian law (IHL). Governed under the principle of *ius cogens* (obligations that are seen as universally fundamental and that cannot be derogated from in international law), it deals with matters concerning protection of cultural property in the event of armed conflict. It applies to what is in the convention referred to as *cultural property*, and not cultural heritage.

The Hague Convention protects items of tangible, movable and immovable cultural property considered to have a symbolic value for a specific community or of having a great importance for the international community as a whole. Cultural property is defined in art 1 as being:

33 See e.g. Prott, 1996.

a *movable or immovable property* of great importance to the cultural heritage of every people, like monuments, archaeological sites; works of art; manuscripts, books and other objects of artistic, historical or archaeological interest; as well as scientific collections and important collections of books or archives or of reproductions of these;

b *buildings that preserve or exhibit the movable cultural property* such as museums, libraries and depositories of archives; and

c *centres* containing a large amount of cultural property.

The Hague Convention recognises that cultural property has a high dignity as a constituent of a people's communal identity. As such, cultural property very often runs the risk of being targeted, damaged or destroyed during armed conflicts. The convention is explicitly connected to the human rights regime and the UDHR, as well as other IHL conventions, e.g. the 1951 Convention on the Prevention and Punishment of the Crime of Genocide and various other military conventions (Genocide Convention). As Blake points out, while the General Assembly of the United Nations decided not to include a "cultural genocide" crime in the drafting of the convention, the idea that any destruction of cultural property is tantamount to genocide still has a significant contextual meaning for the 1954 Hague Convention.[34]

As symbols for local and national identities, items of cultural property have indeed historically served as direct targets in wars. One of the examples of such cultural destruction is the bombing of the Al-Askari Mosque in Samarra (Iraq) in February 2006, a Shiite holy place of high religious and cultural importance.[35] Damage and destruction of cultural property as defined in the Hague Convention is therefore seen as a grave wound afflicting both current and future generations to whom such property is seen to belong, or whose identity it signifies.

The extreme and large-scale destruction and dispersal of cultural property that took place during WWII gave rise to this convention, and the international community recognised the importance of providing regulation that would explicitly protect cultural property in the future during times of war. A spirit of the 1950s post-war humanist, universal responsibility to protect set the tone for this convention. It became the first treaty of its kind that formulated a universal legal obligation among the states to protect cultural property in the event of armed conflict.

The 1954 Hague Convention has two Protocols. The first Protocol (1954) prevents export of cultural property from an occupied territory, and it also states that any unlawfully exported property must be returned to its original territory. The second Protocol (1999) elaborates further on important legal terms such as "military necessity" and "preparatory measures" and also establishes an enhanced protection of cultural property during times of peace, for instance by keeping and maintaining a list of national cultural property and by criminalising, in national law, any deliberate destruction of cultural property in times of both war and peace.

34 Blake, 2015:284, see also Novic, 2016, as well as Chapter 6.
35 Blake, 2015:285.

The Hague Convention explicitly prohibits the use of cultural property as targets or for any act of hostility directed against it that might damage, destroy or in any way endanger it during an armed conflict. The convention even goes so far as to say that all state parties must foster within their armed forces a spirit of respect for all people's cultural property (art 4).[36] It further suggests that cultural property can be marked in order for it to be identifiable in an armed conflict. By placing the "Blue Shield" emblem on these items of cultural property, they can easily be recognised and identified even in times of war. I will discuss this convention in further detail in chapters 3 and 4.

Here, we can highlight the close link between the Hague Convention and the 1970 Convention on the Means of Prohibiting and Preventing the Illicit Import, Export and Transfer of Ownership of Cultural Property. This is the second instrument we will look at. The 1970 Convention was the first *lex generalis* convention of its kind. Whereas Hague regulates armed conflict, the 1970 Convention regulates illicit movement of cultural property during times of peace. It also uses the term "property" and not "heritage", which is utilised in later, more recent, conventions. The 1970 Convention governs illicit trafficking of movable cultural property. "Movable" here can mean more than what are generally considered to be movables in law. This convention considers for instance property that is, or that at least once was, attached to buildings or its grounds, as movables. One such example is the Zodiac Ceiling from the Egyptian Temple of Hathor, which is now on display at the Louvre in Paris. This and similar properties would normally be considered to be immovables in land law, for example. There are many examples of objects in museums today that technically would be considered as immovables in law, such as the Parthenon Marbles, which were once attached to a building.[37] Unlike Hague, the 1970 Convention does not cover immovable property, but it covers things that are removed from immovable property. This convention thus concerns more than chattel but less than what is protected under Hague.

The 1970 Convention provides an extensive list of things that are considered to be "cultural property" within its scope:

(a) Rare collections and specimens of fauna, flora, minerals and anatomy, and objects of palaeontological interest;
(b) property relating to history, including the history of science and technology and military and social history, to the life of national leaders, thinkers, scientists and artist and to events of national importance;
(c) products of archaeological excavations (including regular and clandestine) or of archaeological discoveries;

36 See e.g. the recent training of female militaries by UNESCO in protecting cultural property: https://en.unesco.org/news/female-military-trained-unesco-protecting-cultural-property
37 Merryman, 1999.

(d) elements of artistic or historical monuments or archaeological sites which have been dismembered;
(e) antiquities more than one hundred years old, such as inscriptions, coins and engraved seals;
(f) objects of ethnological interest;
(g) property of artistic interest, such as:

  (i) pictures, paintings and drawings produced entirely by hand on any support and in any material (excluding industrial designs and manufactured articles decorated by hand);
  (ii) original works of statuary art and sculpture in any material;
  (iii) original engravings, prints and lithographs;
  (iv) original artistic assemblages and montages in any material;

(h) rare manuscripts and incunabula, old books, documents and publications of special interest (historical, artistic, scientific, literary, etc.) singly or in collections;
(i) postage, revenue and similar stamps, singly or in collections;
(j) archives, including sound, photographic and cinematographic archives;
(k) articles of furniture more than one hundred years old and old musical instruments.

It has around 130 state parties, which is a considerable amount, but still fewer than the 1972 World Heritage Convention or the 2003 Intangible Heritage Convention, for example. The reason for this might be that this convention draws up onerous rules and puts obligations in place that for some states can be difficult to realise or impossible to enforce politically. Notable state parties of the convention are: the earliest member states – Cambodia (1972), Egypt (1973), Italy (1978), Canada (1978), Greece (1981), followed by later signatories such as the USA (1983), Australia (1989), the UK (2002) and New Zealand (2007). Cambodia was an early signatory because it had an interest in protecting its ancient culture of Angkor, and it is a typical example of a so-called "source state"/"state of origin"/"exporting state".[38] On the other hand, many of the "market states"/"importing states"[39] were late in signing the convention. This second group of states are represented by the likes of the UK and the USA. These are states usually understood to be the primary buyers and importers of cultural property, and that house large museums such as the British Museum or the Metropolitan Museum.[40] The market states also tend to have substantial antiquity markets with large-scale auction houses such as Sotheby's and Christie's. Some notable states that are missing or yet to sign the convention even though they are considered to be large import or export states are

38 Here and in cultural heritage research generally, these terms are used as synonyms.
39 Here and in cultural heritage research generally, these terms are used as synonyms.
40 Merryman, 2006.

Austria, Ireland and Malta in Europe; Indonesia, Malaysia, the Philippines and Thailand in Asia; and Kenya, Mozambique and Namibia in Africa.

Like the 1954 Hague Convention, the 1970 Convention can be described as a convention that codifies the sentiments of the post-WWII era. Both conventions, in different ways, specifically regulate illicit import and export of cultural property when they are taken from their places of origin. The central article of the 1970 Convention is art 3, which proclaims the general prohibition in a seemingly very simple manner:

> The import, export or transfer of ownership of cultural property effected contrary to the provisions adopted under this Convention by the States Parties thereto, shall be illicit.

In his comments to the 1970 Convention, Patrick O'Keefe highlights how this short article may be more complicated than it seems. He recounts how it has given rise to many discussions as well as how it has been referred to as not just a difficult but also a "mysterious" legal clause. There are a number of reasons why this could be the case, and some of those reasons will be stressed soon and throughout this book. One of the reasons why it may be considered as mysterious is probably that it is extremely, for these contexts, short. How come? Another reason might be the choice of the, for the English language, rather unusual word to be employed in legal texts, namely "illicit".[41] Alternatives such as "unlawful" or "illegal" might have been more idiomatic or even preferred. The word "illicit", O'Keefe notes, "has an aroma of immorality that is not present in the more neutral terms 'unlawful' and 'illegal'".[42] The provision in art 3 should be read, he points out further, with the preamble of the convention in mind that cites that the cultural property's "true value can be appreciated only in relation to the fullest possible information regarding its origin, history and traditional setting". The reference to illicit handling seems to be inferring that any removal of something from its place of origin might be problematic, even immoral, if the preamble and art 3 are read together. As mentioned in the introductory chapter, such provisions could potentially have grave consequences for certain unrecognised transnational heritage because it might not have been nominated by the state as heritage, as we will see in more detail in Chapter 3.

Art 4 of the 1970 Convention is formulated with the assumption that "belonging" within its context means a physical as well as a metaphysical connection to a country of origin, and this reveals the statist nature of the regulation. Art 4 seems to imply that both legitimate, as well as *moral*, belonging must directly be connected to the territory of a nation state. The cultural property that is attributed to a nation state is defined within the scope of this convention as cultural property that is:

a created by individual or collective genius of nationals of the State concerned, and cultural property of importance to the State concerned created

41 See also Gordon, 1971.
42 O'Keefe, 2007:41–43.

within the territory of that State by foreign nationals or stateless persons resident within such territory;

b found within the national territory;

c acquired by archaeological, ethnological or natural science missions, with the consent of the competent authorities of the country of origin of such property;

d which has been the subject of a freely agreed exchange; and

e which was received as a gift or purchased legally with the consent of the competent authorities of the country of origin of such property.

Interestingly, cultural property that is attributed to a state can come from a private acquisition too, 4 (d) and 4 (e). The statist notion that cultural property belongs to the state on whose territory it is created or found is thus widened to also include private property. As a result, the convention text seems to be catering for the international market for private transactions in cultural goods, and it even provides an exception for "freely agreed exchange" in art 4 (d) or where cultural property has been received as a gift or purchased legally with the consent of the competent authorities of the country of origin of such property, as in art 4 (e).

Article 4 of the convention in many ways summarises why both the 1954 Hague Convention and the 1970 UNESCO Convention are interesting to study further when it comes to the regulation of transnational heritage. Both clearly acknowledge and recognise that heritage moves across borders, and while movement can be both legal and illegal, private and public, an *in situ* logic is preferred in regulation. Furthermore, both conventions reinforce the state-based authorised heritage discourses, as they emphasise the idea of cultural heritage as *a priori* tied to a state territory, to a national soil. As mentioned, this logic can be problematic when it comes to certain transnational heritage, as will be explored further in chapters 4 and 5.

The last regulatory instrument for the purpose of this section is the 1995 UNIDROIT Convention on Stolen or Illegally Exported Cultural Objects. Even though it is not a UNESCO convention, it is still relevant to the discussion as a complement to international public law and the UNESCO legal framework. UNIDROIT is regulated under international private law and dedicated to the unification of private law. It is an organisation that is not part of the UN system. The organisation has a seat in Rome and it is an independent, intergovernmental institution, founded in 1926 under the auspices of the League of Nations. Currently it has 62 member states.

The 1995 UNIDROIT Convention deals with stolen cultural objects,[43] and came into force in 1998. It regulates the return of objects, more specifically the return of objects that were taken out of a state, contrary to the 1970 UNESCO Convention, for example.[44] Therefore, UNIDROIT must also be read together with the 1970 Convention.

43 See e.g. Fox, 1993.

44 See generally Prott, 1996.

The 1995 UNIDROIT Convention regulates the "illegally" (NB! not illicitly) removed or dislocated cultural objects, taken from one state to another. Unlike the UNESCO legal framework, which does not have a tribunal where disputes can be brought, UNIDROIT has a tribunal for conflict resolution. While all breaches of the UNESCO legal instruments must be resolved either in voluntary mitigation or on a political diplomatic level, the 1995 UNDROIT Convention provides a litigation route within its own unified dispute resolution procedure and tribunal.

It refers to culture under its scope neither as "cultural property", the term used in the 1954 Hague Convention and the 1970 Convention, nor as "cultural heritage" used in the later UNESCO conventions. Rather, it employs the term "cultural objects". Cultural objects are defined in art 2 as:

> those which, on religious or secular grounds, are of importance for archaeology, prehistory, history, literature, art or science and belong to one of the categories listed in the Annex to this Convention.

The categories listed in the Annex are extensive and I will not repeat them here. Suffice it to note that the list in the Annex effectively follows the categories of the 1970 UNESCO Convention, as listed above. Why the word "objects" instead of "property" was chosen for the 1995 Convention, even though the two conventions are so closely linked, remains unclear.

However, while the 1995 UNIDROIT Convention, based on private law, is an important addition to the UNESCO framework, based on public law,[45] and even though UNIDROIT has a tribunal, the 1995 Convention must still be considered as having a rather weak legal standing. UNIDROIT on the whole does not have many signatory parties, as we saw above, and the 1995 UNIDROIT Convention even fewer. The 1995 Convention has, at the time of writing, only around forty signatories. The member states of the convention are currently both source states and market states; of course, the majority of the signatories are source states. Unsurprisingly, the USA is not a signatory to the convention.

Regardless of its seemingly weak legal standing and given its private law context, the 1995 UNIDROIT Convention is interesting as a political proclamation as well as for its symbolical value. Firm legal language can be found in the convention, and questions regarding, for example, jurisdiction, conflicts of law and choice of forum are among some of the measures set out in art 8 of the convention. Art 9 makes provisions for the recognition of court decisions from other member states.[46] It also states that:

> Nothing in this Convention shall prevent a Contracting State from applying any rules more favourable to the restitution or the return of stolen or illegally exported cultural objects than provided for by this Convention.[47]

45 See e.g. Prott, 1996.
46 Art 9 para. 2.
47 Art 9 para. 1.

The Convention thus allows for a choice of forum of convenience where the rules for restitution or return are the most favourable; i.e. either in national or in foreign courts, and in the interim art 8 also lists provisional measures such as injunction. The closer connection between UNIDROIT and the 1970 Convention will be discussed further in Chapter 3.

Conclusively, and before we leave this section, let us summarise why these regulatory instruments are important and how they fail to safeguard transnational heritage. They are important because they recognise the worth of cultural property in both times of peace and times of war. The conventions also recognise that cultural property is a direct constituent of peoples and communities, and even though none of the instruments goes so far as to define the destruction of a community's heritage as a genocide, they still uphold that any destruction and illegal movement of culture must be treated as grave crimes, violations of human rights, that can have a profound effect on a community. But that is also why they are problematic in terms of the regulation of transnational heritage. With the Hague, 1970 and UNIDROIT conventions we can see how community is often defined or legitimised by a nation state. All three conventions focus on the community with the highest dignity, namely the sovereign nation state. In Hague it is the nation state that selects property to be protected by being marked with the Blue Shield; in the 1970 Convention it is the nation state that is seen as the moral and legal owner of heritage that is created or found on its soil and that nominates and selects objects to be safeguarded; in UNIDROIT proceedings can only be initiated once cultural objects cross state lines illegally. Nonetheless, all of these instruments open up avenues for further regulation and for the recognition of transnational heritage. Hague now acknowledges all types of destruction of heritage, even of internal heritage within a state, which might open up the recognition of the transnational within national heritage. Art 4 of the 1970 Convention recognises the many cultural activities that take place within a state which are also conducted by people that are not citizens of the state. And UNIDROIT allows not just states but also individuals to bring actions, it provides a tribunal,[48] and it recognises court decisions from other member states, which can be extremely significant for the future regulation of transnational matters.

Special interest based: declarations and recommendations

Lastly, we arrive at the final category of the ten instruments that govern the regulation of cultural heritage, namely the *Declarations & Recommendations*. The regulatory instruments that I will discuss here are not conventions *per se*, and as such it might be argued that they have a lower legal standing. However, these two instruments are important in international law, and as we will see later on they may be particularly significant when it comes to the regulation of transnational heritage. The regulatory instruments that we will look at here are the

48 Shyllon, 2000.

2007 Declaration on the Rights of Indigenous Peoples (DRIPS) and the 2015 Recommendation concerning the Protection and Promotion of Museums and Collections (the 2015 Recommendation).

DRIPS is a UN declaration recognising Indigenous peoples' rights, including the right to their own culture.[49] In the preamble the declaration is described as setting a "standard of achievement to be pursued in a spirit of partnership and mutual respect". Among other things, it recognises the rights of Indigenous peoples for, e.g., self-determination (art 4), culture (arts 13 and 15), and land and resources (e.g. arts 25 and 26).[50]

It is not a convention, and declarations are formally not considered as sources of international law. But declarations can and do play a significant role in the development of customary international law. This means that if an instrument is considered to be expressing already existing customary law, then such customary rule will bind all states, regardless of whether they are part of a convention or whether they have in any other way ratified an instrument that may codify said rule. Customary obligations are in that sense the most powerful instruments in international law. Whether DRIPS confers such obligations on states is disputed and unclear.

Some argue that DRIPS is now indeed part of customary law because it is directly connected to many of the UNESCO conventions as well as other human rights instruments.[51] For instance, the 2005 Cultural Diversity Convention declares its link to DRIPS in its preamble, recognising and highlighting "the importance of traditional knowledge as a source of intangible and material wealth, and in particular the knowledge systems of indigenous peoples". The 2005 Convention also makes express references to the role Indigenous cultures play for cultural diversity in its articles 2 and 7. Furthermore, DRIPS is connected to the 2003 Intangible Heritage Convention. In the preamble as well as in articles 15, 18 and 19, the 2003 Convention directly references the inclusion of Indigenous communities and their rights, within the scope of the convention.

Outside the UNESCO framework, there are a number of other instruments that acknowledge the rights of Indigenous peoples, e.g. the International Labour Organization Convention on Indigenous and Tribal Peoples, Convention No. 169 of 1989 (ILO Convention No. 169), which is considered to be an important material source of an established international customary principle on respecting Indigenous rights to ancestral lands. Then, there is the UN International Covenant on Civil and Political Rights[52] as well as the American Convention on Human Rights,[53] which are also considered as material sources

49 See e.g. arts 13 and 15. I will also discuss these in more detail in Chapter 3.

50 See further e.g. Edwards and Stewart, 1980; Anaya, 1991; Coombe, 1993; Thornberry, 2002; Anaya, 2004; Brown, 2004; Blakeney, 2009; Blakeney, 2013.

51 Blake, 2015:279. See also Vrdoljak, 2014.

52 Mainly art 27.

53 Mainly art 21.

of international customs protecting and/or referencing Indigenous rights to ancestral lands.[54] All these together indicate that DRIPS might be part of an already existing customary practice, and therefore *erga omnes*.

Others argue that DRIPS is not part of customary law. The second line of argument claims that even though a vast majority of states have voted in favour of DRIPS, a number of states with the largest Indigenous populations such as Australia, New Zealand, Canada and the USA have voted against it. As mentioned at the beginning of this section, DRIPS is formulated as an aspirational document that declares a "standard of achievement" to be strived towards, and not as codifying customary law. Because DRIPS contains new principles, as opposed to old, customary principles, it cannot be understood as a codification of an existing customary practice.

While it is disputed whether DRIPS is customary law or not, it has a wide support globally, even among the countries that have voted against it. The declaration is already, in one way or another, embedded in the existing UNESCO binding legal regime, and it is the only regulatory instrument that has the special nature that outlines the governance of Indigenous cultural heritage.

DRIPS is interesting to mention here, among the ten core instruments, for a number of reasons that have to do with transnational heritage. The Indigenous communities are recognised as nations, as political entities, in international law, and in that sense DRIPS does not deal with unrecognised transnational communities. Still, it advances and gives materiality to the discussion concerning what it means to "protect" a culture in instances where the nation state does not correspond to the community in question, e.g. as in DRIPS where the state community is not the same as the Indigenous community.

Furthermore, DRIPS deals with matters of authenticity, beliefs and conservation of traditions that are often of an intangible nature and that do not fit easily inside the "Western" legal paradigm, as we will see in the next chapter. All these matters will need to be taken into account when it comes to further regulation of transnational heritage, as well as the fact that DRIPS provides workable definitions of terms such as "property", "self-determination" and "recognition".

With DRIPS and with the heritage of Indigenous communities, the connections between heritage and the theory of state building become much more apparent. Cultural heritage becomes tied to a political identity, which in turn becomes directly recognised as a community within a state, even if it exists across state lines. In extension, this leads to political rights to self-determination of a people that is not the nation state. DRIPS as well as the other UNESCO legal frameworks clearly and strongly recognise Indigenous peoples as nations and as communities in law. Therefore, this is also where the Indigenous heritage differs from transnational heritage, in that it at least has a definable and recognised community to which it can be attributed. Nevertheless, as a regulatory instrument it provides valuable insights in terms of community formations, and serves as a precedent in terms of how non-state-based communities can be, and are, envisioned legally.

54 Cf. art 25 DRIPS. See also Nykolaishen, 2012.

The last regulatory instrument that we will look at here before concluding this chapter is the 2015 Recommendation Concerning the Protection and Promotion of Museums and Collections. The 2015 Recommendation deals with the question of museums and their role when it comes to the handling of cultural heritage.

Like DRIPS, it can be argued that the 2015 Recommendation is part of customary international law, but the instrument is not a convention and it does not have the legal status of a convention. Equally, again like DRIPS, it is an important document that is embedded within the context of other conventions and within the UNESCO legal regime, and therefore it has an indirect legal and a direct political value.

As we have seen so far, all the ten instruments that form the core of the current regulation provide their own definition of "cultural heritage", "cultural property", "cultural objects", etc. There are no unified definitions, not even within the UNESCO legal regime itself, and my view is that this is not an oversight, but it is something that has been done on purpose. In this way, all the conventions, recommendations and declarations have their own unique frameworks, showing the flexibility and indeed diversity of what is here broadly called "cultural heritage". In that vein, the 2015 Recommendation also has its own definition, which can be found in its paragraph 6. Objects falling under its scope are referred to as "cultural heritage", but it also mentions specifically "cultural property" and "cultural objects" – i.e. it refers to all three existing terminologies that can be found in the instruments that make up the core cultural heritage regulation. As such, the Recommendation is inclusive, defining cultural heritage in a very modern way as:

> a set of tangible and intangible values, and expressions that people select and identify, independently of ownership, as a reflection and expression of their identities, beliefs, knowledge and traditions, and living environments, deserving of protection and enhancement by contemporary generations and transmission to future generations. The term heritage also refers to the definitions of cultural and natural heritage, tangible and intangible, cultural property and cultural objects as included in the UNESCO culture conventions.

This definition is clearly one of the more contemporary ones, as it inscribes itself in current discussions concerning "living environments" as well as refers back to earlier legal instruments. Heritage is described as values and expressions that are independent of ownership. The 2015 Recommendation does not mention the past, it focuses on the present, on living heritage. Therefore, the potential tension that might exist between history and the present is avoided too, and the aspects of constructed narratives, dominant discourses, etc. that we will look at in the following chapters are underplayed. This instrument does not divide tangible from intangible either, as we have seen in the previous sections, at least not directly. And in the last sentence of the definition, it explicitly inscribes itself within the context of all the UNESCO conventions.

The 2015 Recommendation is thus a significant document for this discussion and will play a large part in the coming analyses in the forthcoming chapters.

UNESCO recommendations tend to be the forerunners of conventions to come. Sometimes it may take longer for a recommendation to become a convention for a number of reasons, for example the political climate is not favourable for such a convention. We will see below why a museum convention may not be coming any time soon, and why the political climate on the matters that concern museums is currently inflamed. Still, a very interesting legal technicality must be mentioned here. While other UNESCO instruments generally address states as the legal subject in international public law, the 2015 Recommendation seems to be also addressing the *museum* as a subject. In a way, it could be argued that museums here gain a special recognition as a legal subject in international public law. The recital of the Recommendation is for instance directed to the states, but it also considers

> museums' intrinsic value as custodians of heritage, and that they also play an ever-increasing role in stimulating creativity, providing opportunities for creative and cultural industries, and for enjoyment, thus contributing to the material and spiritual well-being of citizens across the world.

It is worth pointing out once again that if these instruments can already be part of customary law, that means that in practice the International Criminal Court, for example, could and would consider such instruments in its reasonings and rulings. This means that the 2015 Recommendation may have opened up a recognition of museums as having legal subjectivity. In the next chapter I will focus on this as well as look at how the museum is defined and how the UNESCO definition corresponds with the definition provided by International Council of Museums, and why that is important for transnational heritage and its regulation.

Here we can end on the note that both DRIPS and the 2015 Recommendation must arguably be seen very much as part of the core regulation of cultural heritage law. Whether or not they are considered to be customary law is in a way not that significant. These two instruments are important as they can act as ethical guidelines both in terms of customary practices and political value as well as opening up avenues for future regulation. In that guise they are tremendously interesting within the framework of cultural heritage law for the future regulation of transnational heritage. As we will see in the next chapter, this is particularly clear when it comes to more controversial matters, such as those that challenge the definition and the role of museums today.

All the instruments mentioned throughout this chapter are designed to make cultural heritage law relevant and ethically acceptable. Furthermore, they are in one way or another relevant for transnational heritage. Yet, all of them also fail to directly deal with and define transnational heritage, as well as fail to provide a concrete definition of transnational community.

3 Movement: heritage without borders

Having introduced the ten core instruments, we can deduce that existing cultural heritage law seems to favour the discourses that tie cultural heritage to either specific geographical territories, often in the guise of a nation state, or to smaller communities that are recognised by the nation state and the international community, such as Indigenous peoples and minorities. Transnational heritage is difficult to categorise in any one of these existing community categories that are identified in current cultural heritage law namely the nation state, the Indigenous community and the minority community. This chapter will now advance the argument that by focusing only on these three, there could be a number of other community constellations, and with them their heritage, that might be left out and neglected.

How national heritage is narrated, nominated and selected, internally and externally, can be, and is, significant for communities. Therefore, regulation is always needed because it is so tightly connected to people's self-determination and to their fundamental rights. But also, vice versa, the regulation that does exist is directly framed and created by the states themselves, for their own needs. As such, current regulation can uphold the already dominant authorised heritage discourses. In this chapter I will introduce and follow the three communities recognised in law. I will also highlight how authorised heritage discourses uphold and strengthen the recognised community categories, and argue that these taxonomies exclude transnational heritage, but that they also could be moved and shifted in an emancipatory manner in order to include the transnational.

Authorised heritage discourses: nation state as community

The narratives of origin and the foundational myths of states, the so-called authorised heritage discourses, can become visible in many ways. They can emerge in (1) transitional periods after time of war or occupations when new, or at least reclaimed, national narratives of origin are required. They can be invoked in (2) post-colonial periods when decolonised states are freed and require repatriation or return of heritage taken from their territory by the colonial power. They can also be instrumental (3) during times of peace when they are upheld as the discursive frameworks for larger cultural memory

DOI: 10.4324/9781003212683-3

institutions such as national museums. In all these instances, heritage is employed when envisioning, narrating and strengthening the nation as a community. Let us now look at the most common instances when authorised heritage discourses are invoked, that is, in transitional times, in post-colonial times and within the narratives of national museums.

Transitional times and civilised pillaging

History shows that colonisation and occupation tend to alienate local people from their heritage, while the occupier's culture and identity is held as superior. Colonial ruling practices in this way neglect, damage and destroy local people's customs, property and cultural heritage. When local heritage is spared by a coloniser, it is often essentialised as primitive or exotic, preserved as a relic from a formerly uncivilised past. How heritage is managed and (mis)treated can be, and has been, a direct act towards dispossessing occupied and colonised peoples, overtaking their territory and/or alienating them from their lands, communities, cultures and places of origin.[1] That is why one of the first matters of importance for a newly freed or newly formed state is to narrate, reclaim, gather and articulate its own cultural history and identity through heritage.

It was introduced above that it is important to be recognised as a community in law, as becoming a community is the first step towards self-determination, and eventually statehood. Formerly colonised or newly freed communities thus often have to begin with reconstituting their own communal identity by an inventory of heritage that might have suffered losses or been denied under foreign rule.[2] The cultural heritage of communities plays a prominent role here, in constituting and narrating statehood. Authorised heritage discourses tend to emerge from these periods, when a state's originary narrative becomes necessary during a transitional period after colonisation or occupation and in order to become a free sovereign state.

Showing a common history and a continuous existence as a community is part of the state-building process. As we saw above, a people must claim and articulate its internal identity and first recognise itself as a community. This can be done by identifying shared traditions and culture. The community must also be able to show an external identity, i.e. a cohesion and a oneness that is recognised by other states, in order to politically and legally become a state among others within the international community. For a community to be able to demonstrate a shared cultural identity and a continuity of existence, expressions of culture and common traditions therefore have to be gathered and heritage claimed or when necessary repatriated, salvaged or returned. All of this put together proves and legitimates first an internal identity as a community (where people identify as one internally) and then an external identity as a state

1 Lixinsky, 2015:282.
2 Prott, 2012. See also the 1960 Declaration on the Granting of Independence to Colonial Countries and Peoples (UNGA 1514 (XV)).

(where other states recognise the community as a state). Being recognised as having an internal and external identity as a community in turn leads to becoming a legal community in international law that is a state with self-determination and sovereignty.

Gathering the physical evidence of a colonised or occupied community's cohesion, continuity and existence, as materialised in the heritage that represents it and bears witness to its existence, can be fraught. As often transpires, when formerly unfree, unacknowledged, colonised or occupied peoples become independent, locating such objects required for showing and articulating a cultural identity can turn out to be difficult. Many local items of cultural heritage have often suffered losses, been destroyed, either directly and violently by an occupying power or indirectly due to negation, alienation or negligence over time. The objects that are not destroyed tend to be dispersed – taken elsewhere, often to large imperial museums that belong to former colonial powers or other powerful third-party states. In order to find and constitute an internal identity as a community and thereafter to articulate an external identity as a state, the first step for many decolonised or newly freed peoples often *de facto* involves asking to have their cultural heritage repatriated and returned from former colonial powers or occupiers, or their museums. Returns and repatriations of items of culture are therefore also part of the (re)constitution of a state identity during a transitional period of states in formation.[3]

Once all, most or at least enough cultural heritage has been gathered, reclaimed, articulated, and a communal narrative retrieved, a process of state building can begin. Needless to say, there is always an element of construction and reconstruction in narratives of origin, whether it concerns newly formed states or already existing ones. It has been widely established that heritage is actively used to write and rewrite history. In transitional periods, such as after wars, occupation or colonisation, this becomes truly visible. It is during these periods that the dominant national narratives fully and most clearly emerge. Such narratives eventually become the authorised heritage discourses.

The development of current cultural heritage law follows the general development of international law. As far back as the beginning of the 17th century, Hugo Grotius, the forefigure of international law as we know it today, wrote in the treaty *De Jure Belli ac Pacis* that the taking of cultural objects in times of war could be seen as a permitted act, and that the Law of Nations allowed the taking of war loots and the pillage of cultural items during armed conflict. While anything that allows pillage generally sounds uncomfortable to a modern legal ear, we must begin with the insight that such arguments upheld by Grotius became interwoven in what became international law. However, these practices already existed in law and in military strategy. In fact, the pillage of culture as part of war making was an already established custom, dating back to Roman times at least.[4]

3 A lot has been written on these matters, but see primarily Vrdoljak, 2008.
4 Vrdoljak, 2008:64.

Over time, with the Enlightenment era and onwards, the claim that pillage of cultural objects in armed conflicts can be seen as a permitted act, was nuanced in law. Citing "humanitarian values", "universal beauty" of art and "civilised behaviour" in war, Rousseau and other thinkers sought to "humanise" armed conflict and nuance the unlimited permissions of cultural pillage. The regulation of cultural heritage became in this way inscribed in international law and the laws of war, and to events that take place during transitional and turbulent times. The regulation concerning what eventually became cultural heritage in law stems from the peace treaties entered into during the 19th and 20th centuries. The bulk of the regulatory treaties that lay the ground for the present-day regulation were entered into during this transitional time, among them the 1863 Lieber Code in the United States (art 35) (protecting museums and libraries), the 1874 Brussels Declaration (arts 8 and 17) (protecting religious sites, including Islamic and Jewish religious buildings), the 1899 First Hague Peace Conference (protecting cultural objects), the 1919 Paris Peace Treaties (protecting the integrity of collections), etc. The First Hague Convention would eventually directly lead to the current 1954 Hague Convention and its two Protocols.

That cultural objects tend to be destroyed or pillaged in times of war in order to greatly wound or expel a community is nothing new; and those practices continue to take place to this day. It is still considered uncivilised to destroy or cause harm to other people's cultural property, even during times of war. This sentiment is reflected in current regulation, most evidently in the Hague Convention as well as in the 1970 UNESCO Convention on illicit import and export of cultural property. But it is also through these instruments that the notion of a nation state as the core community in cultural heritage law emerges and becomes reinforced. The legislation envisions a state community, one that can act as a subject in its own right, claim restitution, repatriation and return as well as damages for destroyed or looted cultural objects after times of war. This also gives the impetus to communities to strive to formulate a cohesive identity in order to eventually become recognised as states. By being able to show such constitutive togetherness, a recognisable community emerges in the end. As such it gains legal subjectivity, and with that self-determination and legal agency that allows it to protect itself, its people and property from being harmed.

Authorised heritage discourses tend to therefore overemphasise the sameness, or oneness, of a people in order to show a constitutive existence of a cohesive community. This can also mean having to deny or blur out internal differences within communities that might co-exist in states in order to clearly show an identifiable community formation. But, such overemphasis of the sameness can lay the ground for future nationalist or discriminatory practices directed against smaller minority communities within the states that remain unacknowledged, which in turn can lead to internal tensions and to the denial of internal transnational heritage.

State as origin: post-colonial assumptions for legal and moral belonging

Current international law in many ways has a Eurocentric or Western regulatory history, and a number of alternative regulatory visions from, for example, Africa, Japan or the Islamic world have been downplayed. What it has laid ground for is a Western notion of "civilised behaviour" in a Rousseauian spirit in times of war. Perhaps unsurprisingly, "civilised behaviour" in this sense mainly concerned the armed conflicts conducted on the European continent and did not include the acts of war committed in the colonised territories outside of the "civilised world". The nation state, imagined as a "civilised nation", and in extension as the moral and legal owner of culture on its territory, bears a colonial burden in how it was conceived. The very community that the heritage regulation therefore builds on is a Western, or even Westphalian, idea of a nation state that is often homogenous and unified in a Western sense, as well as geographically closed off.

This understanding of the nation state is still reinforced through regulation. As the core subject of international law to which cultural heritage is attributed, a nation state is the community with the highest dignity that can protect and claim the heritage on its soil as its own. This is evident in most current legal instruments, but it probably emerges most clearly within the context of the 1970 UNESCO Convention on illicit import and export on cultural property. The 1970 Convention strongly envisions and assumes a (civilised?) nation state, to which cultural property can be attributed morally and legally. This means that if cultural property is taken from a state of origin to another state, such act is *a priori* considered to be undesirable and uncivilised. The 1970 Convention in that way infers that decontextualisation and removal of cultural property from a place of origin to elsewhere must be seen, at least from a strong legal, ethical and political starting point, as problematic and perhaps even immoral. For instance, art 5 (d) of the 1970 Convention states that the parties of the convention are obliged to organise "the supervision of archaeological excavations, ensuring the preservation '*in situ*'". This means that any excavated property must not be moved from where it is found.[5] The *in situ* requirement was introduced in Chapter 2. It reappears in several of the UNESCO regulatory instruments, such as the 2001 Convention on Underwater Cultural Heritage. However, within the context of the 2001 Convention the *in situ* requirement plays a different role as we saw, since in that context the question of jurisdiction functions differently at sea. In that way it does not reinforce the importance of the state as a community as strongly as the 1970 Convention.

As a regulatory tool, the *in situ* requirement is common and it appears in most of the core regulatory instruments. Philosophically and politically, such provisions indicate that the *in situ* preservation must always be preferred over other types of preservation because cultural items can be destroyed or damaged if moved, but, more importantly such culture must be seen as belonging to and

5 [my emphasis].

therefore best kept in the place where it was made or where it was found. It is naturally directly connected to the idea of the nation state as being the civilised subject, the community that has sovereignty and jurisdiction over its territory.

Let us stay here for a moment, namely that the *in situ* requirement is tied to territorial sovereignty. This is a very important provision, and it should not be minimised. Strong territorial sovereignty has a tremendous value for all states. Most importantly, gaining sovereignty has been hard won for former colonies or for many newly formed states. It gives communities self-determination and legal agency. But also, as we soon shall see, such territorial sovereignty can often only be symbolical in nature, especially if it is a question of a former colony. The geopolitical powers that operate might sometimes invisibly undermine a certain state's territorial sovereignty on a political level. This is often evident when it comes to the return and restitution of cultural property found or made in a formerly colonised territory that has been taken to an imperial state. The new states tend to have lesser bargaining power when their governments are asking for the return and repatriation of cultural property, for many reasons. Therefore, the *in situ* requirement is many times symbolical in nature, the right might be there, but the return might be hard to achieve, as we will see in Chapter 5.

Given the colonial history and the still very much ongoing asymmetrical power distribution between the former colonisers and their former colonies, and given how hard it still is to get Western colonial countries to agree on return of looted cultural property that was once taken from their colonies, the matters of decontextualisation are both moral and legal in nature. Current regulation is often very weak, not to say toothless, when it comes to actually enforcing the decolonial return of colonial loots. The toothlessness of current regulation in terms of colonial returns can be deduced from studying, e.g., art 7 of the 1970 Convention. It states that each state has to

> take the necessary measures, consistent with national legislation, to prevent museums and similar institutions within their territories from acquiring cultural property originating in another State Party which has been illegally exported *after entry into force of this Convention*, in the States concerned.[6]

Provision like these can be legitimate and they are part of established legal practices, adhering to the strong legal principle that prevents retrospective legislation. Apart from some very rare exceptions, the Nuremberg trials being among the most famous ones, retrospective provisions are generally avoided in law. That the 1970 Convention is not retrospective means that it regulates illegal movement of cultural property that has taken place after the year in which the convention came into force. For this convention it is 1972. What this means in practice is that any cultural property taken from states of origin and brought to other states will not be covered at all by the scope of the

6 [my emphasis].

convention if it was taken before 1972. Given that the bulk of the problematic colonial looting took place before the 1970s, i.e. before the convention came into force, the convention's strong wording loses the power to actually enforce the return of cultural property that happened before that date. What the convention fails to do, and one could argue that this is perhaps one of its major political failures, is to grant provisions of retroactivity for post-colonial returns of cultural property taken from colonies in, what today would be deemed, an illegal manner. As most of the looting or dubious export of cultural items took place before the 1970s, the convention does not apply to these acts.

Furthermore, even when it comes to matters that fall under the scope of the 1970 Convention, i.e. illegal acts of looting or export undertaken without permission that have taken place after the year 1972, the convention still fails to safeguard *all* types of culture. The only cultural property that falls under the scope of the convention is the one that has specifically been designated by the nation state as being of importance in order for it to be safeguarded (art 1). Cultural property that does not comply or goes against the authorised heritage discourse in a state is almost never, or at least very seldom, nominated and selected as having such high importance. By not being selected by the state, such cultural property is therefore denied importance and becomes directly excluded from the scope of the convention. This can for instance be the case with various items of minority cultural property such as Roma heritage, or cultural property belonging to a small, or expelled, group of people, such as the Uyghur heritage in China or the Rohingya heritage in Myanmar, or it could even be a question of Indigenous cultural property when nominating and selecting it would affect land rights or valuable natural resources, such as the Amazonian rainforests.

The 1970 Convention thus reinforces the nation as a community with the highest dignity in law, and as such having the right to reclaim illegally exported cultural property. But this of course only applies to cultural property that has been designated by the state as important and that was illegally taken out of the country after the year 1972. The convention does not provide an answer to how to handle cultural property taken or illegally exported before that date, or transnational cultural property that exists inside the state but that is not designated as important and/or recognised.

This is also true for the sister convention, the 1995 UNIDROIT Convention, which, like the 1970 UNESCO Convention, has no retroactive provision either (art 10). The UNIDROIT convention came into force in 1998, and only the displacement of cultural objects that has taken place after that date can fall under its regulatory sphere (art 12). It means that the 1995 UNIDROIT Convention is even more limited in scope than the 1970 Convention, which at least goes back to 1972. Politically, the timeframe for the 1995 UNIDROIT Convention was the very obstacle that needed to be overcome when it was being negotiated, and it was expected that a provision on retrospectivity was always going to be difficult to agree on. The member states worried that any provisions on retrospectivity might undo or pry open transactions that had taken place a long time ago as well as provide uncertainty for already established practices.

Other than the bar on retrospectivity connected to the date when the convention came into force, there are a number of other important timeframes that must be kept in mind when relying on the 1995 UNIDROIT Convention. These are provided mainly in art 3, which states that

> any claim for restitution must be brought within a period of *three years* from the time when the claimant knew the location of the cultural object and the identity of its possessor, and in any case within a period of *fifty years* from the time of the theft[7]
> and
> a claim for restitution of a cultural object [...] shall not be subject to time limitations other than a period of *three years* from the time when the claimant knew the location of the cultural object and the identity of its possessor[8]
> as well as
> [...] any Contracting State may declare that a claim is subject to a *time limitation of 75 years* or such longer period as is provided in its law.[9]

Timeframes are thus even more important for the 1995 UNIDROIT Convention as they govern and further limit an already narrowly circumscribed possibility to bring forth a legal action for return.

Even though the UNIDROIT Convention gives a legal standing to natural and juridical persons that are not states, it must still be seen as operating under a strong nation state assumption. This means that the nation state is premiered within this context as the core community to which cultural objects are seen to be tied, morally as well as legally. And as we saw in the previous chapter, an object needs to cross state lines for the convention to become applicable, which further stresses the centrality of the nation state. Nonetheless, what is important to highlight here with the 1995 UNIDROIT Convention is that it opens up the possibility to recognise other claimants as well as widening the type of cultural objects that can be included within its scope, objects that otherwise might have been neglected or denied by states, such as transnational heritage, as this instrument does not require any nomination or selection process as the UNESCO conventions do, most notably here the 1970 Convention.

Finally, it is worth reminding ourselves of the legal technicality at play in the UNIDROIT Convention, and the overall important distinction, namely that actions for *restitution* of stolen cultural objects can be brought by anyone, a natural or juridical person, (regulated in chapter II of the convention). When the term "restitution" is used it thus denotes a process by which cultural objects are returned to an individual or a juridical person like a company or an organisation, or a community. Whereas when it comes to actions concerning the *return* of wrongfully exported cultural objects (regulated in chapter III of the

7 [my emphases] art 3.3.
8 [my emphasis] art 3.4.
9 [my emphases] art 3.5.

convention), such action can only be brought by a nation state. When a process for "return" is initiated under UNIDROIT or any other of the ten core regulatory instruments, it means that the object will be returned to a nation state at the request of a government.[10]

Many of these regulatory instruments are cumbersome, difficult to enforce or quite simply legally inapplicable in this way. They still serve as moral commitments, allowing and urging states to act in their spirit, even when they are not directly applicable. For instance, the recitals of the conventions are seen as stating generally agreed-on ethical positions. There are a number of voluntary returns taking place, and former colonial powers are indeed returning some items even though the conventions are not retrospective. But this is not happening at such a speed or a degree as many of the source states would have wished. The voluntary actions are simply not enough, and often they do not include the most valuable items. Even further, the recitals stating the moral and ethical commitments to return do not mention transnational heritage at the same time as the nation state is constantly reaffirmed as the main and often the only legal subject that can have rights and obligations. Therefore the nation state is reinforced as the only community that is able to select cultural property to be protected through the scope of international public law and its regulatory frameworks.

Obviously, current regulation does not cover cultural heritage belonging to transnational communities that are not recognised in a nation state. Transnational communities are in fact not recognised at all as communities in law, and as such transnational heritage only has as much standing as the nation state within which it finds itself chooses to grant, or as much as the international community is interested in protecting and fighting for it on a political or diplomatic level. Keeping heritage *in situ* without further nuance or provision for transnational heritage, and always preferring that it stays within its original context, is not necessarily a straightforward commitment when it comes to transnational heritage. In fact, allowing for the opposite, i.e. not keeping transnational heritage *in situ,* or granting a more or less temporary removal of it from a state of origin that does not recognise it or its community, to another place that does, could mean that endangered heritage can be safeguarded and better preserved if it is taken elsewhere. Let us be reminded of the high-profile destructions of Jewish heritage during WWII, the Buddhist Bamiyan statues in Afghanistan, Palmyra in Syria or more recently minority cultural heritage in Eastern Europe. These have all been damaged, neglected, dispersed or ruined, *in situ.*

When it comes to multicultural heritage or transnational heritage, heritage stemming from communities that are not recognised or that are persecuted within a nation state, it is not as simple as claiming that the one (original context) is always preferable over the other (decontextualisation). Where something should be kept is certainly an argument that must be allowed to differ over time, depending on the item in question. We will return to this discussion in the next section when we

10 Op. cit. note 7.

discuss the role of museums in these matters, as museums are negotiating between adopting post-colonial positions (always return), positions of international responsibility (always act as the protector or as a safe harbour) and sustainability goals (concerning the long-term handling of global heritage). How this affects transnational heritage, for example how to deal with heritage belonging to unrecognised or multicultural communities that can be under threat, remains unclear. What we can see from this section is that even post-colonial regulation can contribute to reinforcing the idea of mono-cultural nation states and their authorised heritage discourses.

Museums

The last and third instance where the regulation can reinforce authorised heritage discourses and the nation state as the core community is when it comes to the organisation of national museums. Vrdoljak writes that national museums are normally seen as having two roles:

1 The education of the general public; and
2 As storehouses of unique and authentic objects for the purview of the connoisseur or the scholar.[11]

How to define a museum, and its roles, is unendingly difficult and vastly disputed. Most, not to say all, founding texts in museology begin with precisely this lamentation, that the museum, as a cultural memory institution, is almost impossible to define. Many scholars tend to begin with the definition of the museums that stems from the ancient concept of *mousieon*, the temple dedicated to the nine muses of the epic, music, poetry, oratory, history, tragedy, comedy, dance and astronomy.[12] Perhaps there is something to this approach, to think of the museum as a temple for beauty, perhaps it is yet another Eurocentric, Western definition that from the outset misunderstands the many roles of the museum. Here, however, I would like to explore the regulatory definitions.

Firstly, as we in saw Chapter 2, the 1970 Convention mentions museums in one of its most important articles, art 7. There, the museums are envisioned as key agents in safeguarding cultural items. However, the 1970 Convention does not provide a definition of the museum.

The 2015 Museum Recommendation on the other hand provides a definition. A museum is defined in paragraph 4 as a:

> non-profit, permanent institution in the service of society and its development, open to the public, which acquires, conserves, researches, communicates and exhibits the tangible and intangible heritage of

11 Vrdoljak, 2008:9 citing Cameron, 1971.
12 Alexander and Alexander, 2008:3.

> humanity and its environment for the purpose of education, study and enjoyment. As such, museums are institutions that seek to represent the natural and cultural diversity of humanity, playing an essential role in the protection, preservation and transmission of heritage.

Another important regulatory definition of the museum can also be mentioned. It is provided by the non-governmental organisation International Council of Museums (ICOM). ICOM has had a prominent and leading role in the drafting of the 2015 Recommendations; it oversaw the museum definition as well as the 2015 Recommendation's correspondence with the ICOM Code of Ethics. All ICOM instruments are voluntary industry codes that have been agreed on by its members, that is, the museums, and not the states. It means that the museums themselves draft and agree on what the definition of the museum should be.

Because of the close link between ICOM and the 2015 Recommendations, the two definitions ought to be read together. The current ICOM definition is from 2007 and defines a museum as follows:

> a non-profit, permanent institution in the service of society and its development, open to the public, which acquires, conserves, researches, communicates and exhibits the tangible and intangible heritage of humanity and its environment for the purposes of education, study and enjoyment.

The two definitions are evidently quite similar. However, in the summer of 2019 ICOM put forward a proposal for a new definition for its Code of Ethics. It was argued that the definition from 2007 might have become outdated. After actively preparing and considering a new definition for a year and what the role of the 21st century museum would be, an updated version was set to be put forward and agreed on at the Extraordinary General Assembly of ICOM in Kyoto, Japan, in September 2019. The suggested version, prepared by a Danish ICOM curator, included a new conceptualisation of the museum that would take into account issues of inclusivity and cultural democracy. It reads:

> Museums are democratising, inclusive and polyphonic spaces for critical dialogue about the pasts and the futures. Acknowledging and addressing the conflicts and challenges of the present, they hold artefacts and specimens in trust for society, safeguard diverse memories for future generations and guarantee equal rights and equal access to heritage for all people.
>
> Museums are not for profit. They are participatory and transparent, and work in active partnership with and for diverse communities to collect, preserve, research, interpret, exhibit, and enhance understandings of the world, aiming to contribute to human dignity and social justice, global equality and planetary wellbeing.[13]

13 Available at the ICOM website: https://icom.museum/en/news/icom-announces-the-alternative-museum-definition-that-will-be-subject-to-a-vote/. See also

This draft definition turned out to be too controversial, and a backlash to the Danish-led proposal came quickly. The draft was called "ideological", "political" and even "over inflated verbiage". Because of the controversy, and presumably because it was apparent that it would not be agreed on by the museums, the scheduled vote did not take place in September 2019 and was postponed until a later unspecified date. At the time of writing, the 2007 definition of museums is still upheld by ICOM in its Code of Ethics.

Why did this happen? Why is it important to talk about the definition of the museum and the role of the museum in the 21st century when discussing the regulation of transnational heritage? These are perhaps rhetorical questions, as it is quite clear that museums have a privileged role when it comes to safeguarding, explaining and narrating the objects they hold, or the people and communities such objects can be attributed to.

National museums can provide information about the state and its history, its people as well as the objects exhibited, through so-called "object biographies".[14] Object biographies[15] are the more or less constructed genealogies of the objects in the collections, their contexts, how they were made, what their significance is, or was, and how they came into to the museum's possession, and why. However, these narratives are often in full accordance with the authorised heritage discourse of the state, and they tend to overemphasise the national, and the sameness and homogeneity of the state as a community. The two roles of the museum highlighted by Vrdoljak above, as educator and as a storehouse, imply that museums are cultural memory institutions that record an "objective" historical process and that safeguard heritage.[16] By being presented in that way, it underplays the fact that museums often have an uneasy dependence on the state. Object biographies have in fact been used to reinforce authorised heritage discourses, and to side-line alternative contextual information or dissenting voices.

This was probably what led to the controversy surrounding the new ICOM draft definition. Today museums clearly have enormous challenges to overcome in terms of how to account for and ethically handle the various conflicting narratives concerning, e.g., nationality, belonging, colonial and imperial history that are connected to their collections. I will discuss this in much closer detail in Chapter 5.

Furthermore, intensive discussions concerning how museums ought to be governed and funded ethically, as well as who should be invited as a board member or a trustee in a museum, abound as we will see in Chapter 5. Criticism regarding their lack of diversity and representation is also intense. Naturally, museums have much potential, and their role cannot be easily discarded as outdated. People care profoundly about museums. They are the environments

https://icom.museum/en/resources/standards-guidelines/museum-definition/ and Wakefield, 2021.

14 Geismar, 2018.

15 *Necro*graphies instead of *Bio*graphies, see e.g. Mbembe, 2003.

16 Vrdoljak, 2008:9.

that frame the narratives of living heritage, and as such they might be instrumental in safeguarding transnational heritage.

The link between the 2015 Recommendations and the ICOM Code of Ethics is important to highlight here. It cannot be pointed out enough that ICOM's Code of Ethics is a voluntary industry code, developed by the museum sector itself, and the 2015 Recommendations a UNESCO instrument. Both types of instruments can have a very strong tone giving value, but they can also be seen as self-serving; museums will only agree on something that suits them and not necessarily something that criticises their established practices or challenges their core activities. This will in turn be reflected in the UNESCO instrument because they are linked. Of course, the ICOM ethical code has a more than substantial impact on how museums conduct their business in practice, and therefore all provisions put forward to be included in the Code of Ethics will be of utmost importance for the museums, and as such potentially controversial and difficult to agree on.

The UNESCO Recommendations and the ICOM Code of Ethics seem to suggest that museums have a fundamental role in the administration and handling of cultural heritage. For instance, in art 1 of the 2015 Recommendations it is stated that museum collections constitute the primary means by which to protect and promote cultural and natural diversity of tangible and intangible heritage. And as already mentioned, the Recommendations lack the force of state law and international law. Still, it can be argued that this instrument is part of international customary law, and therefore it might be legally stronger than it seems. Both the Recommendations and the ICOM Code of Ethics are considered to be hortatory instruments and as at least encouraging commonly agreed-on standards and commitments. Both are also designed to highlight the importance and relevance of museums globally and make them ethically acceptable.

Museum have for instance explicitly agreed on and committed to voluntarily returning human remains, regardless of when they were acquired, before or after the coming into force of any convention. But the museums do not have an equally clear position when it comes to the return of historically acquired cultural heritage or colonial loot. The commitment that does exist is in line with, for example, the 1970 Convention, i.e. that the museums will not acquire any new items that in any way have an uncertain provenance.

Another interesting question is whether the museums are the addressees of the 2015 Recommendation, or whether the Recommendation only addresses states. The preamble of the recital reads:

> ***Considering*** that it is the responsibility of every Member State to protect the cultural and natural heritage, tangible and intangible, movable and immovable, in the territory under its jurisdiction in all circumstances and to support the actions of museums and the role of collections to that end

This seems to directly be addressing the states. At the same time a paragraph below states:

> ***Recalling*** that a UNESCO recommendation is a non-binding instrument that provides principles and policy guidelines addressing different stakeholders

What this means is that the Recommendations might be widening the role of the state as the community with the highest dignity in international law to also include its museums as stakeholders. It could also mean that this formulation legally strengthens the state-based narratives and authorised heritage discourses that are enabled through the practices of the museums. How museums should be defined, organised, and their role in the constitution of the community as well as the enormous critique currently directed at museums is something that I will discuss in detail in Chapter 5. Suffice it to conclude here that the three instances mentioned: transitional times, post-colonial regulation and museum-based national narratives are key instances where the state is premiered as the community with the highest dignity in law that can have heritage attributed to it.

In summary, the 1970 Convention and 1995 UNIDROIT Convention, as well as the 2015 Recommendations, can underscore the authorised heritage discourses by designating the nation state as the main community and as such the core legal and moral owner and protector of heritage. This community type is currently seen as the strongest iteration of community, as it has the highest status in international law. The idea of the nation state being the ground for legal and moral belonging of heritage is a post-colonial one, and it is strengthened through current international law. However, this conception of the nation state as the highest community also leads to politically cumbersome, difficultly negotiated regulation that is weak and almost impossible to enforce in practice as it does not cover colonial looting or the protection of transnational heritage, for example. It also premiers the idea that the communities that are protected in international law are first and foremost the states, and the way in which they envision themselves and their museums. Obviously, this can be problematic for alternative formations of communities that do not fit in within the dominant conceptions of the state, or for people that are stateless, or unacknowledged within the state, as well as for all types of transnational communities.

Multilocal: heritage sites and the Indigenous communities

The next community constellation that is recognised in regulation is the Indigenous community. An Indigenous community is a nation but not a nation state. Discussing Indigenous cultural heritage involves analysing the role of "ancestral territories" that existed before the nation state existed, and how a community can be tied to a territory, emotionally, politically and, in the end, legally without being a state are some of the questions relevant in this context. At the heart of the discussion lies the question: Who is included as a member of, and stakeholder in, an Indigenous community? Here the connection to territory plays a key role. Emily Donaldson writes for instance that

> [t]hough the meaning of ancestral places may be ambivalent and fraught, a shared approach to these challenges can bind communities together, overcoming historic violences and generations of silence. The uncomfortable, even painful nature of the resulting bond is radically different from what phenomenologists have cast as a nurturing relationship between people and land.[17]

Let us begin with the legal instrument briefly presented above, namely the 2007 UN Declaration on the Rights of Indigenous Peoples, or DRIPS. In Chapter 2 I discussed its legal status in international and customary law and will not repeat it here. I will instead focus on the express discursive links made between the Indigenous communities and two interesting aspects here – the connection first to territory and "ancestral lands", and second to the community's "traditional knowledge" or "traditional cultural expressions". These two aspects lay the foundation for the recognition of the Indigenous community as a community in cultural heritage law.

The discussions concerning cultural heritage and the rights of Indigenous communities abound and need not be repeated here.[18] There are many conversations going on in terms of how to ethically and sufficiently protect Indigenous heritage. Some of them are difficult. One of the most recent controversies included a discussion concerning a mural in San Francisco called "The Life of Washington".[19] It depicts the American Indigenous people in a derogatory manner. The direct question in that case was whether to demolish the mural, and more broadly, how generally to treat heritage that is offensive to Indigenous peoples. There is a lot of positive development too, in terms of progress and recognising and protecting Indigenous heritage. In Australia, a ban on ascending the iconic rock of Uluru was finally granted in 2019.[20] In Canada, an Indigenous legal practice was established as being legally binding, meaning a recognition of Indigenous law as Canadian law.[21]

What I want to explore here is the construction and recognition of the Indigenous community in regulation. When it comes to cultural heritage regulation and Indigenous rights, it tends to be a question of the local rather than the national. How the local is constituted through regulation and how it subsequently forms the base for recognising an Indigenous community is one of the core issues here. As mentioned, I will particularly focus on the connections between territory and community,[22] and then turn to the traditional

17 Donaldson, 2018.

18 See for instance some, in my view, of the most interesting contributions (in chronological order): Edwards and Stewart, 1980; Anaya, 1991; Assembly of First Nations and Canadian Museums Association, 1994; Simpson, 1997; Thornberry, 2002; Anaya, 2004; Lewinski, 2008; Macmillan, 2012; Blakeney, 2013; Lai, 2014.

19 Bryson Taylor, 2019.

20 Warne, 2019.

21 Liderman, 2019.

22 See e.g. the landmark case *Mayagna (Sumo) Awas Tingni Community vs. Nicaragua (2001).*

knowledge and cultural expressions and how they narrate the community. Towards the end of this section, I will return to the more explicit transnational matters and how the transnational can correspond to the Indigenous.

Ancestral lands: the spatial formations of Indigenous heritage sites

In Western popular culture the image of the desert symbolises empty space, death, danger. There is a romantic notion of the desert as magic, alluring, bewitching, vast spaces invoking fantasies of free spirits and captured genies. Perhaps this is why deserts often figure as, or as part of, sites that are selected and designated as world cultural heritage, and why so many deserts have been inscribed on the World Heritage lists.

One of the deserts that is listed as World Heritage is the M'Zab Valley, inscribed as a cultural site. Situated in the Saharan desert, it is registered as Algerian heritage. It contains five perfectly preserved *ksours* (fortified cities) that are adapted to the environment. At the same time its architecture respects the community living there and the traditional structures of the family. Dating back to the year 1012 AD, it serves as a source for inspiration for architects and urban planners to this day. There is also Tsodilo, the so-called "Louvre of the Desert", situated near the Namibian border in Okavango Sub-District. It encompasses a small area of large quartzite rock formations that rise from its sand dunes to the east and a dry fossil lake bed to the west in the Kalahari Desert. It is registered as a cultural heritage site for Botswana. Then there are the large transcontintental and transnational sites such as the Silk Road and the Qhapaq Ñan, Andean Road System that contain deserts. These are just some of the many cultural sites that are deserts or that contain deserts that are registered as World Heritage.

The desert invokes a timelessness, a collapse of the past and present, a convergence of nature and culture and of space and time.[23] With the desert, as with the sea, the notion of a static territory is inherently questioned and challenged. In the desert the national, the local, the natural and the cultural converge. A desert, when designated as a cultural heritage site, becomes a spatio-legal entity that is both constituted and framed by regulation. Before regulation, it is nature, or somewhere where people live, or a place which people have cultural and/or ancestral ties to, or an occupied area… With deserts as heritage site, all these layers of meaning are stacked on top of one another.

A desert can thus be a number of things at the same time: a cultural site, when focusing on its manmade structures like buildings and temples; a natural site, when focusing on its quality as wilderness or its unique flora and fauna; or a resource, when focusing on, e.g., its oil reserves. The desert is all these at once, or just one of them, depending on how it is regulated, or not regulated.

It also depends whether there is a national regulation or whether a desert site is somehow inscribed on an international heritage list, as a cultural, natural or

23 Bruncevic, 2018.

mixed heritage site in accordance with, e.g., the 1972 World Heritage Convention. This idea that places become constituted through regulation, convention, written accounts and narratives is already well established and one that we are exploring here.[24] When it comes to the heritage sites registered on the World Heritage lists, the idea of becoming-heritage through regulation, recognition and registration is particularly interesting. In that moment the local (e.g. the Indigenous), the national (e.g. the selected site as heritage) and the global (its outstanding quality as World Heritage) converge.

Becoming heritage through inscription and registration also allows, according to Ganapathy, a distant public to "think about and lay claim to places about which they would otherwise not be concerned"[25] as well as for them to understand the narrative accounts that "serve to frame geographically distant 'others' – both people and the landscapes they inhabit".[26] In this way it can be argued that the regulation contributes to envisioning, narrating and in the end constituting a place as heritage. By becoming inscribed as World Heritage, the global is brought into the local, as the local becomes the concern of humanity as a whole. Such spatialisation and placemaking of heritage will be discussed in the last chapter. Here I want to highlight the concurrent ideas of the desert both as heritage and as playing a constitutive role in the formation of communities, e.g. as "ancestral sites". To illustrate this movement, let us look more closely at Death Valley and its many spatio-legal incarnations.

Death Valley is a famous desert site situated on the outskirts of Eastern California. It lies some hundred kilometres west of the Sierra Nevada mountain range, and it is referred to as a rain-shadow desert, meaning that the rain stays on the shadow side of the mountain range and does not reach the Valley. First and foremost, it is the ancestral home of the Native American Timbisha Shoshone tribe, who have lived in the area for hundreds of years. Secondly, its unique fauna and flora are protected under national law, as the Valley is a national park. It is also a site that has had a prominent place in popular culture. Back in 1922 the feminist adventurer Edna Brush Perkins described it in her book *The White Heart of Mojave*.[27] For Vincent Bugliosi and Curt Gentry, it has served as the scenic backdrop for their iconic book *Helter Skelter*,[28] which describes the Manson family murders. After the murders, the members of the Manson family hid in the Barker Ranch, situated in the Valley's south-west corner. It is no doubt at a mythical place, one that has many meanings as a space.

In spatial theory, spatialisation, or becoming-space, explains how space is constantly constructed and reconstructed relationally.[29] That means, a place is a matter of constant negotiation, an endless *becoming*, where a number of parallel formations occur simultaneously. I have written about such formations in more

24 See Ganapathy, 2013, and more generally Cronan, 1992; Slater, 1995.
25 Ganapathy, 2013:97.
26 Ganapathy, 2013:98.
27 Brush Perkins, 2001 [1921].
28 Bugliosi and Gentry, 2018 [1974].
29 See e.g. Lefebvre, H., 1991; Massey, 2005; Massey, 2007.

theoretical detail elsewhere,[30] and, building on that, what I am interested in here is to show the various instances of *becoming-Death-Valley*, which in turn happen through an interplay of regulation and the stacked layers of ancestry, culture, nature, narrative and time.

Its first formation as space and its most important constellation is as the ancestral territory of the Timbisha Shoshone tribe and as such it is a constitutive element in the formation of this Indigenous community. The Timbisha Shoshone community builds its ethical and political demands as a community on its connection to the ancestral territory and through a claim on land rights by their historical existence on the site. Here, claims for reparation, recognition and redistribution of land become on the one hand constitutive of the community and on the other a challenge to the sovereignty of the nation state and its territory.[31]

It is an act that can be described as internal decolonisation, i.e. reclaiming a territory within a nation state. This is common practice for Indigenous communities, involving recognising the ancestral homes of people that were at one point colonised. It also means reclaiming more than land rights. Interestingly, for example, and perhaps unsurprisingly, the people of the Timbisha Shoshone tribe find the Western name, Death Valley, given to the site by white settler colonialists to be immoral and evil. In fact, Death Valley consists of a number of sites with names that follow a similar colonising theme: Funeral Mountains, Devil's Golf Course, Hells Gate. For the Timbisha Shoshone tribe, the place is anything but connected to death, and as such the resistance to the colonial names is also part of the repatriation of the land – in this way the material land rights and the symbolical name rights of the land converge.

The other spatial framing of the site is as national park. It is designated as such through national regulation because of its unique climate and ecology. As the Valley is situated in the region of the Basin and Range, between the Rocky Mountains and the Sierra Nevada, in a place where the Earth's crust is being pulled apart, it has a unique ecological landscape. Through this formation, the interest of the nation state is stacked on top of the interest of the Indigenous community.

There are other less obvious spatial formations of the site, e.g., those connected to the manmade structures and the representations of the Valley in popular culture. There is for instance the ghost town Leadfield, which has figured in jazz music lore. There is the yearly MarsFest event held in the area that consists of presentations on extra-terrestrial life given by NASA's Search for Extraterrestrial Intelligence Institute.[32] The park's post-apocalyptic scenery figures extensively in popular culture, in a number of novels and films, most notably in *Star Wars* where R2-D2 can be seen wandering down its canyons.

Even though it is the largest national park outside Alaska in the United States, and even though it is regulated in national law as a national park like a number of other similar national parks, the Valley has not been nominated and

30 Bruncevic, 2018:129.
31 Bhabha, 1994:xv.
32 Ross, 2016a. See also Ross, 2016b.

registered as a World Heritage site under the 1972 Convention. Conversely, Yellowstone and Yosemite national parks, that are very similar in nature, have been registered as World Heritage sites. Neither has the Valley been discussed as a potential or prospective nominee, as have the Petrified Forest National Park in Arizona and Central Park in New York, which are both currently on the tentative list for registration. The tentative list for registration is an inventory of cultural properties that each State Party compiles and that it intends to consider for nomination as registered heritage in the future. Why the Valley is not on such a list is not known. Both Yellowstone and Yosemite national parks are, like Death Valley, directly connected to Native American communities, so it being an ancestral territory does not in itself prohibit registration and nomination. The fact that Central Park is on the tentative list and considered for nomination probably has to do with its cultural rather than natural outstanding significance. The prominent cultural position that the Valley has had, and continues to have, is thus not considered as something that would bar it from nomination either.

What we can see here is, first of all, how heritage sites, and particularly sites that are connected to Indigenous communities, can be spatialised by being conceived of or framed by regulation, national as well as international. They also become-space through other systems, e.g., by figuring in popular culture and folklore, and as such become iconic and symbolic spaces in people's minds. For instance, when prompted by the Timbisha Shoshone tribe to consider changing the name Death Valley, allegedly the Park Service claimed that it would be impossible to do so now as the name Death Valley has become part of the *folklore*. But to which *folk* such lore is attributed to, and how such a community is framed and envisioned, is a different matter altogether, one that brings out the multicultural and transnational layers of this site. Furthermore, the constitution of space does not only happen through regulation but also through the imaginings, and authorised heritage discourses, that are disseminated, e.g. through registration or conversely by popular culture. Therefore the aspect of folklore is directly connected to the constitution of space and the communities that claim that space as their own.

Folklore: traditional cultural expressions and intellectual property

This means that, other than claiming land rights, the Indigenous communities often also have to reclaim their folklore, that is, their narratives, internal cultural practices and traditions that contribute to constituting an Indigenous people as a community. In regulation, folklore is usually referred to as traditional cultural expressions (henceforth tce), and other practices are referred to as traditional knowledge (henceforth tk). The use, access to and ownership of such cultural expressions and traditional knowledge form one of the key components in DRIPS. Both are defined in art 31, which states that the Indigenous peoples:

> have the right to maintain, control, protect and develop their cultural heritage, *traditional knowledge* and *traditional cultural expressions*, as well as the

> manifestations of their sciences, technologies and cultures, including human and genetic resources, seeds, medicines, knowledge of the properties of fauna and flora, oral traditions, literatures, designs, sports and traditional games and visual and performing arts. They also have the right to maintain, control, protect and develop their intellectual property over such cultural heritage, traditional knowledge, and traditional cultural expressions[33]

It is claimed that what singles out DRIPS as a regulatory instrument is its carefully worded terminology, formulated without falling back on or relying on what can be deemed as Eurocentric or Western taxonomies. The definitions of tce:s and tk:s in DRIPS do not for instance separate natural resources from cultural resources, land rights from cultural rights, tangible from intangible, written from oral, etc. However, it could equally be argued that it is precisely this type of wording that upholds a colonising narrative that envisions the Indigenous as something exotic and foreign and therefore its heritage remains not as strongly protected as other similar "Western" expressions.

Such reading of DRIPS can for instance indicate the reason why Indigenous cultural expressions and knowledge as tce and tk are regulated within the scope of this comparatively weak regulatory instrument, rather than understanding such expressions and knowledge as falling under the scope of much stronger regimes such as the intellectual property regulation. The division between intellectual and physical property is of course a Western one, and not consistent with Indigenous understandings of tce and tk. Maybe the tce:s and tk:s were never envisioned or meant to be falling under the commodifying, proprietary structures in intellectual property law.

Still, it is almost impossible to disregard the intellectual property framework and how it works together with DRIPS, and what role it plays in terms of the construction and the protection of Indigenous communities' folklore. Intellectual property can function as a contextual background for comparison, particularly as it is often invoked in many instances of misappropriation of Indigenous heritage.

Macmillan points out for instance, that both tce and tk could in theory be framed as intellectual property, and that attempts have been made to claim it as intellectual property, when it has been misappropriated. These attempts have not been widely successful. Blakeney also points out that there have been attempts to claim Indigenous heritage as intellectual property, both to counteract misappropriation and as a prohibitory measure taken by the communities in order to protect it from being copied or misused. Doctrinally, DRIPS and the intellectual property regimes have different rationales and are in principle incommensurable. Yet, there are many examples where intellectual property and Indigenous heritage have been placed side by side, often in the claims for protection of tce and tk as intellectual property. In such instances intellectual property law and DRIPS converge in and through a claim for a communal intellectual property right.[34]

33 [my emphasis].

34 Many of the objects and practices defined as cultural heritage and cultural expressions in e.g. DRIPS could very well fall under the scope of trademarks or be

While the idea of a communal intellectual property right is foreign to the intellectual property regime, many Indigenous communities have nonetheless tried to turn to intellectual property law in order to attempt to claim protection for their tce:s such as their traditional symbols and images, arguing that these constitute communal works that can and should be protected by copyright law. Maybe this has been done since DRIPS is in itself a weak legal instrument that fails to enforce such claims. Indigenous communities have therefore turned to "harder" regulation, such as intellectual property, that provides sanctions and enforcement possibilities.

However, turning traditional cultural expressions into private intellectual property rights in order to protect them from misappropriation is not a straightforward endeavour either, since the construct of intellectual property does not directly lend itself to claims of communal rights.[35] This became obvious in a number of cases involving cultural appropriation, e.g., in the case of the appropriation of a traditional Indigenous image, the so-called "Wandjina", that was used as a logo by an Australian surfboard manufacturer.[36] When the surfboard manufacturer attempted to appropriate the cultural symbol as a trademark, the Indigenous community fought back in order to counteract the commodification and misuse of the traditional imagery. This is fully understandable as Indigenous cultural expressions are connected to wider, more fundamental, claims than merely the possibility of commercially exploiting and controlling a communal cultural symbol. For the Indigenous communities, the traditional cultural expressions are also tied to the political recognition as people and to fundamental rights to, e.g., self-determination and legal recognition as communities.[37]

It could therefore also be argued that DRIPS has been formulated to resist the commodifying categorisations of Indigenous intangible heritage, and that both tce and tk have been defined much more broadly than what would usually fall under the scope of the intellectual property regulation. The definition in art 31 DRIPS encompasses heritage and practices that would not normally fall under any of the existing intellectual property regimes. This is also clear from articles 11–13 in the declaration. Art 11.1 mentions for instance the right to "practice and revitalise", art 12.1 the right to "manifest, practise, develop", art 13.1 the right to "revitalise, use, develop and transmit" to future generations Indigenous peoples' histories, languages, oral traditions, philosophies, writing systems and literatures, etc. None of these fall under current intellectual property regimes. Whether this way of regulating Indigenous tk and tce has an emancipatory or a re-colonising effect, I will leave to each reader to consider for themselves. It is also important to note that art 12 in DRIPS, in my view rather unexpectedly, mentions the repatriation of human remains, which goes beyond intellectual property.

claimed as intellectual property, e.g. "oral traditions, literatures, designs, sports and traditional games and visual and performing arts", see art 31 DRIPS.

35 Rahmatian, 2007; Blakeney, 2009; Blakeney, 2013.

36 Janke, 2003; Janke, 2005. See also the Australian case *Neowarra v State of Western Australia*, [2003] FCA 1402 (Austl.) as well as Blakeney, 2013.

37 See e.g. Anghie, 1992.

Clearly, relying on intellectual property law alone to protect outputs of communal practices is not enough and definitely not without friction, to say the least. A communal intellectual property right does not exist in intellectual property law, at least not yet. The lack of it opens up a fetishisation of the individual as the author of culture and therefore as the rights holder and legal subject that carries rights. An autonomous individual (either as a human being or as a juridical person like a company) must be identified as the proprietor of the intellectual property, in order for it to be safeguarded as *property* under the intellectual property regimes. This can be seen as colonising, as taking traditional knowledge out of the Indigenous common pool and into a private sphere. Conversely, cultural heritage law in turn gives rise to a fetishisation of a community: an identifiable (legally recognised) community is needed in order to identify to whom the heritage can be attributed in order to be protected as heritage. When such community cannot be defined, or when the Indigenous is in itself diverse, the transnational is revealed. In this way, we can see that transnational heritage cannot be covered by regulation that deals with Indigenous communities, and therefore it remains unprotected, and not envisioned, at all.

Heterogeneity: minorities and the migrant community

So far, we have seen how the transnational is revealed in many places, yet how it is also excluded from regulation when it comes to the regulation that defines both the state as community and Indigenous people as community. Let us now look at the last community formation that is recognised in regulation, namely the minority.

Art 27 of the International Covenant on Civil and Political Rights (ICCPR) deals with minority rights. It concerns groups of people that are not defined either as the majority in a nation state or as an Indigenous community.[38] ICCPR was briefly mentioned in Chapter 2, but it was not listed among the core ten instruments. Here it is important to mention ICCPR as an instrument that will be connected to one of the core regulatory instruments, namely the 2005 Cultural Diversity Convention. Art 27 ICCPR states the following:

> In those States in which ethnic, religious or linguistic minorities exist, persons belonging to such minorities shall not be denied the right, in community with the other members of their group, to enjoy their own culture, to profess and practise their own religion, or to use their own language.

This is a significant provision when it comes to studying community formations in regulation. What is interesting to highlight here is that a minority is formulated and recognised as a community through its ethnic, religious or linguistic commonality and marked by the fact that a group's belonging differs from the dominant, or the majority, community.

38 Nykolaishen, 2012. See also UN HRC, General Comment No. 23, Art 27 (Rights of Minorities), para. 7.

It is also important to remind ourselves that minority rights are placed among civil and political rights, i.e. rights that are of the highest dignity in human rights law. This is a mandatory provision for states.[39] The provision should be read together with art 15 (a) of the International Covenant on Economic, Social and Cultural Rights (ICESCR), which states that everyone has the right to take part in cultural life. The provision does not refer only to national culture but to all cultures, including the minority cultures, that exist and are exercised on a territory.

Furthermore, Art 15 ICESCR has been interpreted as including a duty for the state to protect the cultural heritage of all citizens belonging both to its national community and to its minorities, as well as to protect all cultural heritage that can be deemed cross-cultural and as such to be of benefit for humanity as a whole.[40] ICESCR is thus also directly connected to the UNESCO framework and to the 2005 Cultural Diversity Convention.

The 2005 Convention is a significant instrument that mentions minority communities and their cultural rights. In order to protect the diversity of the global cultural output, it is stated in the preamble to the 2005 Convention that it is expressly:

> taking into account the importance of the vitality of cultures, including for persons belonging to minorities and indigenous peoples, as manifested in their freedom to create, disseminate and distribute their traditional cultural expressions and to have access thereto, so as to benefit them for their own development

Art 2 of the 2005 Convention also recognises "equal dignity of and respect for all cultures, including the cultures of persons belonging to minorities and indigenous peoples". This means that the Convention recognises the importance of diversity for the conception of community and that a minority can be such a recognised community. Let me put the 2005 Convention in context.

We already saw in Chapter 2 that the 2005 Convention inscribes itself in the human rights regime and within the context of the UDHR, most notably article 27. Art 27 UDHR mentions cultural rights. The 2005 Convention is not equally focused on the nation state as the core community to which rights are attributed, and cultural heritage is treated as being the driving force for global cultural diversity. However, art 2 in the 2005 Convention still reiterates the centrality of the sovereignty of states, with the nuance that states cannot uphold diversity if they are only protecting national culture by keeping it "pure" and closed off. Instead a multicultural line is premiered where states are

39 See e.g. CERD, General Recommendation No. 32 on "The meaning and scope of special measures in the International Convention on the Elimination of All Forms [of] Racial Discrimination". See also *Khurshid Mustafa and Tarzibachi vs. Sweden*, the European Court of Human Rights (ECtHR).

40 O'Keefe, 2008.

encouraged to interact with each other, without prejudice against any one cultural output. Equal dignity and respect for all cultures as well as allowing the developing states to safeguard their own cultural expressionism are thus highlighted.

As mentioned in Chapter 2, the 2005 Convention has around 140 signatories. It expressly references global poverty, traditional knowledge, the position of women in society, the importance of the free flow of ideas subscribing to multicultural views of the world in terms of peoples, linguistic diversity, globalisation, culture – simply put, cultural diversity. Cultural diversity is defined in art 4 of the convention as

> the manifold ways in which the cultures of groups and societies find expression. These expressions are passed on within and among groups and societies. Cultural diversity is made manifest not only through the varied ways in which the cultural heritage of humanity is expressed, augmented and transmitted through the variety of cultural expressions, but also through diverse modes of artistic creation, production, dissemination, distribution and enjoyment, whatever the means and technologies used.

Conclusively, the minority and the Indigenous communities are considered to be similar yet have different regulatory framings. Both are mentioned in the preamble of the 2005 Convention. But unlike art 27 ICCPR, which expressly mentions religion, language and ethnic belonging as markers of community identity, the same is not the case for the 2005 Convention. It more generally refers to tce:s, which we saw above in, e.g., DRIPS.

The minority is thus the third and last recognised community in regulation. This community category's regulatory standing can also be deduced from a number of other legal instruments such as UDHR, but also the 1970 World Heritage Convention, the Framework Convention on National Minorities, and the Faro Framework Convention on the Value of Cultural Heritage for Society. Finally, before we conclude this chapter on the three main community categories, let us look at the migrant community. The migrant community is a type of community that cannot be directly defined as a minority as it is too diverse. Here, however, it can be approached as an unrecognised transnational community.

Poetics of exile: cultural heritage of the émigrés in diaspora

To conceptualise the provisions concerning recognised minorities, and how they affect transnational communities, we can briefly look at the conception of minority as a community in practice. As we saw above, a number of the legal instruments stress the importance of an ethnic, language or cultural commonality as being a constituting element for the minority community. One particular group that is interesting to look at in this context because it cannot easily be framed within the conception of a recognised minority is the refugee or migrant community.

I want to turn to the cultural works created by people in exile. We can begin the discussion by looking more closely at two works of art by the artist, ceramist and writer Edmund de Waal. Both examples investigate the issues of migration and memory. The first deals with the fate of an heirloom, a Japanese *netsuke* collection, that de Waal inherited from his maternal family, the Ephrussi family. He wrote about this collection, its fate and meaning in his memoir *The Hare with Amber Eyes*.[41] The second is one of his latest works. It is from 2019 and it deals with similar issues of migration and memory, called *Library of Exile*.

The story of the Japanese *netsuke* collection, including the titular hare with the amber eyes, encompasses European history, a family saga, issues of identity and questions about the geographical and moral belongings of artworks. It begins with de Waal's great-grandfather Viktor von Ephrussi in turn-of-the-century Vienna, a city that was turning nationalist. The story then goes by way of Japan, France and the UK, among many other places, to once again return, temporarily at least, to Vienna.

De Waal, a British national, inherited the collection of traditional Japanese figurines, *netsuke*, carved in wood or ivory. The collection was initially acquired by Charles Ephrussi, a cousin to his grandfather. Ephrussi was a writer and art collector, living in Paris at the turn of the century. Collecting Japanese *netsuke* like these was fashionable at the time, and such small sculptures were very sought after by art buyers in Europe. Charles Ephrussi gave the collection he acquired to his family in Vienna as a wedding gift. It was later brought to the UK by de Waal's refugee father in 1939. Eventually, it found its way back to Austria in the late 2010s as a long-term loan from the de Waal family to the Jewish Museum in Vienna.

The collection first comprised 264 figurines. As a travelling collection of objects, it became a symbol of migration. Its movement from one place to another tied it to nations, communities and individuals in different ways. Recently, some seventy of the figurines from the collection were auctioned for the UK charity Refugee Council – particularly for the benefit of unaccompanied refugee children coming to the UK. Another part of the collection was given as mentioned on a long-term loan to the Jewish Museum in Vienna.

The loan to the museum in Vienna was considered a controversial decision as the family had almost been destroyed by the Nazis less than a hundred years before. It went against the now-established practice of resituating Jewish art to Jewish families, and not the other way around. When asked to comment on the decision to allow part of the collection to return to Vienna, de Waal referred to the loan as "invert restitution". This was a way of taking back objects that embody migrant stories in order to reclaim their place in Viennese history. In current Vienna, the objects could acquire a new symbolical meaning. Such invert restitution, de Waal claims, highlights the cross-cultural experience of the past and the present that is embodied in art.[42]

41 de Waal, 2011.

42 The Art Newspaper Podcast from 17 May 2019: https://www.theartnewspaper.com/podcast/should-museums-sell-works-of-art-plus-activism-at-the-whitney-biennial

In this context, the notion of "invert restitution" is interesting as it challenges many of the established practices and notions of community. As we saw above, restitution to individuals within the scope of the 1995 UNIDROIT Convention concerns the return of artworks stripped from people during, for instance, the Holocaust. Restitution has to do with healing or at least soothing the losses suffered in times of war, and here it is directly connected to the Shoah and the Jewish diaspora.

The 1995 UNIDROIT Convention has few signatories, as we saw, and therefore it is considered a weak regulatory instrument to rely on for restitution. The restitution of specifically Nazi looted art is further regulated in the so-called Washington Principles outlined at the 1998 Washington Conference on Holocaust-Era Assets (Washington Principles). Eleven principles were agreed on in Washington regarding how to deal with Nazi confiscated, or looted, art. The principles state that the countries must acknowledge that: (1) art has been confiscated by the Nazis, (2) relevant records and archives should be open to research, (3) resources should be made available to facilitate the identification of all art that had been confiscated by the Nazis, (4) consideration should be given to unavoidable gaps or ambiguities in the provenance in light of the passage of time and the circumstances of the Holocaust era, (5) every effort should be made to publicise art that is found, (6) efforts should be made to establish a central registry of such information, (7) pre-war owners and their heirs should be encouraged to come forward and make known their claims, (8) if the pre-war owners can be identified, steps should be taken expeditiously to achieve a just and fair solution, (9) if the pre-war owners cannot be identified, steps should be taken expeditiously to achieve a just and fair solution, (10) commissions or other bodies should be established to identify such art, and (11) nations should be encouraged to develop national processes to implement the principles.[43]

The Washington Principles have led to positive developments in terms of return, even though they have been criticised for being neither binding nor a strong legal instrument. They have also been criticised for a number of other shortcomings, e.g., that they address public institutions and museums only; that there is a lot of vagueness in terms of terminology; and that they particularly focus on confiscated artworks and not on other forms of dispossessions.[44] Like many instruments that we have seen so far, the Washington Principles were entered into in a voluntary fashion, and there is no legal way through which institutions or nations can be forced to comply with the principles other than on an ethical and political level of commitment. Here too, there are very few signatories to the principles; at the time of writing only some 46 governments have signed the commitment.

43 Washington Conference Principles on Nazi-Confiscated Art (1998).

44 Art Law Blog, 2019. https://www.artatlaw.com/blogpost/architect-washington-principles-takes-stock

Therefore, it was all the more interesting, not to say controversial, when the de Waal family returned their art (that was not looted *per se*, and as such the principles are inapplicable, but that was still in grave danger during the Nazi era) to Vienna. Such acts can be significant to mention when regulation of transnational heritage is discussed. Even though this can be seen as a controversial decision, it forces us to consider what a migrant community is, what the traumas of the Jewish people during the Holocaust can symbolise for the current refugee community in Vienna, and why returns like these can instantly serve as a transnational symbol for the living, contemporaneous heritage that is created by migrants and people in diaspora. We are confronted with modern-day Vienna, a city that is now multicultural, globally oriented and welcoming of refugees at the same time as the country is experiencing a new politically conservative climate with a young generation drawn to far-right extremism. To place such historical heritage in that context gives the items the possibility to invoke the past and maybe serve as a warning to the present. As such, the collection is significant to many, recognised and unrecognised, communities.

Continuing to explore a similar topic, in 2019 de Waal created the work *Library of Exile*. It is a "space to sit and read and be"[45] – an installation that exhibits and makes available books written by people who have been forced into exile through persecution on the grounds of religion, race, gender, beliefs, etc. *Library of Exile* is a work of art as well as a working library, stacked with books that can be taken down, browsed, discovered and read. There are over two thousand books in the *Library*, including classics by Ovid, Dante and Victor Hugo, books written by prominent women authors in exile such as Marina Tsvetaeva and Judith Kerr, and by non-Western authors such as the Zambian author Kayo Chingonyi, the Syrian author Samar Yazbek, the Albanian author Ismail Kadare, and other less expected books such as the one written by de Waal's grandmother Elisabeth de Waal about her experiences as a refugee.[46] Some 1500 authors and books written in eighty-eight original languages altogether have been included in the *Library*. The books are in translation and not in their original language, highlighting the migratory and diasporic role of language.

De Waal constructed the walls of the library as a porcelain slip that encloses the library. The slip is layered with sheets of gold. It is engraved with the names of the lost libraries of the world, from the ancient library of Alexandria and the university libraries destroyed in Europe during WWII, to the libraries more recently destroyed in Sarajevo, Aleppo, Timbuktu, Mosul, etc. The installation is framed by the history of lost and migrant culture, the work itself trying somehow to repair some of the forcefully forgotten stories and memories. De Waal provided 'ex libris' labels, and the visitors were invited to write their names in the books that mattered to them the most, enabling them to also inscribe themselves in the histories of the lost libraries, as well as his artwork.

45 British Museum website. Edmund de Waal: *Library of Exile*. https://www.britishmuseum.org/exhibitions/edmund-de-waal-library-exile

46 Full catalogue available at *Library of Exile*: https://libraryofexile.infoteca.it/start

The books included in the library have been written by authors that have had to move across borders in order to write, and the work itself is also a migrant. *Library* was first shown at the Venice Biennale in 2019 and then sent to the Japanisches Palais in Dresden. Thereafter it was installed at the British Museum in London, and it will eventually travel to Mosul, where all the books will be donated to the new library of the University of Mosul with the help of Book Aid International.

In both *The Hare with Amber Eyes* and *Library in Exile*, de Waal engages with culture in transit – culture that moves from one place to another, that crosses borders, that collects stories of migration, loss and hope. The idea of exile shapes memory and belonging, but it also adds the multi-lingual, multicultural, transnational, to the places to which culture travels by way of migration. Such cultural richness and diversity is the very essence of transnational heritage. Cross-cultural pollination is the core trait of transnational heritage.

In this chapter I have presented three types of communities that are recognised in regulation as able to have culture attributed to them. To recapitulate, in order of regulatory importance these are: states, Indigenous peoples and minorities. However, what has transpired throughout the chapter is that while much of the existing regulation is progressive in many ways, admirably dealing with post-colonial heritage, inscribing itself in the discourses of human rights and global diversity, striving towards ethical and just practices, there is so much of the transnational that is not recognised. The three community categories still rely on some type of assumption of sedation, static territory and mono-culture conceptualised through three differently sized communities of the same type. But, and as is apparent in the work of de Waal, for example, these assumptions can be detrimental for the transnational, that is, the itinerant, the deterritorialised, the migratory, the culture that is multicultural in nature. In that way, the transnational does not fit any of the existing community categories and is therefore left out of the regulation.

4 Diversity: transnational cultural heritage

Acknowledging the core regulatory instruments and the UNESCO legal regime as presented above, this fourth chapter now concentrates on the three recognised categories of heritage: tangible, intangible and digital heritage. This chapter discusses three case studies in order to point out in more depth the transnational in heritage as well as analyse the challenges to existing heritage categories.

We saw how international public law relies on three categories of community. In this chapter we will now study the three prevalent categories of heritage. Tangible heritage is regulated in, e.g., the 1972 World Heritage Convention and in the 2001 Underwater Heritage Convention; intangible heritage in the 2003 Intangible Heritage Convention; and digital heritage in the 2005 Cultural Diversity Convention as well as in the 2003 UNESCO Charter on the Preservation of the Digital Heritage.

Here, we will see how the recognised categories of heritage are strengthened in law and how this categorisation affects transnational heritage. This chapter focuses on three case studies:

For tangible heritage:
- the demolition of a Soviet building in post-socialist Lithuania;
For intangible heritage:
- tasseography as intangible heritage in modern-day Turkey; and
For digital heritage:
- the hack of the Nefertiti bust in Germany and the creation of the work *The Other Nefertiti.*

Tangible heritage: building memories

All eyes of the art world turned to Lithuania when its Pavilion was awarded the Golden Lion at the 2019 Venice Biennale. Until then, its art, architecture and cultural heritage were still being side-stepped, treated as not the most obvious choice for exploration and study. In the aftermath of the Golden Lion award, there was a collective understanding that Vilnius was being neglected both in terms of its artistic significance and as a treasure trove of the cultural and architectural heritage of north-eastern Europe. Historically, it is one of the most

DOI: 10.4324/9781003212683-4

important cities in the region, but in terms of being recognised for its art and heritage Vilnius has remained comparatively in the background, maybe because the bulk of its more recent modern cultural history played out behind the Iron Curtain. Lithuania gained independence from the Soviet Union in 1990.

My work often takes me to places that I may not necessarily have found on my own. Vilnius turned out to be one such place. It is the home of a unique historical Old Town, which is listed as World Heritage under the 1972 World Heritage Convention. It is also the home of a number of contemporary galleries and art spaces. In addition, Vilnius has an impressive architectural heritage, both historical and modern. One of its most notable contemporary architectural sites is the MO Modern Art Museum designed by the renowned architect Daniel Libeskind. In 2008 Zaha Hadid won an international competition to design the Vilnius Guggenheim Hermitage Museum, but unfortunately that project was scrapped and never materialised.

My host and guide in Vilnius was a lady who is an architect and lawyer, whom I had met in Riga a couple of years before when I was teaching a post-graduate summer course in Art Law. She invited me to Vilnius to give a talk on cultural heritage, architecture and law. When we met in Vilnius, I had just finished writing a book on access to art and cultural commons. One thing she and I shared was a passion for art in public spaces and the expressions of cultural heritage and identity that happen there: in the streets, under the skies, without walls or boundaries. As we walked through the old streets of Vilnius, we talked about the right to the city, and how the urban space is best experienced as an open-air gallery.

Vilnius was founded in the early 14th century by the Grand Duke of Lithuania, Gediminas. Legend has it that an iron wolf came to the Duke in a dream and told him to build a city on that very spot. And so much has happened there since the 14th century, all of which is wonderfully reflected in the city's buildings and architectural heritage. On our tour through Vilnius I saw the extravagant Gothic Church of St. Anne, the Baroque rolling gate of the Basilian Monastery and the Gate of Dawn, the neoclassical Vilnius Cathedral inspired by the ancient Greek temples and the derelict but still impressive Soviet-era building, Palace of Sports. There was so much architecture to be experienced, such as the National Gallery of Art, as well as street art by legendary artists such as Millo, Os Gemeos and Tankpetrol. I was even taken to the little-known Independent Republic of Uzupis within the city, which is not unlike Christiania, the independent free-town and international commune in Copenhagen, with its famously tolerant attitude towards drugs and alternative ways of life. Uzupis, as I was shown, has its own Constitution, which is written on its city walls, and it states in its opening paragraph that "Everyone has the right to live by the River Vilnelė, and the River Vilnelė has the right to flow by everyone." This, for me hitherto hidden, independent republic was inviting me and all its visitors to follow its three mottos: *Don't Fight, Don't Win, Don't Surrender.*

So much of Lithuanian history is exhibited in Vilnius and its architectural heritage. Yes, it has had a turbulent history. With Riga and Tallinn, the capitals of Latvia and Estonia respectively, Vilnius is one of the three capital cities of the

Baltic states that symbolise the mosaic of traditions and indeed shared memories of the area, through their historical transnational connections to the Nordic countries, Poland and, of course, the Soviet Union. Like its neighbouring cities Minsk, the capital of Belarus, or Baku, the capital of Azerbaijan, Vilnius will surprise its visitors with its progressive and modern use of the urban space that sits comfortably side by side with well-preserved historic buildings and local heritage. Or like Tbilisi, the capital of Georgia, it grapples with the architectural remnants from the Soviet era: what to preserve and what to demolish, what to keep as memory, and what to remove and forget.

It struck me that the history of the city is told through the fate of its impressive Baroque Church of St. Casimir. The Church is the first and oldest Baroque church in Vilnius. It was built in the early 17th century. It had been a Roman Catholic church until the late 19th century, when it was first converted to an Orthodox church under Russian occupation and then to an Evangelical Lutheran church in 1915 under a brief German occupation during the Great War. It was damaged during WWII, and for a couple of decades it was even turned into the Museum of Atheism during the Communist era. It went back to being Roman Catholic in 1989, shortly before the country gained its independence. The symbolism is undeniable, the transnational almost palpable.

I was in Vilnius to take part in a roundtable discussion on cultural heritage and architecture. A representative of the Lithuanian Chamber of Architects on the same panel presented a case concerning a building that caught my attention. What had happened to that particular building, much like with the Church of St. Casimir, bore a similar testament to the city's history. The building, one of the most impressive Brutalist Soviet-era buildings in Vilnius, had once housed the traffic police, but it was now due to be demolished. However, protests had erupted from the general public and the Lithuanian Union of Architects, demanding that it be safeguarded.

The old police building was understood to be one of the best examples of the work by the Lithuanian architects Gytis Ramunis and Kestutis Pempė, both winners of many distinguished architectural awards. It had been built in 1982. It had also been awarded the very prestigious accolade Best Design by the Soviet Union's Union of Architects in 1986, the Lithuanian National Culture and Arts Prize as well as the Lithuanian government's Art Prize. It was already listed as a cultural monument; however, it was not listed as World Heritage like the buildings in the Old Town of Vilnius.

In 2015, the German supermarket chain Lidl had purchased the police building solely in order to acquire the land, a striking riverfront site. Lidl's plan was to demolish the building and then build the Lidl Lithuanian headquarters on the site. Nonetheless, the plans for demolition were vehemently opposed by the community of architects and the Lithuanian public. It was claimed that demolition would greatly affect Lithuanian architectural heritage because of the building's unique artistic value, as well as what it represented historically. Initially, the government of Lithuania stopped the plans for demolition, but after negotiation the demolition was then granted.

Under Lithuanian copyright law and its detailed architectural code, architects are allowed to document their buildings before demolition. They are given the possibility to record, photograph and measure the buildings one last time for archival purposes and for their own records. This is done for artistic and historical reasons as well as to keep the memory of demolished sites alive. Since the architects Gytis Ramunis and Kestutis Pempė were both deceased when the Lithuanian government granted demolition, the Lithuanian Chambers of Architects organised instead a communal event, where the architects that were members of the chambers were called to record the site for archival purposes together, in an act of solidarity. They documented the building and then it was demolished.

Still, questions were raised by the community of architects regarding what modern architectural heritage is, what makes it valuable, as well as how (and whether) it should be protected and listed as World Heritage.[1] It was obvious to everyone that demolishing buildings like these with a unique story can be problematic, that it could be seen as silencing them from testifying to the historical events they have witnessed. But in this instance, it was also a question of a Soviet building, representing the tormented history that many of the Lithuanian people would rather not be reminded of or remember.[2]

With the police building, the integrity of architecture as art and as cultural heritage was called into question. The proprietary rights of the multinational corporation Lidl and its operational and commercial use of the site were placed opposite the interest of preserving a Soviet-era building in now-independent Lithuania. The discussion concerned the balance between the intellectual property rights of the original architects, the cultural heritage rights of the Lithuanian people and Lidl's private land rights to the immovable property that they had purchased.

Let us disentangle the various arguments stacked up so far. First, there are the sovereign rights of the nation state Lithuania, which gained independence from the Soviet Union in 1990. The public spaces throughout the country, but most prominently in its capital Vilnius, and much of its cultural and architectural heritage reflect this fluctuating history. The urban space represents the Lithuanian people and the claims they have on their public space and cultural heritage.

Then we have the intellectual property rights of the architects and their heirs which were in some way respected. And finally we have the rights of Lidl, the new property owner, that prevailed and in the end decided how the site should be used and what should be kept on it, or demolished.

As we saw with the Church of St. Casimir, it is not unusual for buildings to change guises and functions over time. These buildings change their meaning as

1 Archmap: http://archmap.lt/en/articles/lietuviu-keliu-policijos-pastato-virazai/
2 The Baltic Course Online, 17 October 2016: http://www.baltic-course.com/eng/real_estate/?doc=124818. See also Archmap; Archmuziejus: http://archmuziejus.lt/en/about-architectural-communication-and-the-case-of-the-police-building-at-gira ites-street-3; Pakulniewicz, 2017.

the outside conditions change – they morph, transform, they are usurped, simply used as canvases onto which ideology can be projected. Unlike the police station, the Church of St. Casimir was spared from demolition. The two buildings are of course in many ways different – the first one a church that has historically been used for both religious and secular purposes, the second a building built as a seat of an occupying state's power, symbolising its violence and authority. Still, a comparison is not unwarranted. The police station was designed by local architects even though it was commissioned by the Soviet Union. As such, it had a cultural, and political, significance. Even though local people and Lithuanian architects fought hard to save the building as a cultural monument and even though it was no longer in use by the police, they could still not protect it from destruction. Whether the decision to demolish has to do with a general lack of appreciation of Soviet architectural heritage in Lithuania, the public's "inability to appreciate it due to its characteristics, compared to the heritage from previous periods of time",[3] or because of the traumatic memories it represents for the people, remains unclear.

That the architectural can be political, and that it is directly connected to the production of public space and with it the community, is obvious.[4] The design of buildings and public space governs how people can move, what they see on a daily basis and how they can interact with the space and each other. This can have a direct effect on how the public is represented and constituted, how it understands itself. A transnational building like the police station is therefore particularly interesting to analyse in this context.

Relevant case law and additional regulatory measures

Some remarks that concern international law and its doctrines will need to be made here. I have already obliquely talked about the doctrine of *sovereign equality of states* in international law, which commits all states to respect and recognise each other's sovereignty, independence, territorial, integrity and national unity.[5] We have also discussed peoples' right to self-determination.[6] The requirement that a state needs to select and nominate its important heritage in order for it to be protected under the 1972 World Heritage Convention has also been mentioned.

There is a substantial body of case law in this area.[7] There are, furthermore, some particularly interesting cases from the European Court of Human Rights (ECtHR) that can be mentioned in connection to the Vilnius case. In one of these cases the ECtHR was asked to consider a right to property that concerned issues of cultural heritage. In this case, from 2008, *Debelianovi vs.*

3 Archmap.
4 See e.g. Sorkin, 2018 and Pallasmaa, 2012.
5 See e.g. Ansong, 2016. See also Parfitt, 2018.
6 Declaration on the Granting of Independence to Colonial Countries and Peoples (1960).
7 See e.g. Jakubowski, 2016.

Bulgaria, two brothers claimed violation of the right to property in accordance with Protocol No. 1, Article 1, of the European Convention of Human Rights (ECHR). The government of Bulgaria had expropriated a house belonging to their father. The house had been selected as national cultural property, as a historic monument, and after its expropriation it had been turned into a museum.

In its ruling, the ECtHR argued that the preservation of cultural and architectural heritage can be a legitimate reason for expropriation, and that it can legitimise a state's interference with the right to property. However, in this particular case, the Court stated:

> In spite of the legitimate aim, the duration of the interference together with the uncertainty experienced by the applicants, who were effectively prevented from enjoying their right to property, further aggravated the detrimental effects of the interference on the applicants. The Court found a violation of Protocol No. 1, Article 1, in respect of Bulgaria.[8]

Interestingly, in this case the ECtHR also stressed the importance of the 1985 Convention for the Protection of the Architectural Heritage of Europe, particularly articles 3 and 4. Article 3 states that each member state must take statutory measures to protect its architectural heritage such as monuments, groups of buildings and sites; article 4 among other things allows the states to conduct compulsory purchases of protected properties. What is also noteworthy is that the same article requires the member states to prevent any disfigurement, dilapidation and demolition of protected properties.

What can be reaffirmed from *Debelianovi vs. Bulgaria* is that only the heritage selected and designated as heritage by the state can fall under the scope of regulation that protects heritage. We already saw this tendency in the previous chapters, and here it becomes all the more visible. Even though the ECtHR highlights the importance of cultural heritage as a matter of public interest that can even justify compulsory purchases and expropriation of private property, this regulation becomes irrelevant and inapplicable when a site is not nominated as such.

Placing the *Debelianovi vs. Bulgaria* case side by side with the case of the police building in Vilnius, we can deduce that they are in many ways similar, but that in many other ways they are each other's mirror opposites. With the police building, we have an architectural site that was listed as a cultural monument, but that the state did not designate as heritage. The private ownership rights of Lidl were seen as overriding and prevailing over the cultural heritage interest, and the demolition could be granted. In the Bulgarian case on the other hand, the brothers' ownership of the house was deemed as less important than the protection of the property that the Bulgarian government designated as national heritage. In that vein, even though the brothers were compensated in the end for the expropriation of the property due to the

8 *Debelianovi vs. Bulgaria.* See further Claridge and Xanthaki, 2016:69.

circumstances of their individual case, the house itself remained protected as heritage, and it was spared from demolition as well as from being used privately by the family.

In another interesting case from 2002, *Podkolzina vs. Latvia*, minority rights and cultural identity were at issue. In this case, a member of the Russian-speaking minority in Latvia had been struck from the list of candidates in the elections to the Latvian parliament. The individual in question was said not to have sufficient knowledge of the Latvian language. The question was whether a violation of the right to free elections under the ECHR Protocol No. 1, article 3 as well as discrimination under article 14 had taken place. The individual, Mrs Ingrīda Podkolzina, had been born in Latvia and was a Latvian citizen.

The court recognised that, while the right to vote and stand for election is important, it is not absolute. The states are given broad latitude to establish constitutional rules and limits to such rights. In this case, Mrs Podkolzina did indeed speak Latvian. However, she had taken a language test and not scored sufficiently high. The court ruled that a language requirement in itself must be seen as a legitimate request for people who are standing for election. Such a requirement is needed in order to have a functioning administration and institutional system. Still, they ruled, when all the circumstances were considered, the elimination of this applicant from the list was seen as not proportionate, and the court deemed that the right to free election had been violated. The court did not examine a breach of article 14.[9]

What this case brings to the surface, and what is relevant for our Vilnius case, is that a Russian-speaking minority seems to be established and recognised in the Baltic region. While Latvia and Lithuania naturally have two different national legal systems, their history is sufficiently similar as a matter of comparison here. What is interesting is that the minority community and here their language is highlighted as being a constituting factor of this group. If we compare the argument raised here with the discussion on migration and language that was raised earlier in conjunction with Edmund de Waal's *Library of Exile*, a similar pattern can be discerned. Here it is not a question of a refugee community and its heritage, but of a community that has been "left behind" or that has not moved, that has stayed in one place, but where the national constitution and make-up of the nation state have changed over time. These matters lie at the core of a community's existence, self-determination and recognition.

We can begin to see more clearly how the contours of a community are narrated and built through regulation. Being recognised as a community means having to navigate through what Parfitt refers to as "a set of separate but equivalent scales" that include the *sovereign* state, the *self-determining* people, the groups that make up the *recognised minorities*, as well individuals that make up *humanity*.[10]

9 Claridge and Xanthaki, 2016:65. See further *Podkolzina vs. Latvia*.
10 [original emphasis] Parfitt, 2018.

In the Vilnius case, all of these scales are present: the *sovereign* (Lithuanian nation state), the *minoritarian* (the Russian minority), the *self-determining* people (Lithuanian citizens) and the *universal* (the unique Brutalist building as global architectural heritage). What also emerges from the Vilnius case is the way in which architectural heritage can act as constituent of the transnational community. Buildings and architectural heritage can become the expressions as well as extensions of both the occupier's body and the minoritarian community.

Employing architecture as an instrument for occupation and colonisation is unfortunately a common practice. Whether it has to do with raising monuments that represent the dominant power, or building institutional buildings, or in other ways organising space, is irrelevant here. What matters is that this is something that goes to the core of the understanding and regulating of heritage. How suppression can play out in the public space has to do with how dominant power is exercised, and this brings out the spatiotemporal aspect of transnational heritage.

From the Vilnius case we can deduce a number of interesting insights. First of all, in order for any heritage to become at all "heritage" in the regulatory sense, it must be nominated as important by the state. In cases like these, transnational heritage is almost never nominated, and as such it never becomes formally heritage and never reaches the high stature of being worthy of protection. It is always at risk and can be more easily removed, changed or demolished. Secondly, we can see how Smith's argument that the tangible only gains its importance as heritage by its symbolical and intangible values is also evident here. It is not just a matter of a building understood as a tangible cultural expression; what is required, additionally, is that a symbolical value is conferred onto it by the national community in order for this something "tangible" to become listed as national heritage.

This case shows directly how the regulatory frameworks fail to acknowledge, and in the end protect, transnational tangible heritage. Here we can also see how the logic that comes from the core ten regulatory instruments also trickles down to regional law and case law, and repeats the same principles and patterns most notably here that the transnational community is not acknowledged as a recognised community and that regulation fails to recognise transnational heritage even in times of peace, because there are no systems in place to protect heritage that is not designated as important by and for the nation state.

Intangible heritage: commodifying divination

Intangible cultural heritage must also be selected and nominated. In this section we will look at how the intangible is equally dependent on the tangible, in order to be able to be recognised and to gain protection as heritage. The 2003 UNESCO Intangible Heritage Convention provides a definition of intangible cultural heritage in article 2 as:

> the practices, representations, expressions, knowledge, skills – as well as the instruments, objects, artefacts and cultural spaces associated therewith – that communities, groups and, in some cases, individuals recognize as part of their cultural heritage. This intangible cultural heritage, transmitted from generation to generation, is constantly recreated by communities and groups in response to their environment, their interaction with nature and their history, and provides them with a sense of identity and continuity, thus promoting respect for cultural diversity and human creativity.[11]

As with tangible heritage, each year UNESCO updates a list of World Intangible Heritage.[12] Member states apply for registration, and if the nominated intangible heritage is deemed to be of sufficient merit it will be included on the list, thus becoming recognised and protected.

When it comes to tangible heritage there appears to be a, many argue Western, preference in terms of what tends to be registered as outstanding. There are many monuments that are listed, and monumentality in general seems to be the guiding principle when it comes to the types of tangible heritage and landmarks that tend to be registered as World Heritage. However, the majority of the listed intangible heritage comes from the Global South. Therefore, with intangible heritage a "Western" bias does not seem to prevail in the same way. At least on the surface, most of the intangible heritage can be described as distinctly non-Western. For instance, there are a number of what would from a Western point of view seem like surprising entries for heritage, for instance divination or rituals such as fortune-telling. Listings involve registrations for Morocco,[13] the Republic of Korea,[14] Armenia[15] and Turkey,[16] to name a few. If we also add rituals for good fortune, then the list grows even further to include listings for China, Japan and Vietnam, among others.[17]

One particularly interesting example for such entries is Turkish tasseography. The practice involves reading and interpreting images left in the coffee grounds in a coffee cup. The Turkish coffee culture goes back to the 16th century when coffee started to be served at coffeehouses in Istanbul. In its application for registration Turkey describes its coffee culture in the following way:

> Turkish Coffee is not only a beverage but also a communal practice that brings together cultural spaces, social values and beliefs within a context of

11 2003 Convention for the Safeguarding of the Intangible Cultural Heritage, I General Provisions, art 2.

12 For the full list of registered intangible heritage, see http://www.unesco.org/culture/ich/en/lists

13 Morocco: Cultural space of Jemaa el-Fna Square.

14 Republic of Korea: Jeju Chilmeoridang Yeongdeunggut.

15 Armenia: Vardavar, summertime water festival.

16 Turkey: Turkish coffee culture and tradition.

17 Republic of Korea: Cheoyongmu; China: Farmers' dance of China's Korean ethnic group; China: Manas; Japan: Chakkirako; Vietnam: Xoan singing of Phú Thọ province.

> socialization process. Its role [...] can be traced back to opening of the first coffeehouses with its noticeable decorations in Istanbul. Coffee houses were then, and still are the places where people drink coffee, converse, share news, read books and socialize.[18]

The socialising that happens as part of the coffee culture includes the act of fortune-telling, which is further specified in the Turkish application:

> As a widespread tradition, after finishing coffee, the cup is rotated, a wish is made, the cup is turned upside down on the saucer, left for cooling. Apparent images are interpreted in the coffee cup according to the "rules" of fortunetelling as a part of entertainment.

This entry for Turkish coffee culture and tradition was approved and registered on the UNESCO list of intangible heritage in 2013.[19] Reading someone's fortune in the coffee grounds is an integral part of the Turkish coffee tradition.

It came as a surprise to me when, in the course of my research, I found that this very practice, fortune-telling in coffee, is criminalised in Turkey: conducting fortune-telling is a crime under current Turkish law, at least when undertaken as a commercial activity or an occupation.

The commercial practice of fortune-telling was banned back in 1925, by the nationalist, yet secularly oriented, Kemalist reformists widely known internationally as the Young Turks. The group emerged from the ambitious nationalist and modernist project that came after the fall of the Ottoman Empire. This republican elite sought to protect and guard what they saw as the boundaries of national culture.[20] Ideologues for such growing "Turkism" made a distinction between what they referred to as national "culture" (*hars*) and international "civilisation" (*medeniyet*). A new secular republic, a nation state, had emerged after the empire, which we know today as Turkey.

As a nation state, Turkey aspired to become more international, yet nationalised, more like the Western nation states. *Becoming*-nation state, as we saw in the previous chapters, requires that an internal and an external identity can be formulated. For Turkey this meant among other things claiming, narrating, showing and in the end protecting a decidedly Turkish national culture. According to Korkman, this national Turkish culture was not seen as something new, but as a revival "of a pure, ancient Turkish culture, which [had been] under the corrupt influence of Byzantine and Arabic civilizations".[21] It needed to be, to use provocative language, purified of the

18 The Turkish nomination: Nomination file No. 00645.
19 See further Bruncevic and Almenstrand Linné, 2018.
20 Korkman, 2015:327.
21 Korkman, 2015:327.

multicultural element that had been imparted on it by other cultures. Fortune-telling thus became illegal, seen as a remnant of traditions that relied on superstition and irrational folk beliefs that were neither tied to a "pure" Turkish national culture nor desired as part of any internationally oriented, enlightened, Western-like nation.

Becoming puritan and mono-ethnic

In this way, the Kemalist reformists reconstituted, as well as policed, what they considered to be the boundaries of a national culture that belonged to the new republic. Fortune-telling was not the only profession that suffered by being criminalised. A number of other spiritual and religious beliefs and practices were banned at the same time and with them their practitioners and their communities such as sheiks, dervishes, caliphs, sorcerers, healers and amulet writers.

Before we look closer at the Turkish application and registration for coffee culture and tradition as national intangible heritage and the role fortune-telling plays in that tradition today, it is worth having another look at the UNESCO list of intangible cultural heritage and other listings connected to coffee and coffee traditions. At the time of writing, there are nine other entries which include coffee in some way, that are listed as intangible heritage. The first entry was listed in 2008. Beginning with the most recent and working backwards, the registered listings are:

In 2015:

- *Arabic coffee,* as a symbol of generosity; and
- *Majlis*, a cultural and social space where the coffee drink is an integral part.

These are both registered as joint cultural heritage of the United Arab Emirates, Saudi Arabia, Oman and Qatar.

In 2013:

- The Turkish coffee culture and tradition, which we are discussing here, was registered this year, as were
- The *Âşıklık* (minstrelsy) tradition, a performance at weddings, in coffee houses and during public festivals; and
- *Karagöz*, a shadow theatre once played at coffee houses, gardens and public squares, especially during the holy month of Ramadan.

All three are registered for Turkey.

In 2008:

- *Arts of the Meddah*, public storytellers, usually performed in coffee houses: registered for Turkey;
- *Iraqi Maqam*, a type of music often performed in coffee houses: registered for Iraq; and
- *Oxherding and oxcart traditions* used to transport coffee beans: registered for Costa Rica.

There is also another, third list, which has not been mentioned so far, namely the list of Intangible Cultural Heritage in Need of Urgent Safeguarding. This list comprises the intangible heritage that is seen as being at risk of peril if it is not widely practised or that might, with the passage of time, be forgotten. There is one entry on that list that includes coffee: *Naqqāli*, listed in 2011, Iranian dramatic storytelling, a performance art once performed in coffee houses, tents of nomads, houses and historical venues.

It can be noted that many of these listings, somehow connected to coffee, are practised and performed in spaces like coffee houses, theatres, gardens, squares and tents, adding the tangible and spatial aspect to the intangible. Even though the listings are for "intangible" heritage, there is a tendency that sees the experience of intangible heritage as directly tied to material, often public, spaces and tangible objects.

The distinction between the public and the private space when it comes to fortune-telling as cultural heritage is very significant, as it denotes the difference between legal and criminalised activity. For instance, Korkman highlights that a variety of such practices "have flourished within private spaces of [Turkish] domesticity, the very gendered habitus enabled and sustained by the nationalist project".[22] Therefore, a coffee cup reading in a gendered, domestic space of a home or garden, a space of domesticity that is often largely female in nature, a private sphere, is not considered as criminal. However, public, commercial readings of fortune are still prosecuted to this day as criminal activity, and seen as profane, even though the ritual at the same time forms the base for a registered practice of World Intangible Heritage. This paradox is revealing and interesting, as coffee fortune-telling continues to exist in, e.g., the cafés of Istanbul. The criminal prosecution is circumvented by offering fortune-readings as complimentary with a purchased cup of coffee.[23]

This non-secular ritual that is an active part of the coffee tradition is at the same time treated as something foreign, "Arabic" or "Byzantine" and not purely Turkish, as well as integral to Turkish national heritage. The practice in its commercial guise therefore remains criminalised as imagined by the cultural elites that were building the Turkish nation state at the turn of the century.

22 Korkman, 2015:328.

23 This could of course be explained by a public policy rationale that is aimed at preventing fragile people from being exploited or taken advantage of by ruthless vendors in order to have their fortunes told. In this way, when the fortune-telling is anchored to the cost of a cup of coffee, such risks are at least minimised. Presumably, these activities are not perceived as dangerous in a private or family setting.

This othering of the Arabic and the Byzantine influences provided the moral and political justification for criminalising fortune-telling in the public sphere or as a commercial activity, as well as formulating the authorised heritage discourse concerning the registration of national intangible heritage.

Now, some hundred years later, this *transnational* practice has been reframed and included in Turkish coffee culture as part of its intangible cultural heritage. Not only does this call into question the larger meanings of fortune-telling as a constitutive social practice, it also highlights the treacherous nature of authorised heritage discourses that construct the state community while they at the same time attempt to hide, or exclude, the othering practices required to articulate and narrate the same.

How the national is constructed, narrated, and how it changes over time depends on the dominant power. Here we can see how that can directly affect cultural heritage. One obvious aspect is the apparent nation-building and how the authorised heritage discourse has given rise to narratives that in turn frame what is considered to be the national community and its cultural traditions. What also becomes increasingly apparent is how some traditions are actively included while others are excluded in order to present a unified idea of a national community. This means that the transnational, that is always already there so to speak, is purposely silenced, othered and excluded by advancing the authorised heritage discourse as the historical narrative of the nation.

Augmented heritage in the cup

A group of Turkish interactive designers decided to study the practice connected to coffee cup readings. They were looking to create a smart "augmented cup" able to "interpret" signs in the coffee and add a digital dimension to this social interaction. The designers sought to create a product for cup reading and fortune-telling and give it a digital layer.[24]

In this project, an *augmented cup* is described as a physical device that has a non-interactive display that shows images, or that provides information about the liquid content, for instance the temperature of the contents in the cup. The augmented cup also has an interactive element, and in order to programme the cup the designers investigated the rituals connected to Turkish coffee fortune-telling. Seen as a socio-cultural practice based on physical interpersonal interaction for readings, the idea was to capture the ritual in a device, including the stories that are narrated by the fortune-teller by interpreting the formations and shapes formed in the coffee grounds.[25]

The design team began their investigation with the interactive element of the practice, namely the moment when the advice is given by the fortune-teller to the client. Focusing on "spontaneous social interaction" that is not obvious or predictable, they set out to explore how it could be designed into a smart

24 Börütecene, et. al., 2016; Börütecene, et. al., 2017; Börütecene, et. al., 2018.
25 Börütecene, et. al., 2018.

device that would be able to provide fortune readings on its display: a cup that by design becomes the fortune-teller. The traditional fortune-telling practices were translated into a digital interactive handheld device where the coffee grounds became the content, the fortune-tellers and the clients became users, and the communication between them became advice interaction.[26] In this investigation the design team organised and studied sessions with over thirty fortune-tellers in order to understand the verbal and non-verbal interaction that took place between the fortune-tellers and their clients during one session.

The traditional cultural practice of coffee fortune-telling became integrated into the interactive cup design. Here, coffee transformed from being a hot, invigorating beverage, to becoming a mediator in a conversation, first as a social, then as a digital, practice. The grounds left in the cup became the *content* to be interpreted that can have meaning, and that can be "read", by the fortune-teller face to face with the client, or by the augmented cup when there is no fortune-teller present. I will not go into further details of the interactive design study, including how the research team incorporated hand gestures, body posture and other non-verbal aspects of the communication into the design of the augmented coffee cup. I refer the interested reader to the published articles where the study and the design procedures are described in detail.[27]

What I want to highlight here is firstly the added intellectual property (the digital design element) that is layered on top of the intangible heritage (coffee fortune-telling). We have already seen how heritage and intellectual property can, and do, converge in the discussion concerning Indigenous traditional cultural expressions and traditional knowledge. A similar remark can be made here when "authentic", "national", "traditional" heritage becomes framed and narrated first under the UNESCO regulatory framework, and then becomes re-narrated by the "modern", "commodifying" regulatory framework by being framed as intellectual property. We will look at the digital layer that is added onto heritage in much more detail in the next case study. The second thing that can be highlighted before we conclude this section is how fortune-telling has been both excluded as "foreign" and included as "national" simultaneously – showing how the third option, the recognition of the transnational, remains inconceivable still.

The augmented subjectivity with the digital layer is also interesting to point out, as we have seen with the example of the interactive smart device that is able to provide fortune-telling. Heritage is commodified by being digitalised, and then it moves away from its communal contexts experienced in, for example, Turkish cafés or the private, often gendered and female, "national" Turkish spaces, and moves into the commercial context, of the digital, international sphere.

This framing and reframing of heritage through constituting and reconstituting the national is of course omnipresent in this particular case. It comes down to a matter of narrative, authorised heritage discourses, and negotiations as to what is included and what is excluded from heritage.[28] What emerges from this discussion

26 Börütecene, et. al., 2016.
27 Börütecene, et. al., 2016; Börütecene, et. al., 2017; Börütecene, et. al., 2018.

is that the regulatory framework fails to cover the transnational in intangible heritage. Furthermore, with this case we also see how the category of "intangible" in practice can include and rely on both the tangible (such as the space of the café and other tangible objects) and the digital (here smart, interactive devices), which in turn is a challenge to the three recognised heritage categories. This case also highlights questions that are transnational, and where the core regulatory instruments fail to a certain extent, such as UDHR (that does not necessarily protect the right to participate in one's own transnational culture), the 1972 World Heritage Convention (that does not necessarily protect transnational heritage that is not selected and nominated by the state), the 2003 Intangible Cultural Heritage Convention (that fails to acknowledge the dependence on the tangible and digital for the intangible), the 2005 Cultural Diversity Convention (that still relies on the state-based recognition of communities) and other heritage regulation.

Digital heritage: dream Nefertiti

As the blockbuster touring global exhibition *Tutankhamun: Treasures of the Golden Pharaoh* was taking place in 2019, with over quarter of a million presold tickets for its London leg alone, I looked over at my yellowing copy of *Loot: Tomb Robbers, Treasure and the Great Museum Debate* by Sharon Waxman. I had read the book so many times, for leisure, for work, for inspiration. In front of me on the other side of the desk, I had just opened on the computer screen a file that I was not entirely sure what to do with, or even what it was. The colourful bust of Nefertiti on the cover of Waxman's book on the one side and a white, colourless but extremely detailed scan of the Nefertiti bust on the other, spinning around on the computer screen. It was like Nefertiti was there in the room, granting me royal audience. I had decluttered the desk for her, invited her in. Maybe she would speak to me, tell me the story in her own words? I looked at her looking at me from the cover of the book while also emerging from the black background that was framing her digital rendition on screen. Yet nothing, silence.

What is there left to say or write that has not already been written millions of times about this fantastic piece of art and cultural heritage? There has always been enormous interest in Ancient Egyptian heritage. Ancient Egyptian artefacts still generate so much interest and revenue. The reason why so many heritage scholars do what they do is because they once read about the pyramids, or saw an image of Tutankhamun's Golden Mask, or looked in the eyes of this very Nefertiti, either while standing in front her at the Neues Museum in Berlin, or when looking at her image in some book. By now we all know how contested and fraught Egyptian heritage can be, we have read about the battles taking place between Egypt and many a large museum around the

28 Cf. the most recent Turkish re-definition and re-narration of Hagia Sofia in 2020, where the categorisation of the building was reverted to a mosque, after having once also been a church, then a museum, then a cultural memory institution.

world, including the Neues Museum. So how could I possibly begin the story of the Nefertiti bust anew?

My case here is also not about *that* Nefertiti. It is about "The Other Nefertiti". *The Other Nefertiti* is an artwork that emerged after the so-called Nefertiti hack. The hack is sometimes dubbed as the art heist of the century, one that involved stealing but not taking, or even moving, the bust. The German artists Nora Al-Badri and Jan Nikolai Nelles clandestinely scanned the bust in the Neues Museum, without anyone's permission or notice, and then publicly released the 3D data of the bust under a Creative Commons Licence. The artists also exhibited an exceptionally detailed 3D print created from their newly acquired data. It was one of the most precise facsimiles of the Nefertiti bust ever to be shown in public, the first of its kind to be exhibited in Egypt.

There is no natural beginning to begin from. The Nefertiti bust, the Original, if we must fetishise the original as opposed to its archetypal dichotomic copy or facsimile, the version currently housed under the protective glass panes in the Neues Museum, is one of the most famous items of cultural heritage in the world as well as one of the most contested items of heritage in cultural heritage law. To tell Nefertiti's story of how she ended up where she is now, how she survived more than three thousand years, how she travelled from the dusty Egyptian Nile delta to where she now dwells in her privileged, professionally lit, extremely guarded, well-visited, gilded cage, involves having to carefully navigate the authorised heritage discourse, and a polyphony of other voices: local voices, global voices, artistic voices, activist voices, scientific reports, diplomatic practices, legal arguments and so much more. For me it seems to be a story that is almost impossible to tell linearly, chronologically or, to use a complicated word, "objectively". So here goes an attempt – mine is a version of the story that aims to bring out the transnational in Nefertiti's story and end up in a discussion about digital heritage.

Once upon a time in Amarna

The Nefertiti bust was found in Amarna, Egypt, in 1912 by archaeologists working for the German Oriental Company. Amarna, or Tell el-Amarna as it is known in Arabic, is a city on the Nile delta. It was briefly the capital city built by the Pharaoh Amenhotep IV, who later took the name Akhenaten. Akhenaten was married to Nefertiti. During his rule he moved the capital city and the earlier royal court from Thebes to Amarna. He also changed the pharaonic religion, from polytheism to a quasi-monotheistic worship of the sun, or the disc of the sun, a characteristic of the deity Ra. Even Freud was fascinated by Akhenaten and Nefertiti's story. In *Moses and Monotheism*,[29] Freud puts forwards a hypothesis that Moses might have been born into an Ancient Egyptian family of noble standing, probably followers of the monotheist Akhenaten, and

29 Freud, 2010 [1939].

presumably his wife, Nefertiti. There is, however, no scientific proof that this was the case.

Akhenaten's rule was short, only seventeen years. The exact dates are difficult to affirm, but it is generally placed somewhere between 1350 and 1330 BC. Shortly after his death, and perhaps after a short period of Nefertiti's solo reign, his successors took over and moved the royal court back to Thebes, attempting to erase all traces of him, his wife, their rule and religion from the collective local memory, and from history.

The short story of how the bust of Nefertiti ended up where it is now can be summarised like this. The excavation during which the bust was found, in late 1912, was led by the famed German archaeologist Ludwig Borchardt. The bust was part of the German lot, granted under the process that divided findings from archaeological missions commonly referred to as *partage à moitié exacte*. This was a system that regulated the dividing up of the treasures between the excavation mission and the Egyptian authorities, in equal lots. There is of course a much longer, and much more complicated, story to it.

The longer more intricate story cannot be recounted in full here for many reasons, one of them being that there are many conflicting accounts.[30] Nonetheless, a short overview of the longer story is provided here for the sake of clarity. The longer version usually begins in the late 19th century, or perhaps even earlier that century, when the Napoleonic troops showed interest in conducting excavations in Amarna and when Ancient Egyptian heritage generally became fashionable. The first extensive excavation conducted in the region was carried out by the famous British archaeologist Sir William Matthew Flinders Petrie, equally renowned as Borchardt for his excavations, if not more so. Petrie's assistant, Howard Carter, now the most famous of them all, would some thirty years later become world renowned in his own right when he discovered the tomb of Tutankhamun in the Valley of the Kings.

Recalling the longer, complicated, more intricate version of the story is important in order to account for this arms race of sorts to getting permits for conducting excavations. The prestige of being the one, or the first one, to find ancient treasures in the desert drove this race. Therefore, there were different excavations taking place in the region at the same time, and many nations were fighting to obtain the permissions and access to sites in order to be able to excavate on the territory that is today's Egypt. Everybody wanted to be the first one to find the hidden treasures of the ancient world that would make them famous, send a signal around the world regarding their country's colonial potency and, of course eventually, make them rich.

The political state in Egypt at the time was turbulent. A threatening but unsuccessful civil uprising had just taken place. Egypt was still under the rule of the Sultan, and the Ottoman Empire. A *khedive*, the local ruler, who was loyal

30 The curious reader is referred to some of the books I read while working on this chase: Fletcher, 2004; Waxman, 2010; Lange, 2013; Tyldesley, 2018; as well as Merryman, 2006 and Merryman, Elsen and Ulrice, 2007.

to the Sultan, governed formally, but the territory was *de facto* under British occupation and was thus also subordinated to the British consul general in Cairo. British troops controlled the Suez Canal, and they had helped quell a nationalist uprising against the *khedive*. Because of this, Flinders Petrie, as a British archaeologist, knew that if needed, he would have the protection of the British military during his excavations and obtain access to sites rather easily.

The German Oriental Company also made a play for access to sites, and they gained an excavation permit for the territory of Amarna. The German permit came formally from the *khedive*, and even though the British military knew about it they did not contest it. To make this even more complicated, the German permit was administratively issued by the French-led authority in charge of matters concerning the Egyptian antiquities and excavations, the *Sérvice des Antiquités de l'Égypte*. The French authority was there on the invitation of the Ottoman rulers, as the French had helped formulate a new legislation where the system of *partage à moitié exacte* was legally established. As mentioned, the system allowed all finds from foreign excavations taking place on the territory to be divided in two equal lots, one that could be taken by the foreign expedition and one that would stay in Egypt and, in practice, in Cairo. The German Oriental Company thus had the necessary permit from the French-led administrative authority, which was invited by the formal ruler, the Ottoman *khedive*, under British occupation and with their knowledge.

Borchardt's expedition during which the Nefertiti bust was found was conducted in late 1912. A number of items were found during that particular expedition. The finds were divided under the *partage* system in January 1913. It is vastly disputed how the clearly exquisite Nefertiti bust ended up being awarded to the German and not the Cairo lot. A couple of decades later, Egypt demanded and successfully kept the equally exquisite Tutankhamun Golden Mask when it was found; why did they not do the same with Nefertiti? Some claim that the reason why the Nefertiti bust ended up in the German lot is because Borchardt concealed or underplayed its true value. Others say that this is not true or is at least vastly exaggerated, and that the *partage* happened on proper terms and was fair and legal.

So much has been written about this, and there is no need for me to further account for the various versions of the circumstances around the find, for example the one about Borchardt maybe claiming that the bust was made out of gypsum, or claims that the bust was photographed in bad light, or the claim that the German Oriental Company generally acted unscrupulously in various different ways during the *partage*. Naturally, it is still to this day contested, and needless to say both Germany and Egypt are still claiming moral and legal ownership of the bust.

The bust first reached Berlin in late 1913. It was presented to the founder and financier of the German Oriental Company and the person who had funded the entire excavation in Amarna, James Simon. Simon was an art collector and an archaeological enthusiast. After briefly exhibiting the bust in his private residence, he then gifted it, together with other artefacts from the Amarna excavation, first on permanent loan, then as a gift to the Egyptian

Museum of Berlin, a collection that was then and is now part of the Neues Museum. For different, equally disputed, reasons even though it was the most impressive item in his collection, the bust was not exhibited or mentioned to the public before 1924, that is, more than a decade after it came to Berlin, even though many of the other artefacts from the Amarna excavation were already on show in 1913 and 1914. When the Neues Museum closed in 1939 owing to the imminent war, the artefacts from its collections were taken out and sent to different locations for safekeeping.

There were indeed Royal Air Force bombs that hit the Neues Museum in 1943, but the bust was by then in safe hands, having already been evacuated and taken elsewhere. The American Army found it in 1945 and handed it over to its Monuments, Fine Arts and Archives branch, the "Monuments Men" as they are now known in popular culture. In fact, all the collections that had been housed in the Neues Museum before the war were divided between East and West Berlin. Most artefacts remained in East Berlin and were kept in the Bode Museum. The Nefertiti bust, however, was sent to West Berlin.

Interestingly, as early as 1946 a claim for her return came, not from the state of Egypt, but rather from East Germany, insisting that the bust rightfully belonged to the Museum Island, now East Berlin. It was not returned. The bust, which had been evacuated before the war and was moved to several places in West Germany during the war, was instead returned by the Americans to West Berlin in 1956. Its first place of dwelling after the war was the Dahlem Museum, West Berlin. Then it was moved once again to the Egyptian Museum in Charlottenburg, also in West Berlin, in the late 1960s. A German debate as to who was the true owner of Nefertiti lasted until 1989, as long as the country was divided and until the fall of the Berlin Wall.

It took a while before the whole Amarna collection was reunited even after the reunification of Germany. In 2005, the bust was moved from the Egyptian Museum to the Altes Museum. The Altes Museum is also on the Museum Island, that is, in East Berlin. By 2005 Berlin was united, there was no more East or West in capital letters, just cardinal directions. Finally, in 2009, Nefertiti "came back" to the Neues Museum, newly redesigned by David Chipperfield, when it reopened in October 2009, and the Amarna collection was reunited. Nefertiti was given the privileged place in the Nordkuppelsaal, a dark room, where all light is directed on her. She is behind glass, the sole artwork in the room, in a 12 metre-high floor-to-ceiling space.

The first Egyptian claims for the return of Nefertiti came in the early 2000s. They intensified further in 2003. Two Hungarian artists, András Gálik and Bálint Havas, had created the work LITTLE WARSAW | THE BODY OF NEFERTITI, a bronze sculpture of a nude female body without a head. The artists had then been allowed by the Neues Museum to use the Nefertiti bust and place it, if only for a short while, on their sculpture. This was recorded and the film *The Body of Nefertiti* (2003), directed by Kristóf Forgács, was shown at the Venice Biennale that year. The Egyptians considered this to be vastly insulting, an act of sexualising and disrespecting the bust. A long discussion for repatriation was initiated.

Yet, Nefertiti remains in the Neues Museum. In the book *Loot*, Sharon Waxman describes a conversation between two lawyers who were discussing the return of Nefertiti to Egypt at a conference in 2004. One, favouring return to Egypt, was arguing that the export of the bust from Egypt to Germany in 1913 was not British, or French, or even Ottoman to grant, that Egypt was colonialised and not in charge of its own territory at the time, and therefore the *partage* is not legally valid. The second, favouring that the bust stays in Berlin, advanced on the contrary that the transaction and the *partage* were conducted in the only legal manner available at the time, that a valid *partage* had indeed taken place, and, he added, that a pagan ancient bust stemming from a now-dead civilisation could hardly be directly attributed to the modern-day, predominantly Muslim, nation state of Egypt.[31]

The fact that there is a global Ancient Egypt mania, and that items from that period, like Nefertiti's bust, still to this day inspire artists to engage in conversations Ancient Egyptian heritage, does not make this any less difficult. The Egyptian objects in this way become incorporated in contemporary collective culture, on a global scale, and many feel that Nefertiti and other items like this bust somehow belong, or at least are very important, to us all. Everybody certainly wants what is best for Nefertiti, yet it seems to be very difficult to agree on what that is.

Going back to the touring exhibition *Tutankhamun: Treasures of the Golden Pharaoh*, which I began this section with. This exhibition was set up in order to raise funds for the Grand Egyptian Museum, under construction at the time of writing. Touring exhibitions like this one are enormously instrumental in helping to bring money to Egypt, money that can be used for *in situ* restoration and conservation of Egyptian monuments and artefacts that are still in Egypt, as well as wider purposes, such as for Egyptology research, or precisely to build new, better, museums and art institutions able to safeguard and protect the heritage of Ancient Egypt. Exhibitions such as *Tutankhamun* frequently raise hundreds of millions of dollars each time they tour the world. Even though tickets to these blockbuster shows tend to be very expenseive, they still attract millions of visitors. The Egyptians feel that these artefacts are in this way their international ambassadors, that they bring tourism, acclaim and money back to their country. Needless to say, many objects, like the bust of Nefertiti and other artefacts of similar stature, such as the Rosetta Stone in London and the Dendera Zodiac ceiling in Paris, remain housed in Western museums. And above all, they continue to be financially valuable to the institutions that hold them, but hardly to Egypt.

31 Waxman, 2010:61.

The Other Nefertiti

Then there is *The Other Nefertiti*, the artistic work created by the artists Nora Al-Badri and Jan Nikolai Nelles. By using a hidden, hacked Kinect Xbox controller, which is a portable scanner, they were able to scan the bust and obtain its digital data. The scan was conducted by hanging the scanner around Al-Badri's neck and hiding it under a scarf that she was wearing. Walking around the bust and at key points scanning it from all angles, the artists were able to gather the necessary data for their scan. The data makes up an STL file of 100 MB with a density of 9 mil polygons. It was obtained without the knowledge of, or permission by the Neues Museum. The data was at a later stage openly and publicly released at the Chaos Computer Congress 32C3 in 2015. It was also released under a Creative Commons Licence.

Not long after the artist duo's public release of this data, many members of the tech community claimed that the data was too precise to have been obtained in the manner Al-Badri and Nelles had described.[32] They argued that this type of data of such high quality can only have been obtained either by being leaked by someone in the museum who has access to its scans and archives of data, or by hacking the museum servers containing such data.[33] The artists never confirmed or denied this allegation. I will return to this discussion at the end of this section, but it should already be pointed out here that, for the purposes of my analysis, how the data was obtained is comparatively irrelevant. Whether it was obtained by a clandestine scan, or as a leak, or as a larger system hack, matters little for the discussion here. Rather what I am interested in is the very string of performances that Al-Badri and Nelles managed to stage, the awareness they raised and what they artistically created. The focus here is the significance which their performance has for further analysis of cultural heritage law in general and matters of transnational heritage in particular.

After securing the data, Al-Badri and Nelles invited the general public, anyone with access to a 3D printer, to use the data, to print their own Nefertiti, to "recreate", "remix" and "redistribute"[34] the bust. The available data allowed users to print and change the bust. Many people around the globe took advantage of this possibility to interact with it and its data, printing versions of the original and adding funny wigs to it, or placing their own Nefertitis in unusual settings, etc.

Such personalisation of heritage, as Katyal calls it, "challenges the idea of a single, fixed, homogenous curatorial voice, lending much greater legitimacy to multiple interpretations and curations of objects"[35] and frees heritage from its institutional constraints. The idea of freeing Nefertiti in this way from the constraints of a large-scale institution and the narrative created by the Neues Museum is interesting. It does not even necessarily have to do with "freeing"

32 See e.g. Wenman (b): https://cosmowenman.com/2016/03/08/the-nefertiti-3d-scan-heist-is-a-hoax/
33 Voon, 2016. See also Newitz, 2016.
34 See e.g. Simon, 2010.
35 Katyal, 2017:1124.

the object itself, but rather releasing the information which is embodied in it, which is carried within its body. In our case, this was something that the Al-Badri and Nelles encouraged people to do, as well as something that they managed to do themselves by printing their own version of the bust and creating the work *The Other Nefertiti*.

The Other Nefertiti became an artistic intervention that was also shown at an exhibition in Cairo where Al-Badri and Nelles had been invited to present their work in 2015. Their installation was called *Something Else*, and it was shown Off-Biennale in downtown Cairo. *The Other Nefertiti* included one of the most precise facsimiles of the bust ever to be made public, and this was the first time an item like this was exhibited in Egypt.

At the end of the exhibition, when asked to leave their bust in Cairo as a symbolical return, Al-Badri and Nelles declined this too. Instead they chose to "return it to the desert". Resisting the authorised heritage discourses, they wrote in a press release: "we buried the 3D print in the desert in the outskirts of Cairo as a counter-act to the excavation. We delivered it back to the desert as a space, but the coordinates won't be revealed."[36] The press release goes on:

> The artefact is going to be delivered to the desert as an Utopos. The bust is passed on to a bigger temporality as a poetic counter-act to the excavation. The place is loaded with the possibility of a rediscovery in an undefined future. With the data leak as a part of this counter narrative within our investigative practice we want to activate the artefact, to inspire a critical re-assessment of today's conditions and to overcome the colonial notion of possession in Germany's museums. With regard to the notion of belonging and possession of material objects of other cultures, the artist's intention is to make cultural objects publicly accessible and to promote a contemporary and critical approach on how the "Global North" deals with heritage and the representation of "the Other"....[37]

Assembly line

Many believe that the original Nefertiti bust, at the time it was made, may once have been part of an assembly line of sculptures created by an artisan during the rule of Akhenaten and Nefertiti. It may have even been the mould itself (hence the missing eye enabling the artisan to practise inserting the iris).[38] In such a case, it is not at all unlikely that other similar Nefertiti busts could eventually be found somewhere in the desert of Amarna. Engaging with precisely this, and calling to mind the fetishisation of the original object, Al-Badri and Nelles chose to leave their version – copy, facsimile, new original, depending on how we choose to define it – in the desert. If it is found in the

36 Al-Badri and Nelles, 2018.
37 Al-Badri and Nelles, 2018.
38 Gardner, 2006:64.

future, someone might even think that this 3D print is an object that stems from that assembly line. Or even, if it is dated to our period, it could serve as a representative of its own time as digital heritage, as symbolising the digital and augmented relationship to heritage, identity and belonging of our time.

Unsurprisingly perhaps, the work and the performance connected to *The Other Nefertiti* did not even end there. After the desert burial of *The Other Nefertiti*, Al-Badri and Nelles created a Nefertiti chatbot, a software application used to conduct an on-line chat conversation via text. Challenging the many conflicting narratives and the authorised heritage discourse, the artists aimed to investigate what would happen if Nefertiti was to speak for herself. They developed an artificial intelligence avatar, bringing Nefertiti into the posthuman era, where the (hyper)object[39] and the cyborg exist side by side with the human. Needless to say, *The Other Nefertiti* as well as the chatbot created a media frenzy, resulting in global coverage in *The New York Times*,[40] *Hyperallergic*[41] and *The Independent*, among others.[42]

The latest development in the case happened as this book was being written in November 2019. Another German artist, Cosmo Wenman, won a legal battle in the German courts against the Prussian Cultural Heritage Foundation, which oversees all Berlin state museums, including the Neues Museum, under the Freedom of Information Act. As part of the settlement, the foundation, known in German as the Stiftung Preußischer Kulturbesitz, released its 3D scan of the original Nefertiti bust. Wenman had been one of the first people to claim that Al-Badri and Nelles' clandestine scan might have been a hoax. To prove that, and after a three-year legal battle, he managed to obtain the Neues Museum's own 3D scan. Ironically, before releasing the institutional scan and their data, the Neues Museum chose to place a Creative Commons Licence CC BY-NC-ND at the bottom of the physical, original Nefertiti bust. This license would appear on all data renderings. It allows copying, distributing and adapting the scans, but not using them for commercial purposes. Wenman subsequently released the data he obtained from the museum on his website.[43] It never proved or disproved the provenance of the Al-Badri and Nelles data. But it was not necessary as their goal had been achieved: Nefertiti was now publicly available.

This development brought an additional layer into the cultural heritage discussion, namely how a work that is in the public domain as it is over three thousand years old, becomes re-colonised by digitisation. The institutional ownership of the physical object as well as the intellectual property created in its digital renderings now make it all the more owned for being made digital. Even though the data is under a Creative Commons licence, the intellectual

39 Bruncevic, 2018, Chapter 3.
40 Wilder, 2016.
41 Voon, 2016.
42 Vulliamy, 2016.
43 Cosmo Wenman website: https://www.thingiverse.com/thing:3974391

property is still, technically, legally, formally, with the museum. The move from tangible property and real space into intellectual property and digital space[44] is important to highlight as it is now a very common practice in conservation, and museums do precisely this, scan and photograph the objects in their holdings for both preservation and research, as well as for commercial endeavours such as merchandising. Whether or not the museums then invite the audiences to interact with their data is another issue, but if and when they do, additional derivative works are created, and with them, additional, private, enclosed, commercial, layers of intellectual property rights.

Al-Badri and Nelles' work *The Other Nefertiti* and the performance tied to it has set in motion a new category of heritage that can be referred to as *technoheritage*,[45] rather than digital heritage. Technoheritage is the convergence of technology and heritage that has the unique ability to challenge what the artist duo here are referring to as the museums' "interpretorial sovereignty", and the narratives created by museums as "object biographies". The Nefertiti-Bot is heritage enabled by the added layer of technology to talk. Highlighting the questions regarding who has the right to tell a story and who has the power and the privilege to keep the information that such objects hold, Al-Badri and Nelles thus touch upon some of the core issues in cultural heritage law and particularly manage to show the transnational aspects of ancient heritage.

The Nefertiti bust is a wonderful example of transnational heritage, as its transnational character is undisputed. With the added layer of technology, it also explores what has been touted as possible "solutions" to contested heritage. As part of many mitigation processes, various digital compromises involving the creation of more or less sophisticated technoheritage versions of originals like this one have been presented. However, far from being a desensitising, anaesthetising and soothing solution, something that can be used in dispute resolution, overly relying on technoheritage in this way might mask problematic practices that in actual fact re-colonise physical artefacts through added layers of proprietary frameworks such as intellectual property rights. The digital can in this way also re-colonise heritage and the space in which it is exhibited through intellectual property and the digital data rights that are subsequently created.

Many large Western museums, including German ones, are now introducing policies on how to deal with their colonial pasts and the problematic heritage in their holdings.[46] The technological alternatives have not been ruled out. These discussions go to the core of the regulatory instruments and their challenges, such as the 1970 Convention on Illegally Exported Cultural Property (which does not include the export of data embodied in an object), the 1995 UNIDROIT Convention (can private data cross state lines) as well as the 2005 Convention on

44 Katyal, 2017:1117.
45 Katyal, 2017.
46 Both Germany and France have issued policies and guidelines for the return of the colonial artefacts that are held in their public cultural institutions. In the UK, the V&A Museum has also committed to a position of return and repatriation.

Cultural Diversity (does it include transnational technoheritage). None of these instruments directly discuss copies, facsimiles and technoheritage that intensify transnational heritage.

How this all impacts on wider matters of decolonisation will be discussed in the next chapter. What this case-oriented chapter has shown is how the narratives created around heritage are *de facto* constantly constructed and renegotiated, and how transnational heritage still tends to be excluded from the regulatory frameworks and by extension from protection. We have also seen how, with the advent of the digital and the emergence of technoheritage, the difference between tangible, intangible and digital may have collapsed once and for all.

5 Constellations: the transnational in community

In this penultimate chapter, before we arrive at a conclusion in terms of future possible routes towards regulation of transnational heritage, I will now focus on the transnational in community, that is, the alternative heritage, alternative narratives and alternative community formations, how they are imagined, constructed and negotiated. As we have already seen, many of these "other", "alternative" or "counter" categories are not recognised in regulation. They resist some of the assumptions perpetuated in and through law such as, for instance, the strong requirements in terms of ethnic sameness or connection to a common territory. Many of the formations that will be discussed below do not figure expressly in any of the cultural heritage regulatory frameworks. Focusing on counter-narratives and alternative community formations will help us in further understanding the heritage from groups that have not been given a recognised status in law, at least not yet. Above all, this chapter strengthens the overall argument, namely that a more flexible, constellation-based and diverse notion of community is needed in regulation in order to save and preserve the diverse iterations of transnational heritage that do exist and that are constantly being produced.

What we have seen so far is that the community concepts that are recognised in law seem to favour a conception of communities legitimised through nationalist, mono-ethnic, territorial and authorised heritage discourses. Even Indigenous and minority communities are legitimised by assumptions concerning ethnic or religious homogeneity, or at least territorial connections. In this chapter I will further elaborate on the claim briefly raised in Chapter 3, namely that the three existing community types: the nation state, the Indigenous community and the minority community, are all in fact one and the same type of community, but in different sizes. I have already argued that the Indigenous and the minority communities are, in a way, simply nation states in waiting. Cultural heritage law in that way recognises one category of community but in three different sizes, so to speak, and therefore my claim is that law can only understand this one type of community, namely the homogenous, mono-ethnic, geographically closed type of community, in three different sizes or in its three stages of development.

What I will address here is a radical understanding of diverse, multicultural, multi-ethnic, fluent, location-independent, constellation-based, transnational communities and argue why such constellations are needed in regulation, and

DOI: 10.4324/9781003212683-5

in that vein why an understanding of the transnational community is still seen as comparatively foreign to law.

This chapter further develops the critique of the existing taxonomy of communities by highlighting the imagined,[1] the location independent[2] and the contested[3] in communities and the many counter- or alternative heritage narratives. I will focus on the formations that, by the dominant logic presented here, are yet to be made visible. By adopting a progressive understanding of community, a number of "new" communities will emerge such as the multi-ethnic urban communities or the location-independent lifestyle-based communities. These do not have outspoken political aspirations for self-determination, and they come packaged in ways that law is not used to dealing with. The chapter thus shows why the notion of the transnational community must be studied further in cultural heritage law, even beyond the scope of this book. It will be advanced that the existing, in many ways outdated, static and in the end exclusory community conceptions are far too dependent on ethno-nationalist assumptions. This is simply not enough.

Finally, this chapter discusses how to negotiate the boundaries between communities, and how community membership is claimed, imagined as well as contested and reconstituted. That means reaching beyond the existing community categories as well as the existing heritage categories that are drawn up in regulation in order to envision the possible regulation of transnational heritage. We have seen that the current categories carry colonial, nationalist, imperial and even patriarchal legacies. Now we must turn to exploring the uncharted territories where the categories that we have relied on in regulation must become decolonised.

Diverse community: decolonising heritage

Many recent initiatives have taken up the challenge of reclaiming and reimagining the conceptions and formations of community. We have already seen how every community is in some way constructed through, and dependent on, a dominant, and often exclusory, authorised, state-based, heritage discourse. The new initiatives, however, focus on highlighting the counter-narratives that approach the formation of community differently, more radically. To this end we will see how, for example, museums are now actively re-organising their collections, providing new and more diverse narratives based around their already existing permanent collections, but also how they are actively decolonising their holdings, deaccessioning artworks deemed to be overrepresented and dominant, in favour of less dominant, less visible, structurally excluded works. These initiatives are often the results of and rely on "curatorial activism"[4] where alternative imaginations of museums, their collections and their roles in terms of inclusion in the community,

1 Anderson, 2016.
2 Bhabha, 1994.
3 Nancy, 1991; see also Nancy, 2000.
4 See e.g. Reilly, 2018.

are undertaken. Curatorial activism is a term perhaps mostly associated with Maura Reilly and her book of the same name, used to describe curatorial endeavours that promote visual cultures in and from the margins: that is, culture emerging from artists who are non-white, non-Western-Anglo-Saxon, identifying as women, feminist and/or queer.[5] These are the categories that we now turn to.

All recent decolonising activities have placed original myths, state-based narratives and dominant, excluding, discourses under new and much more profound scrutiny. This means that the issues of historical justice and human rights are placed in the forefront of the ongoing museum discussions, how collections are or ought to be organised and how culture can be curated in new ways in order to imagine and acknowledge alternative, inclusive and diverse community formations. Some of the initiatives have therefore actively involved rethinking the role of national museums or even, as we have seen to a certain extent, how a museum ought to be defined and organised and what its ethical role is. For scholars and thinkers such as Reilly, it is not about giving up on the museum as such, but rather working on ways to make it viable and accessible for everyone.

Beyond authorised heritage discourse – decolonising heritage

Community formations that reach beyond ethno-nationalism and alternative reimaginations of community are the driving forces of the initiatives that aim to decolonise cultural heritage. The prominent role of the *Decolonise Museums* movement can be mentioned, as well as what it signifies in this context.[6] The movement challenges museums to rethink their internal structures and even calls for the museums to, when necessary, deaccession their "mainstream", "Western" or "dominant" holdings.

Deaccessioning means selling off works that are in the public collections and then using the funds gained from the sales to acquire new or to display different types of artworks, e.g. those created by members of marginalised and minority communities. Actively asking the question how to disrupt the dominant and hegemonic practices in curation and museology in order to become more diversified, inclusive and democratised is placed at the core of the decolonising endeavours. The movement encourages museums to acknowledge, engage with and exhibit the multitude of communities and community formations that exist in and around them. The active questioning of hegemonic practices and narratives is in fact one of the core tenets of the *Decolonise* movement. It has to do with taking seriously, acknowledging and dealing with any and all unequal power structures that are at work in society and within the museums and their practices when it comes to heritage, art and curation, and how asymmetrical power is reproduced in and through art and heritage discourses.

5 Reilly, 2018:22.
6 See e.g. Janes and Sandel, 2019.

The call to decolonise museums originates from the wider *Decolonise* movement, a grass-roots movement that has spread across the cultural institutions and academia in the Global North. Many activists have campaigned for a public coming to terms with exclusory, colonial legacies and practices that are recreated and perpetuated in, e.g., cultural, educational and curatorial institutions. Sometimes it has to do directly with the remnants of colonial heritage and historical ties to slavery and territorial occupation.[7] At other times the movement has organised itself around broader themes of curatorial and educational activism that deals with diversity and inclusion. There are also a number of student-led *Decolonise* movements.[8]

The *Decolonise* movement naturally and unsurprisingly inscribes itself in the wider post-colonial and decolonial academic and scholarly fields.[9] It develops the arguments advanced by the forefigures of the movement such as Edward Said,[10] Homi Bhabha[11] and Gayatri Spivak.[12] Building on their arguments that are raised and established in post-colonial studies, the *Decolonise* movement explores the intercultural practices that reach beyond the colonising habitus and focuses on how cultural institutions could be used as platforms better equipped to incorporate the diverse and the inclusive aspects in their practices, and to combat the unequal and lingering colonial power structures that are still at work.

For instance, in *On Being Included*,[13] Sara Ahmed, another key figure in the post-colonial movement, offers an account of the existing diversity and inclusivity initiatives and why they have so far largely failed in terms of creating truly equal opportunities, diversity and equality. She describes the discrepancies that exist between the general institutional symbolic commitments to diversity and the will to include everybody equally, vis-à-vis the underlying, material and practical inequalities that remain in place and are being reproduced in everyday institutional work. This everyday work is what we will focus on here, and how it can be decolonised. Ahmed's studies are guided by her own background in feminist theory and postmodernism, and those theoretical fields frame the argument here too.

More concretely, the *Decolonise* movement is a critical movement, and its practices have to do with the radical revelation of both the visible and the invisible habits of thought and practices that go beneath the surface and are not always visible. It explores the role of the dominant myths and the asymmetric power structures that are at work in society. All this is situated within the wider

7 Cf. UDHR art 4.
8 See *Decolonise UKC*, a project managed and led by students at the University of Kent with the aim to develop a manifesto focusing on Education, Inclusivity & Identity: https://decoloniseukc.org/ and their Twitter account: https://twitter.com/DecoloniseUKC
9 Bhambra, 2014.
10 Said, 2014.
11 Bhabha, 1994.
12 Spivak, 1988.
13 Ahmed, 2012.

framework of critical theory, where structures and memberships of groups or process are studied as ideologically contingent. Therefore, working with the already highly developed critical tools that question ideologies and practices that are considered oppressive (including those at work in schools, in universities, in museums or at home), the idea behind the *Decolonise* movement is to encourage people to actively use emancipatory responses to matters of inclusion and exclusion. Dominant societal structures such as religion, nationality, identity, cultural norms and laws become questioned, challenged, deconstructed and reimagined.

Within this critical context, the cultural institutions, in the term's widest sense, including museums, are encouraged to resist staying or becoming places for "indoctrination" or "colonisation" where unequal power structures are reproduced and perpetuated. Rather, they are urged to become the cultural terrains that enable empowerment and self-transformation.[14] This also means encouraging people to practise and share their knowledge as well as actively work towards changing oppressive norms and structures, or inspire and educate themselves and others to be able to challenge what is presented as the non-negotiable "nature" of society.

In a cultural heritage context, all this falls broadly under curatorial activism. Addressing the decolonisation of cultural memory institutions thus generally means raising questions about dominant power structures concerning issues of race, gender and class, among many others, and how that can and does affect the art world, the heritage sector and museums, and ultimately how the issues of equality, diversity and inclusivity are dealt with. The *Decolonise* movement invites institutions themselves to address the mental health and well-being of people who experience themselves as marginalised. The movement provides activists as well as institutions with tools with which to confront history, imperialism, and other excluding or dominating structural obstacles that may be reproduced in and through culture.

Finally, and most pertinently for us here, the movement raises the question of community building in the sense of how democratic membership and inclusion in a community is imagined. The movement takes a stand against exclusory norms, cultures and practices that exists in one's own community, as well as in education, and how to overcome the estrangement and division that are consequences of habitual, unreflected practices of asymmetrical power distributions.[15] The movement further asks of museums to commit to providing safe, inclusive, democratic environments, and for these spaces to be able to deal with and discuss difficult issues concerning community, identity and belonging.

Even more concretely, scholars have started to draw up practical guidelines as to how the *Decolonise* movement's tenets can be incorporated in cultural practice, including regulation, and how to deal with existing colonising remnants and tackle issues of structural exclusions and domination. As mentioned above,

14 Ahmed, 2012:70.
15 Packer and Goicoechea, 2000.

the movement is a non-hierarchical, grass-roots movement, and there are a number of strategies being employed simultaneously in different ways at different times. All of them are difficult to summarise and present as unified here. However, some general common denominators of the various commitments that hold together the movement can be highlighted:

Enlightenment: the foregrounding of the discussion concerning how certain knowledge tends to be privileged over other by being labelled as "objective" and/or "neutral".
Epistemology: the highlighted discussion on how certain phenomena are presented as being objective knowledge and how knowledge and knowledge sources are structurally defined, simultaneously inspiring reflection over why other contexts or other types of knowledge are structurally and historically left out, excluded and/or deemed as political, biased or non-scientific.
Ontology: the reflection on and questioning of what is allowed to be defined as the cultural field and/or culture in general: what is included in culture and what is left out.

The principles of the *Decolonise* movement can also be tied to the discussions concerning, for example, decontextualisation of works, something that was mentioned in previous chapters. If a work has been decontextualised and placed somewhere outside its place of origin, it also means that the host institution has to be responsible for how such works are presented, described and narrated and what it means to hold them in the collection, how they are understood and framed within the institutional context. Addressing this is not just about regulating the return and repatriation of cultural heritage and works of art to their places or owners of origin, but also about actively diversifying current and existing collections as well as advocating for responsible curatorial practices. It can even mean having to deaccession dominant and overrepresented works, for instance those created by white, male artists in favour of those created by artists that come from marginalised communities. In order for cultural practices not to continue to re-articulate and even reinforce colonialism and colonising practices,[16] these types of strategic undertakings must be discussed and implemented.

The curatorial practices of diversifying and deaccessioning still remain controversial. A number of American museums such as the San Francisco Museum of Modern Art (SFMOMA) and the Baltimore Museum of Art were some of the first large cultural institutions to lead the way by strategically starting to deaccession works. For instance, SFMOMA sold a Mark Rothko painting, and the Baltimore Museum focused generally on deaccessioning "blue chip"[17] male

16 Vrdoljak, 2008:8.
17 The term refers to artworks that are considered to be of great economic value and that can be relied on to be profitable over time as an investment. Such art is expected to hold and increase its value, regardless of general trends in the art market or the financial market.

artists such as Robert Rauschenberg and Andy Warhol. This was done in order to raise acquisition funds that could enable the institutions to acquire and display works from a more diverse set of artists – in this American context, that meant particularly art created by Black artists. Deaccessioning is thus both an act of exclusion (here, excluding works created by blue chip artists: often white, male) and inclusion (of works by members of marginalised communities, e.g. Black women) in order to ameliorate the historical wrongs and exclusory practices, and in order to better reflect and represent the general population as well as the local community.[18] Furthermore, deaccessioning must happen in the general spirit and commitment to promoting diversity and openness. Actively rethinking collections, exhibitions and educational programmes in museums in order to enhance diversity and accessibility is thus part of the *Decolonise* project. It has to do with the commitment to widening the number of perspectives within the collections in order to reach beyond authorised and dominant discourses. Museums enhance their holdings in this way and are able to continually address the existing historical gaps in their permanent collections.[19]

Actively working with equality and diversity in and through curatorial activism has fuelled various deaccessioning initiatives. The fact that most museums still display a majority of art created by blue chip or dominant artists, and that these remain on near-constant permanent view, means that museums are still colonised in a way. Addressing these issues means contributing and playing an active role in the constitution of a diverse community and spaces in which people feel included and invited. This also means connecting the museum collections more directly to the city in which it is located, for example, and the people who live there, as well as the people who visit it.

It is for instance obvious that there is a large and unjustified historical discrepancy between the works shown in museums and the populations where the museums are located. Creating inclusive canons, diversity and inclusivity means that museums need to take equality into account and take responsibility for how art history is exhibited and narrated. Museums are thus encouraged to undertake structural changes with the mission of creating a new relevance as well as broadening their audience in an inclusionary way that reflects the local population and its visitors.

The regulation of deaccessioning

Deaccessioning is a regulated practice, and there are rules on how to create inclusive and ethical collections, including how acquisition and deaccessioning may happen. The main regulatory instruments that can be mentioned here are the ICOM Code of Ethics, introduced above, and the ICOM Guidelines on

18 See also the deaccessioning of the Asian holdings in the Chicago Art Institute: Johnson, 2019.

19 The Art Newspaper Podcast from 17 May 2019: https://www.theartnewspaper.com/podcast/should-museums-sell-works-of-art-plus-activism-at-the-whitney-biennial

Deaccessioning (The Guidelines). There are also a number of other national regulatory instruments that regulate standards for deaccessioning[20] as well as internal regulations for museums.[21] Museum missions and their broader institutional purposes in terms of acquisition and deaccessioning are thus regulated practices.

We can begin with the Guidelines on Deaccessioning, which must be read together with the Code of Ethics, as the first is written with reference to the second. The Guidelines define deaccessioning as the act of lawfully removing an object from a museum's collections and then goes on to state that where the law does not prohibit a museum from deaccessioning, a museum can consider deaccessioning an object from its collection for one of ten listed reasons:

1. Poor physical condition
2. Threats to health and safety of the staff and visitors
3. The museum is unable to care adequately for the object
4. It is a duplicate
5. Poor quality and lacks aesthetic, historical and/or scientific value
6. It is false or fraudulent
7. Another museum could more appropriately care for, display and provide access to the object
8. It is inconsistent with applicable law or ethical principles, including being stolen or illegally exported or imported, or subject to other legal claims for return or restitution
9. It is no longer consistent with the mission or collecting goals of the museum
10. It is being sold as part of the museum's effort to renew and improve its collections.[22]

I will not describe any of the ten reasons in detail here; I think that most of them are self-explanatory. What can be highlighted, however, is that the Guidelines specifically prohibit that any potential monetary value gained from a deaccessioned object be considered as part of the motive for determining whether or not to deaccession. The Guidelines further state, in the section called Disposition, that funds gained from deaccessioning and disposal of an object cannot be used solely for the benefit of the museum's collection, that is, general acquisitions and to care for the collection. It is also stated that the museum may not use the funds for the costs of regular museum administration or maintenance.[23]

20 See e.g. American Alliance of Museums Code of Ethics for Museums (1994). See also AAM Direct Care of Collections: Ethics, Guidelines and Recommendations, 2016:12.

21 See e.g. the abovementioned ICOM regulation, e.g. its Code of Ethics for Museums (2004).

22 ICOM Code of Ethics section 2; articles 2.12–2.17.

23 See also 2.16 ICOM Code of Ethics.

In practice this is usually interpreted as meaning that any proceeds from sales that are part of deaccessioning can be used, for instance, to acquire works from the same period, from a more diverse pool of artists such as women or artists from marginalised communities. It also means that deaccession of duplicates and triplicates in the institutional hold can be allowed, particularly if they

- come from dominant artists, or
- are not on display, or
- are costly to store, or
- if they do not significantly contribute to the overall collection.

Furthermore, deaccessioning of works by dominant artists can also be allowed if the works that are held are not of as high a quality as other works by the same artist. It must also happen in accordance with any other restrictions that may exist, for example restrictions outlined in donation or gift letters, and in conversations with the artists themselves if they are alive or the artist's estates, if they are deceased.

Deaccessioning is discussed and often encouraged by many current curators and museum directors, spurred on by the *Decolonise* movement, the Black Lives Matter movement and other socially engaged movements such as #Metoo, arguing that this is how art history, ethical heritage discourses and collections with social relevance can be embedded in the present practices. It means negotiating how communities are conceived of in the museums, or how marginalised members of communities can be recognised and represented in art history.

Above, we saw how the authorised heritage discourse constructs a narrative of origin, of the state or of any of the other recognised communities. The authorised discourse works as a foundational myth of the community, and this is a practice that eventually leads towards state building and recognition. We also saw that such origin narratives form the discursive frameworks for the states and are particularly visible in larger, often national, museums. This means that how a community is envisioned is a question of power and how a national identity is described, narrated and presented often guides the organisation of national museums and their collections. That means that collections can come to reflect underlying ideologies of dominance in their organisation as well as through their permanent collections, exhibited works and overall holdings. When a dominant narrative is driven by a nationalist or a Western ideal, it means that it can be reproduced in museums and in their practices through, for example, holding a predominant number of works created by white, male, Western, artists, or, not holding works that represent the de facto diversity of a nations population.

This is exactly what the *Decolonise* movement has sought to show as well as to rectify. Infusing the diverse and the multicultural, and dealing with the problematic issues and decolonising museum practices, become the first steps toward moving beyond the mono-ethnic community assumption that underpin the discourse of the nation state.

The *Decolonise* movement has brought forth an inverted paradigm where the dominant white, artistic output that has so far acted as an unquestioned default has shifted, and many dominant voices have been moved to the side or even to the periphery, in order to invert the dialogue and reimagine the community and its constitution differently. Such fundamental shifts can only occur not just by putting on temporary displays and exhibitions, but also by rethinking the deeper structures and organisations of collections all together.

This in turn means that the notion of "community" is opened up, showing the excluded groups, and how their cultural expressions are often omitted. It also means that the conception of community is moved beyond its homogenic, mono-cultural, ethno-nationalist assumptions through curation. In this way, it can be argued that the transnational in heritage emerges as being already there, yet excluded. What is on the surface presented as a mono-cultural community is in fact a construction that relies on an authorised heritage discourse and active inclusions and exclusions. The argument being that transnational heritage is not an "additional" category that needs to be created in regulation, but rather one that already exists but is not acknowledged.

We can be reminded of some of the definitions of transnational heritage presented in Chapter 1, particularly those found outside the regulatory sphere where the term is often connected to, e.g., migrant cultures, or culture produced by migrants in diaspora. We have already touched upon the diasporic communities and how they participate in shaping and transforming the societies in which they settle,[24] such as the Edmund de Waal examples in Chapter 3 where the transnational in culture comes with migrants that move to a new homeland.[25] Understanding transnational heritage in this way as tied to "realms of memory" or *lieux de mémoire*[26] and as shared memories of co-existence, means seeing the transnational in a (decolonised) local or national community.

The "alternative" museum tour, the counter-narrative and the reimagined community

Reframing institutional narratives in this way, and actively focusing on the importance of counter-narratives, serves to advance the discussion regarding transnational heritage. Even though research, theory and activism have challenged the structural, institutional as well as individual exclusion and colonising practices in museums, galleries and other cultural institutions for many decades, narrow curation is in many ways still the dominant practice. Very little change has taken place. Recently, as the *Decolonise* movement gained momentum, intensified by the Black Lives Matter movement and backed by a number of other social movements such as feminist, queer and anti-racist movements. All of them together provided the tools for dealing with and revealing exclusory

24 Beschea-Fache, 2012.
25 Grasmuck and Hinze, 2016.
26 Nora, 1992.

practices, as well as providing up-to-date information and statistics showing how the cultural world is still deeply engaged in "othering" or exclusory practices. For instance, it could be shown that a large number of galleries exhibited and represented only white artists, that a very small percentage of museums' permanent collections included non-white or female artists, that European and North American artists dominated the large majority of blockbuster exhibitions and so on.[27]

As a direct response to this, many alternative museum tours started to emerge, exploring the issues of exclusion, biased narratives, colonial heritage, and racial and gender issues. Confronting the official narratives and the authorised heritage discourses became a strategic step towards imagining new types of diverse community formations. Such counter-narratives and alternative museum tours serve as more than a curiosity here. Their role in educating the public as well as forcing the institutions to radically rethink permanent collections and how art history is represented in general cannot be underplayed. This opens up new, multiple narratives, where the transnational within the national becomes unavoidable. There are three interesting examples that can be briefly mentioned here as being directly affected by this type of awareness: the expansion and reorganisation of the Museum of Modern Art in New York (MOMA); the controversy that surrounded the proposed sale of Kerry James Marshall's painting *Knowledge and Wonder*; and the refurbishment of the Swedish National Museum.

The expansion of MOMA involved extending the museum building and reshuffling the permanent collection. The collection is now organised differently, around themes instead of chronology. Artists such as Picasso are placed side by side with more recent, more diverse artists such as Faith Ringgold. From now on, the MOMA permanent collection will also be rotated every six months, accentuating how narratives in museums are framed, in which contexts art is placed, and how it is presented can be fluid and negotiated over time. This type of insight is at least a first step towards introducing diversity in cultural practices, alternative narratives and becoming a more inclusive, decolonised, institution.

The second example concerns the controversy over the proposed sale of Kerry James Marshall's painting *Knowledge and Wonder*. In 2018 the city of Chicago presented what turned out to be a controversial plan: to sell the Marshall painting, which the city owns. The painting, or rather the mural, was made in 1995. The artist created it for a local public library in west Chicago, which is a predominantly African American, neighbourhood. It was commissioned in the mid Nineties for a fee of $10,000. When the artist's profile rose, particularly with the current and ongoing growing appreciation of Black-American art, the city decided to auction the mural at Christie's in New York. Christie's estimated its value at around $10 million to $15 million, a sum that could bring a large income to the city of Chicago. The idea was to use the proceeds from the sale to upgrade the city library and to establish a fund for

27 For some interesting statistics see Reilly, 2018:22.

public art in underprivileged communities. The artist as well as the people of Chicago were very critical of the proposed sale and vocal about their disapproval. In the end the sale did not take place, partly because many argued that the city of Chicago also owns other works by prominent artists and that are exhibited in the public sphere such as Picasso's sculpture *Untitled* (1967) in Daley Plaza and Richard Serra's *Reading Cones* (1988). These two works were not put forward and considered for sale even though they too could be estimated as having high values. This indicated that there are also differences and (here racial) hierarchies among dominant (male) artists that might be at work, and that must be kept in mind too.

Nationalmuseum, the Swedish National Museum, reopened in October 2018 after having been closed for a five-year period of refurbishment. As part of the renovation project a new wing was added to the building, the technology in the museum updated and, curatorially, the meaning of "national" within the context of the National Museum and Swedish national art and art history was rethought so that it could be presented in a more inclusive manner. The museum chose to directly address issues of inclusion and exclusion in its curatorial vision, which ignited a heated debate as to what national museums should be able to claim about citizenship and inclusion and whether these are the discussions that a national museum should be engaging in at all. Many felt that the National Museum had adopted a "political" tone and moved away from the more "neutral", "educational" narrative that had been adopted before the refurbishment.

The Swedish National Museum is publicly funded and regulated in law.[28] The regulatory instrument that governs it states that the museum has a public remit to promote inclusive art, and to constantly strive towards the renewal of narratives and how art is presented and framed. However, until the refurbishment the museum was steeped in a traditional understanding of what the national is, as well as a dominant authorised heritage discourse as to what is understood as the national, oftentimes meaning the mono-ethnic. In a country like Sweden, with a vast Indigenous community as well as a substantial community of migrants, not to mention its historically multicultural ties, for example to Asia through trade, it became evident that negotiating the formulation and narration of the so-called "national" in a national museum is not at all straightforward.

All three examples are illustrative of the fact that within the mono-cultural there lies something transnational, diverse and multicultural that is not always discernible, not to say excluded. Focusing on the transnational is an act of resistance that can be experienced as controversial, which circles us back to what was described at the beginning of this book as the political and the emotional aspects connected to cultural heritage and its authorised discourses. Many cultural institutions are now moving away from the mono-ethnic conceptions of collections, revealing both local and global diversities that exist

28 Swedish Museum Act, *Museilag* (2017:563).

withing their holdings, and engaging in a number of parallel narratives of identity and belonging that are simultaneously at play. This is the transnational in heritage, even if it now looks different to how it did in the early chapters of this book. Understanding that all heritage is transnational in some way is thus a direct result of the *Decolonise* project.

What we will see in the next section is how global movements such as *Decolonise*, as well as other activist movements like the environmental movements, and various other awareness initiatives have actively been driving the agenda as to what should be exhibited in museums, how museums should be governed and what responsibilities they have in terms of how multicultural, diverse, yes *transnational*, communities are imagined.

Living heritage

In the end, it comes down to the question of "living heritage", of constantly developing communities, of people that co-exist, of understanding community as something that evolves over time, and that never remains the same. To address this we need to return, once again, to the museums – but this time from the point of view of living heritage. Museums are becoming increasingly more responsible for capturing the constantly evolving contours of communities through inclusive curation and diversified holdings.

Throughout this book I have discussed precisely this from various points of view with the insight that cultural heritage is something living, regardless of how old it is. It is something that forms the community. The issue that we have arrived at now is how to safeguard diverse heritage without having to resort to assumptions of mono-ethnicity or nationalist hegemonies in order to imagine a community and in order to narrate its heritage. More concretely, this means that we have to regulate in a way so that heritage or groups of people are never left out because it or they do not fit in within a given definition of community, or heritage.

One direct way to exit from the exclusory authorised heritage discourses is to decolonise the museums by, e.g., returning works connected to colonisation to their places of origin, or by diversifying the collections. But there are indirect ways too, and they have to do with how museums represent, govern and fund their collections and practices. The *Decolonise Museums* movement has therefore urged museums to deal with both direct and indirect colonial practices that are embedded in curation, exhibition and wider curatorial practices. This is in line with existing regulation such as art 4 UDHR as well as the ICOM Code of Ethics. We can be reminded of the 2015 UNESCO Museum Recommendations as well as the ICOM Code of Ethics, that are both hortatory regulatory instruments stipulating similar ethical positions. As we saw in the previous chapters, all regulatory instruments are designed to make cultural institutions and their practices more relevant and more ethically acceptable.

It is now widely held that in order to be truly ethically acceptable the museums must acknowledge and appropriately deal with their direct ties to the colonial past, for example through voluntary returns and repatriation of works, if the legal route is not applicable. At the time of writing, museums have reached a consensus and are committed to returning all human remains held in their collections regardless of when they were acquired. However, there are no similar clear ethical positions and undertakings when it comes to the return of cultural heritage. The *Decolonise Museums* movement has required and campaigned for securing wider promises from the museums in terms of the return of colonial heritage, urging them to go much further than what is legally required under the non-retroactive, difficult to enforce, cultural heritage laws. These campaigns have given rise to some changes and commitments that now function as norms that the museums act in accordance with. One such important step was taken by the French government in November 2019 and December 2020, when the country pledged to permanently return the Benin statues and other colonial African heritage that are held in France.[29]

Secondly, and it cannot be stressed enough, the calls to decolonise the museums do not only have to do with the direct connections to colonisation and the slave trade or diversifying the collections. Decolonisation also means addressing wider ongoing practices of exclusion that give rise to less visible forms of domination. A clear example of a call for indirect decolonisation was a collaborative initiative in 2019 that was organised by *Decolonise Museums* and *Decolonise This Place*. The two activist groups came together for a string of coordinated protests directed at the Whitney Museum in New York. An open letter that was published by Verso prompted the initiative and acted as one of the triggering factors for the protests. The letter was signed by theorists, critics and scholars calling for the removal of a board member of the Whitney Museum who was also the CEO of the company Safariland, a manufacturer of weapons and teargas.[30]

Various media outlets, and artists such as Michael Rakowitz, became involved in the protest, which we will discuss below. Rakowitz, who was selected for that year's prestigious Whitney Biennial, chose to withdraw from it in a show of solidarity.[31] The art and research collective Forensic Architecture, which had also been selected for the Whitney Biennial that year, also took part in the protest. At first they chose to keep their place in the Biennial, and instead submit an investigatory work, *Safariland*, as their contribution to the Biennial, but subsequently they withdrew altogether. The investigation conducted by Forensic Architecture suggested among other things that Safariland gas canisters had been used on civilians at the San Diego–Tijuana border. It was also argued that their canisters had been used on protesters in Ferguson,

29 See e.g. the French commitment to returning cultural heritage to Africa, from 18 December 2020 https://www.elysee.fr/emmanuel-macron/2020/12/18/restitution-des-biens-culturels-une-promesse-tenue-pour-une-nouvelle-page-des-relations-entre-lafrique-et-la-france

30 The letter is available at: https://www.versobooks.com/blogs/4295-kanders-must-go-an-open-letter-from-theorists-critics-and-scholars-updated-list-of-signatories

31 See e.g. Kinsella, 2019.

Standing Rock and in Gaza. These were Safariland products, and their CEO benefited, indirectly, from these activities. As part of the decolonise commitment, the open letter called for his removal from the Whitney board. He eventually left voluntarily.

This was not the only board member whose broader business dealings were investigated by the *Decolonise* movement. The former director of the Serpentine Galleries in London resigned due to an alleged connection between her husband and a controversial cyber-weapons company. The *Decolonise* movement also investigated and called for the resignation of a MOMA board member, but the individual in question remains on the board at the time of writing.

As we can see, to decolonise involves bringing to the surface how museums are governed and funded. One of the more prominent examples of contested museum funding in recent years has involved the Sackler family's philanthropic donations. This American family, who are the founders and owners of the pharmaceutical company Purdue Pharma, which produces the controversial painkiller drug OxyContin, were one of the largest donors for many of the leading and prominent cultural institutions in New York, London and Paris.

The artist Nan Goldin staged a number of protests against the Sackler family for what she describes as their involvement in the opioid crisis due to over-prescriptions of OxyContin. Having personally had experience with the damaging effects of the drug, she urged all cultural institutions globally that are in any way receiving Sackler funds, to boycott their donations on an ethical basis. She was joined in her protests by the *Decolonise* movement as well as a number of other groups that have campaigned against over-prescription of painkillers.

As a direct response to their protests, many cultural institutions that were receiving funds from the Sackler family either terminated or put on hold their collaborations. Among them were the National Portrait Gallery in London and the South London Gallery, which also returned a donation, and the Guggenheim in New York, which decided to no longer accept any gifts from the family.

A larger discussion had already been initiated concerning how cultural institutions should ethically deal with sponsorship and donations from funders that can be considered as unethical in some way. The widely reported issue concerning the donations and sponsorships by British Petroleum (BP) to cultural institutions had already been instigated by environmental activists. In the wake of these protests, the Tate in London had declared an institutional "climate emergency", pledging to reduce its carbon footprint by 10 percent, to switch to green options and to change the travel policies for its staff, among other things. It had already ended its collaboration with BP in 2016 as part of its commitment to climate emergency issues. On the other hand, the British Museum has so far refused to fully terminate its collaboration with BP, which has drawn wide criticism. A board member left her seat on the board in protest.

The *Decolonise* movement is now urging all museums to divest themselves of any unethical funding in this way. It calls for the museums to move away from practices that can be seen as unethical and to carefully consider who is included on their boards, how they are funded and governed, and how they are committing to ethical curatorial practices. This includes questions concerning staff conditions as well as appointments of directors. Furthermore, calls for solidarity with migrants, livelihoods of people in the local communities and discussions of how racial equality can be integrated and included in the everyday practices of the museums are also encouraged as part of the decolonising commitments.

The impossible and the responsible

To decolonise means coming to terms with the existing and ongoing exclusory practices and invisible colonial acts. The artist Michael Rakowitz has explored the decolonise theme in his practice. Rakowitz, who is of Iraqi-American Jewish descent, is accustomed to dealing with and exploring matters of the transnational and how excluded and contested communities are affected and negated by dominant powers and authorised discourses on a global scale.

In his Whitechapel exhibition in London in 2019, Rakowitz studied a number of issues of inclusion and exclusion such as housing sites and urban design and how the creation of living environments creates communities. He focused on how architecture and buildings can embody histories or advance certain community formations while excluding others. We have already discussed the broader significance of architecture as heritage in Chapter 4, and many of the issues raised by Rakowitz in the Whitechapel exhibition will resonate with what was discussed above.

Rakowitz engaged in a discussion concerning the role of architecture in racial inclusion and exclusion, as well as how it contributes towards the construction of suburban areas and ghettos. His work deals with what in this context can be described as internal transnational heritage, or, in the words of Rakowitz himself, what is through the eyes of the dominant power structure seen as an *impossible community*. By paraphrasing Judith Butler, he develops this argument by stating: if a diverse and inclusive community is seen as something impossible, then we must demand the impossible.[32] The impossible of course being a transnational community that is not contested, that is allowed to exist, that is not exclusory, one where everything intersects with everything, a truly multicultural constellation. Such an impossible community lies at the heart of the transnational. It is expressed through inclusive public spaces, and through memory making that reflects co-existence. Rakowitz thus places the issue of transnational in the foreground for the national, local and global.

The issues of the impossible community can be placed under the more established banner of "representation". How diverse and living communities can be constituted, narrated and represented in and through culture is at issue. Rakowitz's work is therefore important to mention here because it highlights the impossible in the formation of the transnational community in a new way,

32 Hyperallergic Podcast, Michael Rakowitz Discusses Withdrawing from the 2019 Whitney Biennial, and His Leonard Cohen Problem, from 17 May 2019. https://hyperallergic.com/500947/michael-rakowitz-whitney-biennial-leonard-cohen/

i.e. it is contested both internally (e.g. who is seen as a member of the local or national community) and externally (whose external culture is allowed into the public space).

Falling monuments – identity, politics and representation

A lot has been written about the constitution of the public space, what it means in terms of the creation of community, as well as the role it plays as a co-constituent of identity, that I need not repeat here.[33] The *Decolonise* movement has interrupted the dominant heritage discourses and grand narratives outside museum walls too. The public spaces have became contested and with them the monuments that adorn them.

Throughout June 2020 public statues and monuments representing or connected to slavery, colonisation or racism were toppled, destroyed, graffitied or disassembled by activists. A number of monuments around the world fell as a result of this, particularly spurred on by the killing of George Floyd. First, confederate statues in the United States were challenged, such as the statue of Robert E. Lee in Richmond, Virginia. It was spray-painted, used as a site for projections of alternative narratives and became the focal point for gatherings and assemblies for the Black Lives Matter protests. Not long after that, the monument of the slave trader Edward Colston in Bristol was toppled and thrown into the harbour by protesters. A Voltaire statue[34] in Paris was defaced. The statue of Leopold II in Ghent was officially and voluntarily taken down by the Ghent city council. And so on.[35] These monuments were seen as directly embodying authorised heritage discourse. As such, they indicated and represented the dominant image of a community, its history, traditions and in the end its (imagined!) constitution.

An unprecedented contestation of authorised heritage discourses emerged in this way throughout the summer of 2020, where the toppling of monuments was seen as the performative act of decolonisation. Many of these obviously very problematic monuments in the public sphere perpetuated dominant and often colonial narratives. The representation and meaning of monuments in the public space was brought into question as well as how a community is constructed and negotiated through its public space. The veneer of transparency that had hitherto shrouded the monuments fell.

What can be deduced from this is that what happens in the public sphere matters to the regulation of transnational heritage too. Let us then, once again, return to the rejected Danish-led proposal for a new definition of museums for the ICOM guidelines mentioned at the beginning of this book:

33 See however Bruncevic, 2018; Bruncevic 2015; Lefebvre, H., 1991; Massey, 2005; Massey, 2007; etc.

34 Braun, 2020.

35 See e.g. the Monument Lab podcast devoted to the decolonisation of monuments: https://monumentlab.com/podcast

> Museums are democratising, inclusive and polyphonic spaces for critical dialogue about the pasts and the futures. Acknowledging and addressing the conflicts and challenges of the present, they hold artefacts and specimens in trust for society, safeguard diverse memories for future generations and guarantee equal rights and equal access to heritage for all people.
>
> Museums are not for profit. They are participatory and transparent, and work in active partnership with and for diverse communities to collect, preserve, research, interpret, exhibit, and enhance understandings of the world, aiming to contribute to human dignity and social justice, global equality and planetary wellbeing.[36]

I hope that it now has a different, more urgent, ring to it. And the fact that this proposal was too politically controversial to pass perhaps makes more sense within this context. The boundary between the museum and the public space became erased in many ways during 2020. Read together with the proposed new museum definition, we now realise that we might have entered Malraux's *museum without walls*.[37]

And, with the insight that the boundary separating the museum space from the public space has been thinned not to say eroded, and now knowing that how museums are regulated and constituted touches on fundamental inclusion and the very tissue of a community, we realise two things. One, how museums are governed, funded and under what ethical rules they operate has to do with more than "just" the return of colonial loots or building diversified collections. And two, we come to the realisation that perhaps all heritage is in one way or another transnational, i.e. inherently multicultural, diverse, changing and movable.

Of course, the activities of the *Decolonise* movement are part of a larger changing cultural landscape in terms of responsibility and accountability that goes further than just how museums are envisioned and organised. This was a moment in history when a number of movements collided with *Decolonise* such as the environmental movements, the Yellow Vests, as well as the intensification of the Black Lives Matter movement in the spring of 2020, all calling for inclusion, diversity and equality inside and outside societal and cultural institutions. They all envision a transnational community. The multicultural, and indeed the transnational, suddenly appears everywhere. In fact it was always there, hidden under the surface, but made invisible. Now, when the transnational community has become apparent, it cannot be put back into the box.

Location independent: in-between communities

I will leave the *Decolonise* movement briefly and return to it towards the end of this chapter. In this final section I want to focus on a last community type, one

36 https://icom.museum/en/news/icom-announces-the-alternative-museum-definition-that-will-be-subject-to-a-vote/. See also Sandahl, 2019:1–7.

37 Malraux, 1967.

that is also invisible to regulation. We have seen how the community categories that exist in regulation tend to require a connection to territory in order for a group of people to be conceived of as a "community". Here we will look at communities without territories – the location-independent communities. I have chosen to focus on communities that emerge from countercultures, particularly the skateboarding and surfing cultures, as examples in order to illustrate the point. Both are location-independent communities whose members identify through common lifestyle norms and cultural codes internally, and are able to show common traditions, history and shared beliefs externally. Yet none of these are considered as communities that can have cultural heritage, partly because they are not location dependent and partly because the community does not look like any of the community types envisioned in regulation.

Community via appropriation

Ask anybody to describe a "skater" or a "surfer" and you will almost certainly get a clear picture of what they are. A skater will probably be described as a young(ish) white, middle-class male with radical beliefs and an adventurous lifestyle. Some may even add to their description items of clothing like types of jeans, sneakers, hats or caps, or accessories like different skateboards and stickers, or certain musical or cinematic aesthetics, or the love of brands like Vans, Volcom or Supreme. A surfer will probably be described as male, blond, middle class, a free spirit that lives for the "endless" summer, and items of clothing, vehicles, accessories and cultural tropes will be mentioned here too. These archetypes, or rather *stereotypes*, are created and upheld through media, branding and member participation, which in turn has given rise to easily identifiable location-independent communities that have formed over time.

While both skateboarding and surfing could be primarily thought of as sporting activities, many of their members will be quick to dispel any such assumption and will proclaim that "it's not just a sport. To one degree or another, [it is also] art, religion, philosophy, and metaphysics."[38] Both skateboarding and surfing can in that vein be described as (counter)cultures with ideals of disobedience and revolt, as well as a commitment to a lifestyle and its community. The two should not be conflated, and it is not the intention here either. However, there are common denominators that are at play within both of these cultures that can aid in illustrating a critique as well as a potential opening of the regulatory community categories. These communities are not tied to any territory, they do not have any political aspiration for self-determination, they are not a minority, yet they identify with communal lifestyles and beliefs as well as produce their own cultural output.

Wave-riding can be traced back to thousands of years BC to ancient Peru among other places. Modern surfing history generally connects the practice to ancient Polynesia and the leisurely activities of the Hawaiians, where it "was

38 Warshaw, 2010:72.

practiced with equal enthusiasm (and class-leveling nudity) by farmers, warriors, weavers, healers, fishermen, children, grandparents, chiefs, and regents".[39] Skateboarding on the other hand sprung up more recently in the early 20th century, in a period of drought when the waves were flat and Californian surfers started to engage in what was often referred to as "sidewalk surfing".[40]

It was Westerners who first started to use the terms "surfer" and "surfing", which replaced the earlier "surf-swimming", "surf-boarding", "surf-bathing", "surf play" and "surf sport". In Hawaiian it is referred to as *papa he'e nalu*, which means "board for wave-sliding". English-speakers had also elaborated other expressions such as "floatboard", "sharkboard", "broad-board" and "bathing-board". The word "surf-board" first emerged sometime in the 1790s, when travelling Westerners came to Polynesia and observed this water activity performed by the natives.[41]

The colonial and racial aspects in surfing history are undeniable. A lot can be said about the settlers' attempts initially to "civilise" the natives and change their local customs such as surfing and hula dancing, as well as the subsequent attempts to ban surfing because it was considered immoral and improper by missionaries in Hawaii. However, in the early 20th century surfing became a tourist activity, and a number of prestigious surfing clubs were created by and for the American wealthy elite. These were whites-only organisations, and the local population was only allowed in the exclusive hotels and their beaches as "beachboys" or as surfing instructors. Matt Warshaw describes the beachboy style that emerged from this as "sexed-up, easygoing, empty-pocket deviancy [which] laid a foundation for what would later be called the surfing lifestyle".[42]

Surfing came to California, then Australia and eventually spread globally. The colonial and segregation aspects connected to it were whitewashed, so to speak, and with time it became an activity connected to a Los Angeles lifestyle that was in many ways privileged, fashionable and coveted. Surfing became popular, and magazines like *Vogue* and *National Geographic* wrote about it. It became at once an urban counterculture that settled in and around Venice Beach, connected to graffiti, drugs and cultural disobedience, as well as a privileged, exclusive activity that required expensive surfboards, wetsuits and leisure time that allowed the surfers to spend their days on the beach, hang out or travel the world in search of the perfect wave and the endless summer.

There is no clear consensus in the skateboarding community as to when and how it started, who invented the first skateboard and who was the first to start "surfing" on land. Some place its beginning in the early 1900s when boards with wheels, resembling kick-scooters, emerged. Others place it in the 1940–1950s as a pastime for surfers who were trying to find something to do while the waves were flat or as an after-surf activity. Skateboards emerged around

39 Warshaw, 2010:252.
40 Borden, 2019:6–10.
41 Warshaw, 2010:446.
42 Warshaw, 2010:823.

that time too, but it is not known who made the first one. Magazines devoted to skateboarding sprung up in the early 1960s. The skateboarder became identified as a member of a counterculture, and this was strengthened by how they were portrayed in the media: as rebels, daredevils and performers. Skateboarding as a culture has gone through a number of transformations: from a land-bound pastime for surfers in the beginning, to becoming a sport in the 1970s, to its decline in the 1980s and its rise and return in the 1990s, to moving into haute couture and fine art in the 2010s.

An unmissable phenomenon in skateboarding during the 2000s has been the meteoric rise of the skateboarding manufacturer turned fashion label, Supreme. It was established in the early 1990s by British-born James Jebbia, marketing itself as a fusion of skateboarding, culture and clothing. It moved from once being a brand on a need-to-know basis within skateboarding community and their followers, to securing a mainstream position in fashion. Supreme manufactures skateboards, accessories and clothes, and is particularly well known for its collaborations with cultural icons such as Harmony Korine, Larry Clark, Jeff Koons, Richard Prince and Damien Hirst, as well as fashion brands such as Nike, Louis Vuitton and Comme des Garçons. Building on a number of values that have their origin in the skateboarding counterculture and its ideals, Supreme has been taking on some of the longest-standing tenets perfected over decades by traditional haute-couture fashion brands, creating a new type of fashion and entirely new fashion followers.

Supreme's "box logo" is now famous: a red rectangle with the word SUPREME written in white letters, in the font Futura Bold. The company has acknowledged that the layout of the logo is directly based on artist Barbara Kruger's famous imagery, widely recognised iconic messages and slogans placed over advertising images written in white Futura Bold font in red rectangular boxes. Some of Kruger's most recognised slogans are "I shop therefore I am", "Love is for Sale" or "Your Body is a Battleground".

Barbara Kruger commented on Supreme's use of her visual imagery in November 2017 during the New York performance art biennial, Performa. She exhibited a series of works, or rather staged a series of life performance pieces, entitled *Untitled* (The Drop), *Untitled* (Skate) and *Untitled* (Know, Believe, Forget). As part of the exhibition, she covered a skatepark with her work as well as created merchandise with her signatory slogans in the white Futura Bold letters in red rectangles. The audience were invited to purchase skateboards and accessories for skateboards bearing her slogans in her visual language, which now has the same layout as the Supreme logo. This performance was done in collaboration with another skateboarding brand, Volcom.

In these and similar ways, both the surfing and skateboarding cultures are connected to a level of direct appropriation of, earlier cultural practices. We saw in Chapter 3 how, to this day, surfing brands and manufacturers easily fall back on the unauthorised use and misappropriation of Indigenous iconography and symbols. This is nothing new.

Any type of (colonial) appropriation of traditional culture is rightly considered to be extremely problematic in cultural heritage law. In this sense, the community categories that exist in regulation can serve as a pivot, for example the Indigenous communities are enabled to protect their communal traditional symbols or traditional cultural expressions. But what is interesting here is that a new community is emerging too, and with it a new cultural identity that is not recognised in law. It cannot easily be identified as a "group" or "community" – at least not within the discourses of doctrinal law. It is certainly not a "community" in the three community definitions that we have explored here. But there is nonetheless an identifiable community that exists and from which cultural practices emerge, let us call it a skateboarder or a surfer community, that is location independent, whose cultural practices are connected to a lifestyle and a set of beliefs.

Community strengthened by branding

In many ways, current surfing and skateboarding cultures are clearly also commercially driven lifestyles, and it is precisely this commercial framing that has strengthened the sense of communal and cultural belonging. What is interesting to point out here is the branding practices from global multinational corporations that are contributing to articulating and creating lifestyles, as well as connecting them to other social movements or trends.

Branded social engagement is very common. Some easy examples are connected to the biggest brands to ever exist, such as Coca-Cola and Nike, that tend to mix commercial messages with social engagement. These are companies that actively endorse and inscribe themselves in the contexts of wider social movements. Most recently, they have chosen to proclaim solidarity with the Black Lives Matter movement, one in a row of many movements that they have historically endorsed and supported. The branding practices rely in this way on their global brand community, which identifies with the lifestyle promoted by the company. The brand creates the community, the consumer community then co-creates the brand, and so on endlessly. Much of this is in fact enabled by law, trademark law more specifically.

These brands are, as Gangjee points out, employing a new type of marketing strategy that can be described as "dialogic" and "conversational",[43] and that draws the community of consumers into a lifestyle, rather than the more traditional "broadcast model" where the consumer is seen as a passive recipient of a brand message and as a purchaser of its products. In the dialogic model the brand relies on consumer cooperation, performativity, and for the consumer to subscribe to a lifestyle that is endorsed by the brand. An immersive experience

43 In the *Sickman* case (*Sieckmann v. German Patent and Trademark Office*, C-273/00), it is stated "A trade mark is in reality communication [...] Communication means *one* person imparting something that he knows to another. Consequently, every act of communication requires *a sender, a message*, a medium or channel for its transmission, *and a recipient* who can decipher or decode it" [my emphasis].

is created where the consumers are co-opted as participators, becoming members of the community.

When reflecting on her book *No Logo*'s second edition, which came out in 2009 on its tenth anniversary, Naomi Klein noted that, since the first edition of the book, such commercial branding practices had expanded even beyond the corporate domain of the late 1990s and moved into politics of the early 2000s. Politicians themselves became super-brands, Klein notes, and even the former US president, Barack Obama, had been turned into one of the biggest brands in the world. She writes:

> Perhaps there is nothing wrong with this. Why shouldn't a president who wants to change the country benefit from marketing as good as Starbucks and Nike. Every transformative movement in history has used *strong graphic design, catchy slogans and, yes, fashion to build its base.* Fifteen years ago, Nike appropriated the imagery of the civil rights movement and the icons of sixties counterculture to inspire cult-like devotion to running shoes.[44]

Self-branding[45] is of course now a practice not only undertaken by politicians and celebrities but also by "regular" people, through the brands they identify with, the curation of their (online and offline) life,[46] through their clothing, social media, affiliations, etc. The so-called individual is now assembled through a selection of lifestyle choices, embedded in chosen brands, and as such individuals are constantly connected to a vast communal multiplicity – a far cry from a mono-ethnic nationalist community.

This also reveals a space, or a *brandscape*, where people live branded lives and identify with the communities that emerge from brands. That is clear from Supreme's branding, for instance, which inscribes the brand in the skateboarding counterculture as well as in contemporary art practices. By participating in skateboarding events or by creating queues outside their shops, or by otherwise occupying public space, Supreme inflates its brand, from its commercial sphere through the public space into the consumers' private lives. It brings in consumers and involves them in the corporate brand and its promoted lifestyle.[47] As such, the consumers contribute to the expansion of the brand. This is now an established practice, and it requires both a product that is marketed one-way from a corporation to a passive consumer, and an interactive practice where active consumers, their movements and lifestyle choices, are captured by the brand. In this way the consumers participate in giving meaning and value to an

44 [my emphasis] Klein, 2010:xxv–xxvi.

45 On the performative self as part of the brand image, see McDonagh, 2015:627: "[…] within this process consumers are often encouraged to engage with brands – effectively to 'perform' them – a creative process within which some elements of the brand appear to remain stable (awareness) while other aspects remain contestable and in a constant state of re-imagination (image)".

46 See e.g. Floridi, 2014.

47 Coombe, 1998:53.

ever-expanding brand. The interesting notion here though is that the very same commercial brand itself relies, builds on and even appropriates already existing heritage, culture and artistic visual language in order to create a branded community.

The branded community is formed when consumers start to identify with a brand and its promoted lifestyle. They become embedded in the corporation as well as in their intellectual property. The consumers are thus inscribed in a proprietary, yet identity-forming, way of life through branding practices. By merely living their life while covering their bodies in a brand's logo, and by identifying with the tenets, lifestyle and practices that a brand professes and promotes, a consumer community is formed. It can almost adopt a (quasi-) religious or political language and as such have implications on people's identity and sense of belonging. But it is not out of a religious belief that the brand-based community emerges, but rather out of trademark law, which enables commercial branding practices that encourage association with the brand as part of one's own identity and belonging. These practices also exploit a new type of "immaterial labour"[48] performed by the community. The consumers are directly asked to participate through work in creating value for the brand, by brand loyalty and by becoming actively involved in brand creation. Their participation is recognised as "fun", "inclusive" or simply as a *lifestyle*. At the same time their "work" is co-opted and monetised by the brand.[49]

Intellectual property law does not *a priori* recognise a communal subject, as we saw in Chapter 3. That is why community as a concept based on branding practices and proprietary law remains out of sight here too: there is no perceivable community to speak of neither in cultural heritage law nor in intellectual property law.

Decolonising the location-independent community

Obviously, these are established branding practices where corporations latch on to countercultures, subcultures or global social movements by appropriation and by including them into a corporate identity. It means that in many ways the location-independent community is also misappropriated and colonised in ways not necessarily apparent to law. So when for instance Nike teamed up with the racial and rights activist and former San Francisco 49ers quarterback Colin Kaepernick for the thirtieth anniversary of their "Just Do It" campaign, his social activism, as well as the anti-racist movement, became incorporated in the Nike branding strategy. Kaepernick famously knelt during the national anthem in protest against police brutality and racial inequality. The "Just Do It" campaign is one of the most successful and lucrative "dialogic" marketing strategies ever to be employed. Through their merger a social movement can be seen as co-opted and appropriated by a commercial actor.

48 Arvidsson, 2005. See also Gangjee, 2013:34.
49 Gangjee, 2013:34.

As Supreme latched on to the skateboarding counterculture or as the Tate declined its BP sponsorship in solidarity with the environmental movement, many an organisation has also been accused of "wokewashing",[50] "greenwashing"[51] or even "artwashing"[52] their corporate and commercial endeavours by engaging with socially engaged communities. These are, in many ways colonising, activities that contribute to the production of new types of authorised cultural heritage discourses, but that emerge not from a nationalist logic but from a narrative that is often created in and through media, and upheld by strong corporate branding interests.

Relying on new types of originary myths as well as inclusionary and exclusory practices, the location-independent groups have been emerging for a long time. Though they resemble the communities that are recognised in cultural heritage law, they remain invisible to legislation. If we return to the skateboarding and surfing communities, we can see the narratives that the communities produce and how they give rise to a community identity that appears as coherent, but also, much more troubling, once again as largely mono-ethnical or homogenous, or both, which is of course very problematic.

In 2013, Supreme was for instance the instigating party to a lawsuit for trademark infringement against the brand Married to the Mob (MOB).[53] MOB had started selling t-shirts for female skateboarders in 2004 bearing the legend "SUPREME BITCH" written inside red rectangles in white Futura Bold font. The legend was very similar, not to say identical, to the layout of the Supreme box logo. Supreme had initially given its consent to the proposed layout and the use of the legend SUPREME BITCH on MOB t-shirts.[54] However, when MOB then offered its t-shirts for sale through larger retail outlets such as Urban Outfitters, Supreme sued for trademark infringement. MOB counter-claimed in its defence that the "Supreme Bitch" slogan did not constitute infringement. It argued that the slogan used on t-shirts made specifically for female skateboarders was in fact an ironic take on the boyish Supreme brand. It was claimed:

> Nine years ago, Defendant Leah McSweeney, founder and CEO of the pioneering woman's street wear brand Married To The Mob ("MOB") began to use the legend SUPREME BITCH (the "SUPREME BITCH Legend") to parody and comment critically upon the Plaintiff's use of the term SUPREME in connection with its *misogynistic and highly demeaning 'boys' club' attitude* and line of street brand wear.[55]

50 Bradshaw, 2018.
51 Miller, T., 2017.
52 Jones, 2016; Dalley, 2018.
53 *Supreme v. McSweeney* (2019).
54 *Supreme v. Mc Sweeney*, para. 133.
55 *Supreme v. Mc Sweeney*, para. 105 [my emphasis].

MOB developed the argument further by explaining that, as a fashion brand, it was founded by a woman and designed for women within a culture long dominated by male skateboarders and street artists.[56] In that vein, it was stated further, the SUPREME BITCH legend was to be seen as critical commentary and "mockery of the marginalization and objectification of women endemic of the skate culture". Supreme as a brand, it continued, specifically perpetuated this male-dominated culture.[57]

The surfing community has also been accused of racial and gender exclusions, not to mention a lack of engagement with the LGBTQ+ community. The photographer and surfer Stephen Milner commented on this by engaging in a dialogue between surfing communities and queer culture. He explores gay identity in surfing culture by recontextualising the many editorial tropes that exist in mainstream, largely heteronormative, surfing photography.[58] Todd Prodanovich, the last Editor-in-Chief of the legendary *Surfer Magazine*, also highlighted issues that concern surfing and maternity, LGBTQ+ surfers and the solidarity with the Black Lives Matter movement in order to be more inclusive as well as to highlight the community's historical engagement with other social movements, e.g. the environmental and anti-war movements. While many people have taken the critique seriously and the community has started to decolonise itself, its dominant homogeneous as well as heteronormative image still remains a problem.

Location-independent cultural communities are interesting formations. On the one hand some of them, like the surfing community, have formed by way of direct colonisation and appropriation of traditional cultural practices. These communities are then strengthened and narrated through internal counter-culture as well as external commercial branding practices. In a way, these communities come to resemble communities that are recognised in cultural heritage law: they have an internal and an external identity, they have an authorised narrative, they have common histories, traditions, beliefs, rituals and cultural output. They identify among each other as belonging together.

These group formations are not tied to any one territory, nor are they claiming political self-determination, at least not yet. However, we know for instance that the surfing community is extremely territorial over certain surfing spots such as the iconic Banzai Pipeline surf break in Hawaii or the big wave spot in Nazaré, Portugal. Together with their environmental commitments and reluctance towards mass tourism, it is not impossible that these communities may someday argue for territorial sovereignty and some kind of political self-determination.

How we conceive of communities that can have cultural heritage is largely dependent on the conceptual frameworks available to us, including regulatory frameworks. Who controls the panoply of narratives and conceptions of communities is a matter of regulation. We have seen in this chapter how heritage is

56 *Supreme v. Mc Sweeney*, para. 107.
57 *Supreme v. Mc Sweeney*, para. 108.
58 Represa, 2020.

always in many ways transnational, and relying on the community taxonomies that exist in current regulation can be fraught, if not impossible. New regulation is needed, one where diverse transnational communities are recognised and their heritage safeguarded. In the next, concluding, chapter, I will explore some potential regulatory routes that will enable us to do precisely that.

6 Memories: new regulatory approaches

In this final chapter, I fuse together what has been said so far in the previous five chapters and discuss possible future regulatory approaches. I conclude on three final remarks or what I refer to as a tripartite regulatory approach. This chapter outlines a potential route for future regulation that emerges from the discussions that have been advanced here. The regulatory approach presented in this chapter will, firstly, return to a notion of cultural commons and discuss the concept of the commons as a possible avenue for further regulation of transnational heritage. Secondly, I will highlight a participatory "responsibility to protect", R2P, approach based on the doctrine in international law with the same name. And finally, I will end with a reminder that as matters of memory are indeed ever changing, constantly negotiated and constructed, they cannot be, nor should they be, approached as static objects in and of law. This means understanding that in the intersection of diversity, identity and belonging there ultimately lies a need to acknowledge everybody's stories, their narratives. Thus, the final approach envisions a "right to narrate", a right that understands that the more or less temporary constellations of transnational heritage cannot and ought not to be systematically excluded through regulation, or lack thereof. In my view, these three approaches together must in some sense frame any future regulatory strategy employed for the administration of transnational heritage. The book finishes on the cautionary note that if we fail to acknowledge the transnational in heritage and the many ways in which communities are inherently transnational, then culture will continue to be exposed to risk, neglect and peril – and with it, the people and the communities that it represents and constitutes.

Co-ownership as co-existence: heritage-in-common

In my previous work I have developed "rhizomatic commons". My work has been, and still is, driven and influenced by the concept of the rhizome developed by the French philosophers Gilles Deleuze and Félix Guattari.[1] In their philosophical framework, the rhizome is a tool that enables a radical formulation of alternative ways of creating network-based organisation, as well as one that opens

1 Deleuze and Guattari, 2004 [1972]; Deleuze and Guattari, 2011 [1988].

DOI: 10.4324/9781003212683-6

up systemic boundaries and envisions constellation-based ways of co-existence. This Deleuzeoguattarian way of approaching law has so far not been mentioned in this book. Or, stated a little more truthfully, it has indeed been present here, but in a spectral way, as an echo that informs the way the realms of memory making and the regulation of transnational heritage have been approached and analysed.

Though I have chosen not to directly engage with the rhizome expressly, I would now like to touch upon it briefly, as well as add a post-colonial reading to it when discussing the regulation of transnational heritage as a global commons. Stated in yet another way, my earlier work on Deleuze and Guattari will benefit from engaging more explicitly in a conversation with Édouard Glissant here in the context of transnational heritage, as well as with some of the other post-colonial thinkers already mentioned, such as Spivak, Bhabha, Ahmed, etc., as well as the *Decolonise* movement. This, in order to discuss how the regulation of transnational heritage can be approached rhizomatically, as a global commons. Regulating transnational heritage in this way means having to address co-existence, or *relation*, as Glissant refers to it.[2] This can be done by imagining a fluent, network-based regulation that is rhizomatic and non-hierarchical in nature. That is, as a decolonised, global, commons.

Commons constructions are traditionally presented as a way of managing resources that are somehow communal and that are either scarce, finite, in danger of perishing, or all of these together. From Garret Hardin's essay on the "Tragedy of the Commons"[3] to Elinor Ostrom's Nobel Prize-winning work presented in *Governing the Commons*,[4] commons has been approached as a way of governing public and communal resources through local or multi-lateral norms, rather than national legislation. Shifting the focus from a nation-state logic towards a local logic, where the local and the decentralised are strengthened, is key here.

Much has also been written on the Deleuzeoguattarian concepts such as the rhizome in law,[5] as well as the concept of commons in law[6]. Through my earlier work I have developed legal methodologies towards conceiving of, creating and acknowledging a rhizomatic cultural commons in regulation, and I refer the interested reader to that work.[7] In this concluding chapter I will build on the idea of the rhizomatic commons in order to pull together the many strands that the discussion on the regulation of transnational heritage has led us to, such as the multi-ethnic and diverse ways of envisioning and regulating heritage from communities that are not homogeneous.

2 Glissant, 1997.
3 Hardin, 2009 [1968].
4 Ostrom, [2011] 1990.
5 See e.g. Moore, 2000; Moore, 2004; Lefebvre, A., 2005; Lefebvre, A., 2006a; Lefebvre, A., 2006b; Lefebvre, A., 2007; Moore, 2007; Murray, 2007; Lefebvre, A., 2008; Mussawir, 2011a; Mussawir, 2011b, de Sutter and McGee, 2012; Murray, 2013; Bruncevic, 2018, etc.
6 Ostrom and Hess, 2007; Bollier and Helfrich, 2012; Bruncevic, 2018; Bauwens, et. al., 2019; Papadimitropoulos, 2020, etc.
7 Bruncevic, 2018; Bruncevic, 2015; Bruncevic, 2014.

The rhizome is one of the more complicated figures in postmodern and post-structural philosophy. I employ it as a device for understanding open-ended modes of organisation and regulation that do not rely on or require closed, exclusory systems, or mutually exclusive and competing interests in law. This means that the rhizome as an organising device is inherently diverse and fluent as a concept and as a radical tool that advances heterogeneous organisation of societies. Therefore, it is particularly befitting to refer to it here when we arrive at the regulation of diverse and multi-ethnic, multicultural, transnational heritage. The concept allows us to conceive of what in other closed, vertical, hierarchical systems would be seen as opposites, for example the citizen and the foreigner, or the insider and the outsider. The rhizomatic approach, instead, allows us to imagine constellations of phenomena that co-exist and that occupy the same space at the same time, on the same level.

When it comes to the regulation of transnational heritage, we do not have to rely on or invoke national(ist), exclusory, abstract, vertical, hierarchical regulatory structures. Instead we can imagine transnational, fluent, constellation-based, inclusive, horizonal regulation. The argument here is that transnational heritage can be regulated as a rhizomatic global commons in this way. For me, this is spatial. That means that heritage stops being an object (tangible or intangible) in law and instead becomes a spatiality where movement and more or less temporary constellations of bodies happen, where memories and narratives co-exist, and where exclusory and adversary concepts that are underpinned by authorised heritage discourses are not necessary. Such an approach opens up law for diversity.

In *Poetics of Relation*[8] Édouard Glissant builds in this way on the concept of rhizome as presented by Deleuze and Guattari and focuses on the pluriverse that is created by the myriad of people globally and their narratives, particularly the ones that have historically been systematically and structurally excluded. Glissant highlights the stories that exist underground, rhizomatically, that are invisible, yet present.

Regulating transnational heritage as a rhizomatic global commons, following Glissant, and reading Deleuze and Guattari, thus means making the invisible visible and coming to terms with what we are willing to allow to exist or to perish, and what we want to safeguard as important for the future. In a diverse global society that is inundated with the parallel and often conflicting ways to remember, heritage is much more heterogeneous than the authorised heritage discourses will allow for. Transnational heritage as a global commons creates dialogues and connections of shared co-existences without othering the excluded voices and different ways of life, without creating discursive hierarchies or territorial dependencies, colonisation or occupation. The events that took place in 2020 and the interventions and interruptions to public monuments was one such example that flattened the dominant voices and included the excluded narratives.

8 Glissant, 1997.

In an article entitled "To Mend a Broken Internet, Create Online Parks"[9] published in October 2020, Eli Pariser suggested that "we need public spaces, [...], that allow us to gather, communicate, and share in something bigger than ourselves".[10] While Parks is addressing the internet and the so-called virtual space, I think that this also describes the idea of transnational heritage as a rhizomatic global commons. It could mean envisioning it as a public sphere, or as a *site of consciousness* as Dan Hicks[11] refers to it, that is, a space that allows us to gather, communicate and share, as well as a space where we can face up to historical injustices, violence and colonialism without dominant or excluding structures that govern the narrative. In such an understanding of transnational heritage it becomes something bigger than ourselves, even bigger than any given community of which we are members.

We have already seen from the beginning of this book that existing cultural heritage law is not completely unfamiliar with the concept of the commons. One instance in which a clear commons-as-a-public-space logic is applied in regulation is the 2001 Underwater Heritage Convention, as we saw in Chapter 2. There, the regulation is formulated as a responsibility of the international community to protect underwater heritage. As an *erga omnes*[12] obligation, this responsibility is owed to the entire global community, meaning all states – even the ones that do not have coastlines. Working in tandem with the United Nations Convention on the Law of the Sea (UNCLOS), the 2001 Convention thus foregoes the "traditional" and "static" notion of national jurisdictions and territories as the bases for responsibility, and instead creates an obligation where states alone or together protect underwater heritage in all five nautical zones. Of course, a nation state's responsibility will differ (i.e. not be static) depending on how far from the coastline the heritage is located. Read together, the UNCLOS and the 2001 Convention even designate, as we saw above, some parts of the sea as having no national sovereignty, most notably the high seas, as defined in art 12 of the Convention. The international community must thus ensure a common and equitable public access to heritage that is located underwater, as well as protect it from commercialisation and privatisation.[13] This regulatory strategy manages both to keep heritage *in situ* while at the same time creating access to it on a non-commercial basis that is open to all. This indicates that an underwater global heritage commons is at work.

Creating these types of fluent sovereignties, or shared transnational responsibilities, is a regulatory strategy that could be possible to employ for transnational heritage on land too. However, using this type of regulatory strategy has not been, at least not yet, tried and tested widely, or at all, for heritage on land. There are indeed some territories that are co-governed multilaterally, e.g., Antarctica, but no

9 Pariser, 2020.
10 Pariser, 2020.
11 Hicks, 2020:4.
12 See Chapter 2.
13 8th recital, see also arts 17 and 18 that grant the sanction to stop private enterprises that seek to commercialise or to remove heritage from the sea.

heritage on land is as yet regulated in a similar manner as underwater heritage in high seas, with a universally joint responsibility to protect a shared resource and a global commons. As such, the regulation of underwater heritage in high seas can be seen as a first step towards creating a global commons for transnational heritage on land. The regulation of underwater heritage at least provides an argument that it is technically possible to achieve such a provision and that it would be possible to apply a similar logic in terms of treating transnational heritage as a global commons.

Another convention that has also been mentioned above as being potentially open to the concept of the commons is the 2005 Cultural Diversity Convention. It adopts a discourse that promotes global interchange and dialogue on an international level, where multiculturalism and *transnationalism* are premiered. Both the 2005 Cultural Diversity Convention and the 2001 Underwater Heritage Convention seem to be based on a logic that is open to regulating heritage in a more multi-lateral way or as a commons. The two conventions are not equally dependent on static regulation that relies on nation states, as some of the other regulatory instruments are as we have seen throughout this book. Therefore, it can be argued that these two instruments actively open up regulatory routes in terms of conceiving of a regulation of transnational heritage as a global commons.

What that could mean in practice is up for debate. And as we saw above, it is still worth pointing out that these two conventions have a comparatively weak legal standing and few signatories, which means that states are generally not eager to agree on these types of obligations. Which in turn indicates that, as long as the stronger, more dominant legal instruments continue to invoke a mono-ethnic, nation state-based logic and to encourage and strengthen the existing authorised heritage discourses, a commons construction will remain unlikely. To sum up, regulating transnational heritage in international public law as a global commons is probably implausible at least in the near future, but theoretically and practically it is a possible avenue for regulation that could be explored further.

There are other potential avenues for regulating heritage as a cultural commons that lie outside international public law and the UNESCO-driven legal frameworks. In the Nefertiti case we saw how artists, academics and museums can actively make data available through the use of Creative Commons licences. Even the Neues Museum as a cultural memory institution, when publishing the Nefertiti data that they hold, chose to do so via a Creative Commons licence model. This seems to be a move that many similar institutions are leaning towards, one that is sometimes referred to as OpenGLAM[14] – here referring to open access and open data platforms where heritage is made digitally available – by widening the public domain and creating access through a contractual or licence-based cultural commons solution.

14 See e.g. the digital resource Open Glam: https://openglam.org

Enabling access through digital commons platforms might become even more utilised and relied on as technoheritage gains more ground, and more and more works become layered with digital structures. This means that regulating transnational heritage as a commons through contract- or licence-based platforms such as Creative Commons is more likely to happen in the future. Even though this is not a solution without problems – still keeping and regulating heritage within a private and proprietary structure – it is at least more likely to be utilised in the near future. Institutions could therefore be advised to familiarise themselves with and use such solutions more actively.

Ours is a generation of people that consider themselves to be digital natives, people that have grown up with technology, digital devices, internet and connectivity. We are familiar with and rely on digital platforms, digital layers and virtual interaction in our daily lives. The generation of digital natives has therefore been successful in employing these skills when creating and augmenting access to cultural heritage. For instance, the *Decolonise* movement and other activist movements have relied on digital interaction and engagement in digital "battles" for diversification and inclusion in museums and in the public space. Some groups have utilised and staged hackathons and other digital interventions. Black Lives Matter activists have created and disseminated counter-narratives digitally, for example by projecting alternative visions on colonial statues. This includes overlaying and stacking up various simultaneous narratives onto each other by digital means. With the increased use of 3D technology and 3D printers and scanners, where physical objects and infrastructures are progressively becoming "smart", constantly infused with live information, and where utilising commons platforms for all types of heritage is employed, simple solutions emerge with strong potential. They allow various interests and points of view to exist simultaneously – as such, digital solutions for the regulation of transnational heritage as a cultural commons abound. Therefore, it can be argued that regulation of transnational cultural heritage as a global commons is strengthened by a digital setting.

Once again, then, we can go back to Pariser's article calling us to imagine transnational heritage as a public space that allows people to gather, communicate and share in something bigger than themselves. To that end, we can also add the post-colonial and decolonise projects that have challenged current public spaces and museums, urging the cultural institutions to come to terms with their violent pasts and dominant heritage discourses. Imagined this way, we are truly able to conceive of how transnational heritage could, and in my view should, be regulated as a global commons.

Furthermore, by moving towards norms that are articulated by local or transnational communities, instead of the nation state, this means that a heterogeneous community can be advanced more easily. This is indicated by e.g., studies conducted on urban commons, where it has been shown that heterogeneous communities in metropolitan cities need and rely on various commons structures.[15] The commons construction is thus appropriate for a diverse community, one that

15 Borch and Kornberger, 2015.

also highlights sustainable development and a just distribution of resources. As such, perhaps inspired by UNCLOS and the 2001 Underwater Heritage Convention, and strengthened by other digital and contractual commons solutions that exist outside international public law, it can be interesting to consider commons when it comes to the regulation of transnational heritage. This is more than a political proclamation. It is a commitment to understanding commons as a way to regulate as well as a way to conceive of new global communities and common resources that are co-governed, co-managed, and where a co-responsibility for heritage is understood as a way of co-existence.

Co-*munus*: remembrance as duty

The second part of the tripartite regulatory approach engages with the doctrine of "responsibility to protect" (R2P) in international public law. As a regulatory framework, it is intended for protection against genocide, ethnic cleansing and crimes against humanity. It reinforces the strong political commitment of the entire international community against all forms of violence, persecution and systemic violations of human rights. Today, it has also been established that destruction of cultural heritage can constitute a first step towards genocide. The R2P doctrine was not specifically created for the protection of cultural heritage, but in many ways it has already been established that it can be extended to include the protection of cultural heritage from a wider destruction. In relying on the general R2P doctrine, a parallel framework can be discerned, one that potentially brings out the international community's obligations to transnational heritage, as part of the R2P doctrine.

The R2P doctrine in the context of destruction of cultural heritage is primarily based on three pillars:

i the primary responsibility of states to protect heritage in their territory;
ii the responsibility of other states to assist in building this protective capacity; and
iii the responsibility of the international community to respond and to protect heritage should the first two pillars fail.

This third pillar, it is argued, can also justify the so-called "boots on ground" approach, which means protection by military intervention.[16] Relying on and using military intervention in connection to cultural heritage is by no means a modern military strategy, as we have already seen.[17] In fact, we now know that colonial and war loots make up the large part of what we today think of as "heritage". Most of these were obtained through military actions. However, the boots on ground approach connected to the doctrine of R2P here invokes an inverted logic, namely to protect something *in situ* from destruction, rather than removing it as part of a colonial practice.

16 Frowe and Matravers, 2019:6.
17 See e.g. Vrdoljak, 2008, etc.

If we apply the already established UNESCO and UN logic that certain heritage is so outstanding that its existence and safekeeping matter to the whole of humankind, this means that its destruction can constitute a violent attack on humanity as a whole. This follows the reasoning that sees heritage as a global commons, and as such there is an argument that the international community as a whole needs to be responsible for it, together. Whether that means putting boots on ground when heritage is at risk is difficult to know and cannot be neither strongly advanced nor dismissed lightly. There have been arguments for both approaches, and the boots on ground approach has recently been called for to protect Palmyra and Buddhist heritage in Afghanistan, to name some obvious examples.

As the destruction of cultural heritage can constitute the first step towards serious humanitarian crimes and violations of human rights such as genocide, then such an approach might not be as far-fetched as it might initially seem – even if it can be problematic, as all international military interventions of course are. Also, even when boots on ground is not a relevant intervention to call for, and when other, softer, approaches can be employed, the protection of heritage must be seen as an ongoing international responsibility. For instance, after atrocities have taken place, heritage might be destroyed in the aftermath of war and when it no longer fits a newly created nation state's originary myth or authorised heritage discourse, *or* even further when it is too painful to acknowledge if it represents a "dark" past. How these situations ought to be handled is impossible to advise on beforehand, but here the responsibility and cooperation from the international community must be seen as being of the utmost importance.

Furthermore, it could be argued that the obligation that is formulated under the current R2P doctrine is heavily state focused. Even though a responsibility to protect directed to the entire international community already exists, it remains as the last resort when the state-based responsibilities have completely failed. It has to do with not interfering in a state's sovereignty, which bars other states from meddling in internal affairs even if it is to rectify wrongs committed against humanity. This state focus is, as we have seen, difficult to uphold for the protection of transnational heritage.

In this book we have discussed how transnational heritage is excluded both from state-based definitions and from state-based protection. The responsibility to protect might never kick in for this type of heritage under current international law doctrines, and the role of the international community becomes all the more symbolical if it is not given a prominent role. Therefore, the R2P doctrine cannot only be relied on as it is. The transnational heritage aspects, with a diverse understanding of what constitutes a community, as presented here, must be added.

Another way of putting it is that transnational heritage risks perpetually remaining in a transitional state, but where the regulation pertaining to transitional justice never fully kicks in. In these cases, regulatory principles and doctrines that emanate from transitional justice might need to be enforced more forcefully, or more rigorously. For instance, the Black Lives Matter movement actively utilised a rhetoric directly connected to transitional law when justice was sought, calling for "truth, accountability, reparation, and non-recurrence in the aftermath of massive human rights violations".[18] This might be an unusual situation in which such rhetoric is employed, i.e. inside a nation state that is not at civil war, yet where transitional justice is directly invoked. At the same time, this opens up a new route towards safeguarding transnational heritage and accounting for colonial legacies.

Chapter 2 described how principles of transitional justice are generally invoked in the aftermath of wars, on territories where crimes have been committed and human rights abused. Within those more traditional contexts, it has to do with how to assist newly formed states during transitional periods after times of war.

The 1954 Hague Convention and its two Protocols were mentioned as being relevant and as being the key legal instruments in those contexts. When territorial borders are redrawn or shifted and a nation state is (re)born, which heritage is left on whose territory becomes extremely urgent to untangle. However, again in the context of Black Lives Matter, none of that had taken place, yet such legal reasoning was invoked indirectly.

Hague is a typical convention that exists within the context of the R2P doctrine, one that opens up additional regulatory routes, through international humanitarian law, for further regulation of transnational heritage. But, and as we saw when that convention was discussed above, this is also an instrument that can be problematic in many ways because it is object specific, as well as being also heavily inscribed in the nation state-based logic.

Invoking the R2P doctrine for transnational heritage thus directly goes to the core of how community can be envisioned and defined in law, if it is moved away from the state-based dependence. Communities are all upheld by authorised heritage discourses, and more often than not assumed to be homogenous and mono-ethnic in one way or another, and as such recognised by the state. In order to truly discuss the relevance of the R2P doctrine for transnational heritage, we must conceive of a heteronomous, diverse, multi-ethnic community that is not dependent on a nation state or its recognition.

The term "community" is, as we know, etymologically derived from Latin and is commonly translated as being connected to the notion of common property or common interest. Roberto Esposito famously reread this etymological understanding in 1998 in *Communitas: The Origin and Destiny of Community*.[19] In the introduction to the book, he advances a conception of community that runs contrary to, or against, the understanding of community as a form of property that belongs to subjects, together.[20] He also renounces the concept of community that is envisioned as territory.[21] Instead he deconstructs the term and connects it to its

18 Miller, Z., 2020.
19 Esposito, 2010.
20 Esposito, 2010:2.
21 Esposito, 2010:3; Esposito, 2010:9, etc.

Greek roots stemming from *koinos* (common) and *munus* (obligation, duty, debt, gift). In this reading, community is understood as a gift and by extension friendship, comradery.[22]

Therefore, in one of the most quoted sections in his book, Esposito writes that:

> the community cannot be thought of as a body, as a corporation [*corporazione*] in which individuals are founded in a larger individual. Neither is community to be interpreted as a mutual, intersubjective 'recognition' in which individuals are reflected in each other so as to confirm their initial identity; as a collective bond that comes at a certain point to connect individuals that before were separate. The community isn't a mode of being, much less a 'making' of the individual subject. It isn't the subject's expansion or multiplication but its exposure to what interrupts the closing and turns it inside out: a dizziness, a syncope, a spasm in the continuity of the subject.[23]

In other words, community is formed by diversity, by that which is seen to "interrupt" a mono-ethnic, homogenous, closing. Understood in this way, and as I have argued here, all communities will always, in one way or another, be transnational.

If we go back to the principles of R2P with this in mind, where number (i) is the primary responsibility of states to protect heritage in their territory, and (ii) that of other states to assist in building this protective capacity, and (iii) that of the international community and its responsibility to respond to protect heritage should the first two pillars fail, then we could argue that (i) and (ii) become fundamentally challenged as they rely on an inside and an outside of a community imagined as a state, where the state acts either as the founding community and is as such the responsible *body* meant to protect its own heritage, or as the Other, meant to protect somebody else's heritage on a foreign territory. But, following Esposito, if the state-community is not a body but rather a gift, and an obligation towards the one that interrupts the understanding of such an exclusory concept of community, then a duty to protect emerges *erga omnes* with R2P understood as a transnational duty to remember each other's shared co-existence and to account for and be responsible for the diverse community, as well as to actively preserve all its memories.

Coming-communities: memory matters

Matters of memory are constantly negotiated and constructed. Myth making and memory making seem to go hand in hand. Numerous simultaneous pasts, presents and futures are flowing side by side. Some are more dominant than

22 See also Sax, 1990.

23 Esposito, 2010: 7. See also Nancy, 1991; Agamben, 1993; Blanchot, 2000; Nancy, 2009; Hardt and Negri, 2017.

others. Some are just emerging from having been silenced for a long time, or from having dwelled in the periphery of authorised heritage discourses. Therefore, matters of memory cannot be treated as a static object in law.

Throughout this book I have presented a number of justifications for further regulation and for clearly acknowledging transnational heritage in law. Transnational heritage serves as a constitutive element in the imagination and creation of diverse societies and heterogeneous, multi-ethnic communities. As we have seen, how we conceive of communities, and how we deal with the concept of "community" when it comes to regulating transnational heritage, is imperative. Simply put: how we conceive of "community" matters to how we can envision future regulation of transnational heritage, memory and memory making.

Trying to envision and define a community in law is of course nothing new. Esposito, while inscribing himself in a general tradition of legal theory, indeed references that the subject(s) of law must be envisioned as existing before the law.[24] In such a vision, the people that make up a community, it must thus be assumed, exist before their law is created. Discussing community means discussing politics of togetherness. As we have seen throughout this book, it is not easy to conceive of what a collective unity means and how heterogeneous societies can be envisioned. The boundaries that distinguish who becomes the member of a group and how such membership changes and can change over time are questions of and for law, how an aggregation of individuals becomes a community, how a we-togetherness is formed and also how a we-togetherness works with other similar communal constellations.

Modern states are built and depend on the construction of communities by narration, and by imaging common denominators that distinguish one community from another. It is a matter, to slightly simplify the complex argument that Benedict Anderson makes in *Imagined Communities*, that has to do with legitimatising something comparatively new or at least in progress (the state) by embedding it in narratives that claim it, the state, to be very old, ancient and perpetual.[25] How a group of individuals is defined, narrated and explained over time, as a community and the constant changes of such communities, has been a core concern for this book. In order to safeguard transnational heritage, we have had to assume that there might not be such a concept as "national" heritage and that instead all heritage is always in one way or another "transnational".

In coming to terms with the national, we have also had to deal with the mechanisms of exclusion and occupation of territory, e.g., by looking at colonial history and creation of heritage through authorised heritage discourses. Do the people who once occupied and colonised other people belong to an "us" that exists now, and how do we take responsibility for their actions? Do future generations belong to that "us", and how do we safeguard their interests? This means that matters of global geopolitics flow into the matters of local memories, and that the so-called present and the so-called future converge when matters of heritage

24 Esposito, 2010:89.
25 Anderson, 2016.

are at hand. What is at stake is what might be called self-government, self-determination, self-rule: democracy. Still, law conceives of and organises communities around the notion of a nation state and that in turn gives rise to an assumption of "national" heritage.

It is also not just a matter of squaring off with the colonial past but of dealing with some of the most pressing issues of our times such as populism, migration, climate change, separatist movements,[26] Indigenous issues, the fight for a just global distribution of wealth and resources, etc.; quite simply, matters of inclusion and exclusion. What communal unity means in these circumstances is in no way anything that is a given. Thus, populism arises as a reaction to a nostalgic lack of an imagined, archaic, *lost*, communal unity. Whether or not such a community ever existed, or whether it has been imagined through narration, becomes irrelevant as the lack of it is profoundly experienced as a loss, one that people genuinely grieve. It explains the emotional and political nature of heritage as it is directly tied to precisely this – a lost community.

Migration in turn does the opposite; it forces communities to rethink their own constitution and boundaries. That we live in an unprecedented time of migration is a fact well established, and the nomadic flows of people give rise to questions such as must one be a citizen, belong to a recognised community, in order to have rights? Who is allowed to speak and take part in the communal matters, and with what right? Who gets to define "national" or, at least, what constitutes "our" common concerns such as that of heritage and whom it represents?

Migration can happen for many reasons, such as political reasons, safety, freedom, but also for economic reasons such as job opportunities. And, as Homi Bhabha writes in *The Location of Culture*

> [this] raises affective and ethical issues connected with cultural differences and social discrimination – the problems of inclusion and exclusion, dignity and humiliation, respect and repudiation. In the context of the world disorder in which we are mired, symbolic citizenship is now principally defined by a surveillant culture of 'security' – how do we tell the good migrant from the bad migrant? Which cultures are safe? Which unsafe?[27]

It is thus not just a matter of inclusion and exclusion but also of diversity and difference. Bhabha is addressing the "right of difference" as advanced by Étienne Balibar.[28] Balibar in turn discusses the experienced or psychological need for the restoration of an essentialist cultural identity, one that existed when there was no diversity in society.[29] By extension, according to Bhabha, this all has to do with who gets to count as a "citizen" in a

26 This focus on populism, migration, climate change and separatist movements was inspired by the lecture "Legal Governance in Times of Crisis" given by Professor Hans Lindahl at the Department of Law, University of Gothenburg on 25 October 2019.

27 Bhabha, 1994:xvii.

28 Balibar, 1994.

29 Balibar, 1994; see also Bhabha, 1994:xvii.

political context.[30] This right to difference-in-equality is essential to point out when we are discussing transnational heritage. Within the context of this book, we have seen that there are recognised communities that differ from the national community, such as the Indigenous community or the minorities. Where we could place global migrants and their heritage is not yet clear, which we saw in chapters 3 and 5.

However, and as we have also seen, a so-called more inclusive society is not necessarily an answer either. Many people are actively refusing to be included in communities that they do *not* wish to be included in. Various separatist movements around the world are, on the contrary, calling for secession, self-determination and exclusion from a dominant and oppressive community. In these instances, inclusion is experienced as the most violent act, and the problem is that groups of people feel they do not desire to be included in a particular community that they consider to be an occupant or a colonial power, for example.

In these instances, imagining a unified, single, global legal order is not an answer either, as we have seen with many of the international organisations and the effects of their frameworks throughout this book. Many of them tend to reproduce and inherit existing global power asymmetries, not to say ongoing invisible colonial practices. The issues of injustices between the Global North and the Global South seem to remain sadly unresolved even within the global legal initiatives.

How the diverse, multi-ethnic, heterogeneous community can be envisioned and regulated was not meant to be the core question of this book, but I have had to address it anyway as it is so tightly connected to the regulation of transnational heritage. Whom to include and whom to exclude from the community, to whom heritage belongs, are all indirectly questions that have to do with how we envision collective co-existence. And if we are to add a non-anthropocentric unity and consider our co-existence with the non-human or the so-called "natural" or "technological" bodies, then perhaps this adds additional layers of difficulty. Whom does the Amazon belong to, or do we belong to it, is it an agent or an object, is it a resource or a living body? Can the Amazon ever be labelled as an object in law, e.g. as a natural heritage site? These are examples of such questions. Labelling in turn upholds the underlying anthropocentric assumptions such as the human–nature dichotomy, that are flawed to say the least, and this has been shown by many others before me.[31] Whether or not we ought to ascribe legal personhood to nature, culture or heritage is something that I have chosen not to develop further here, but this was an issue briefly touched upon in *The Other Nefertiti* case. The political and legal agency and inclusion of non-human bodies thus adds further complexity in terms of who or what we consider as being able to be included in a community. The issues of representation as well as identity politics become relevant in new ways.

30 See further Bruncevic, 2018:149.

31 See e.g. Morton, 2013; Purdy, 2015; Latour, 2017, to name a few.

And finally, there is the question of future generations and how we conceive of inter-generational justice. How do we ascribe and distribute transnational heritage through time? The future generations, we must remember, are potentially also vulnerable group members too whose interests we need somehow to represent in this context: interests that we together have a responsibility to protect.

A right to memory as a right to narrate

In the end, regulating transnational heritage means having to decide which "we" matters. For instance, Chantal Mouffe[32] has discussed this difficulty concerning the addressing and making sense of political emotions that are invoked when it comes to heritage. That becomes even further inflamed when transnational heritage is at issue. The populist movements in Europe and elsewhere have actively used and invoked emotions when presenting nationalist visions of community. This marshalling of emotions, this use of narrative and rhetoric in order to make sense of the emotionality connected to belonging is nothing new. It goes back to more direct forms of emotion-invoking communication such as propaganda. In many ways we have seen here how emotions can be employed and reproduced through authorised heritage discourses. In the end it comes down to a *right to narrate*, a right that allows people to tell their own story. This right is not a legal right, but it is one that allows communities to participate in creating their memory, in recounting their own version of their own (hi)story. Bhabha writes:

> In keeping with the spirit of the 'right to narrate' as a means to achieving our own national or communal identity in a global world, demands that we revise our sense of symbolic citizenship, our myths of belonging, by identifying ourselves with the 'starting-points' of other national and international histories and geographies.[33]

Regulating transnational heritage therefore means identifying these "starting-points" and empowering communities through regulation to be able to envision, and fight for, their own right to narrate.

A right to narrate is directly connected to the preservation of transnational memory and the possibility of a shared co-existence. Taking the anti-colonial ethos seriously means actively continuing to address who has the right to narrate which memories and how we organise, keep and safeguard such memories. The strong connections between memory and heritage cannot be underplayed. As we have seen, heritage is directly tied to the justification of people and their existence, but most justifications of community are still all too bound up in hegemonic authorised heritage discourses that tend to favour the mono-ethnic

32 Mouffe, 2014; Mihai, 2014.
33 Bhabha, 1994:xx.

homogenous conceptions of community. And, as has been pointed out so many times along the way, this puts every other, alternative, counter, conception of memory and community, which we have here referred to as the transnational heritage, at risk.

In the end, it is a question of empowerment, of enabling communities and their members to speak their own truths. This means that all regulation of heritage, however we define it, whether we like it or not, will always be connected to the life and death of a community. Through their heritage, communities are constituted, understand themselves, their members, and what it means to be part of a we-togetherness. And sometimes these understandings will change, they may evolve over time, even become difficult, offensive. What is possible to remember can therefore become challenged when we realise that we have to remember things differently. It is problematic, not to say impossible, to reach a consensus on how to regulate, for example, the heritage that reminds us of dark periods of our history and whether its memory ought to be present or absent from the official accounts of history. Sometimes we will want to forget. And that might be OK too. Regulating transnational heritage will thus always mean having to face these issues head on.

Before we conclude, let me summarise and remind the reader of some the core findings that have emerged from the previous chapters and that have been developed throughout the book, as well as what needs to be kept in mind before the tripartite regulatory approach presented here can be employed in the future.

We opened the book with Chapter 1: *Introduction*, where the different matters of transnational heritage were introduced. There, I accounted for the various possible definitions and approaches to transnational heritage. What all of these have in common is that they tie transnational heritage to shared co-existences, as well as to shared or entangled memories. To understand transnational heritage means understanding multicultural, diverse and heterogeneous societies and their cultures, that change over time. Such a notion of transnational heritage and transnational communities seems not to be sufficiently protected in regulation.

Chapter 2: *Matter* introduced and mapped out the existing regulatory frameworks. In that chapter I focused on what I refer to as the ten core legal instruments in international law that frame and structure global cultural heritage law. The core instruments were then divided in three groups, *General regulatory instruments, Criminal law* and *Declarations & Recommendations*. Introducing the ten instruments both chronologically and thematically, the second chapter focused on the problems as well as saw the existing potential in current law when it comes to regulating transnational heritage.

In Chapter 3: *Movement* I presented the three community categories that emerge from these instruments and that are recognised in current regulation, namely the state, the Indigenous community and the minority community. Discussing various constitutive elements in all three categories, such as authorised heritage discourses, ancestral lands, and ethnic or religious commonality, the chapter revealed that regulation tends to favour three differently sized yet in many ways mono-cultural types of community. This means that while a lot of progressive work is being done in terms of, for example, post-colonial returns and recognition of diverse societies and minority rights, the transnational community remains undefined and unrecognised in regulation.

Chapter 4: *Diversity* focused on three particular case studies that represent the three heritage categories: tangible, intangible and digital. I studied the Soviet police building in Vilnius as tangible heritage, Turkish coffee divination as intangible heritage and *The Other Nefertiti* as digital heritage. All three cases highlighted how the recognised heritage categories are never mutually exclusive and that all aspects of them tend to be simultaneously part of cultural heritage. The chapter also argued that overly relying on the national inscriptions and national claims for these categories of heritage can lead to the exclusion of transnational heritage. In this chapter it was also discussed how digitising culture can both free as well as recolonise heritage as it moves from public law regulation to a proprietary intellectual property structure.

Finally, in Chapter 5: *Constellations*, I presented the diverse communities that are not visible in law. Focusing on the *Decolonise* movement and global counter-cultures, it was argued that the transnational culture is more than a geographical cross-border phenomenon. In fact, the transnational is something that must be claimed, and protected, in our museums as well as through our lifestyles. Heritage was presented as polyphonic in a new way and the regulation of it as having to do with acknowledging the many voices that produce it. How to decolonise and safeguard all types of cultural heritage that exists across the world was thus shown to be at issue too. It was argued that lawyers and legal scholars must once and for all become aware of how (not) to employ the established categories of cultural heritage law, how current law can be colonising and how to reach beyond authorised heritage discourses, steer away from mono-ethnic, nationalist hegemonies, and avoid perpetuating "othering" or exclusory practices.

Thus we have arrived here, in Chapter 6: *Memories*. Here the tripartite regulatory approach was presented as comprising a constellation of commons–R2P–right to narrate. In order to regulate transnational heritage, we must understand diverse societies and regulate in a non-hierarchical way. Such regulation frames transnational heritage as a global commons, that the international community has an *erga omnes* responsibility to protect it, and where a right to narrate is guaranteed to all people as a human right.

A final note on memory making: instead of a conclusion

This study might not have a clear conclusion, but it ends with the understanding that what we regard as our reality is something that is constituted by an interplay of constructed and narrated pasts and presents that shine through heritage. Heritage must always be understood as being co-constitutive of people and their communities, and that the constructions of the past and the present together will eventually give rise to that which is at one point or another referred to as "the reality". That also means that the present, the past and the future are in many ways equally unknown, as they are all constantly constructed and reconstructed, imagined and reimagined, negotiated and renegotiated, narrated and renarrated. Failures to protect transnational heritage can result in a failure to understand each other, our shared pasts, and by extension it might also result in the misinterpretation of the present or the misappropriation of the future.

Memory plays a constitutive role in the transformation of community too. As we have seen, assuming stable and fixed objects of heritage as representing a static communal formation will obviously be problematic. In the very beginning of this book I mentioned the notion of entangled memories, of approaching cultural heritage not as predominantly expressed by narrating an object through authorised heritage discourses, and by embedding it within national contexts, but instead of understanding it as transnational and as such always diverse, changing, plural and as a shared testament of co-existence.

Until now, the word "decolonise" in cultural heritage law has meant returning heritage taken as colonial loot to its places of origin. This type of decolonisation has been discussed for many years in cultural heritage studies, in law and in other disciplines, by for instance Ana Filipa Vrdoljak. She has presented many interesting routes for legally dealing with colonial heritage and the returns of colonial loots, e.g., through arbitration administrated by UNESCO. These processes allow one state to call another into arbitration. Arbitration can also be invoked for cases that relate to the removal of heritage that took place prior to the UNESCO conventions coming into force. Under such procedures, the former colonial state can be ordered to pay for the cost of the transfer of heritage back to its place of origin. But the problems with these types of solutions have been that they are slow, bilateral and, in the end, almost impossible to enforce. Making decolonisation a moral claim instead of a legal claim of course helps, as it deters former colonial powers from continuing to uphold a colonial logic. A lot has been happening when it comes to decolonisation and the return of heritage as understood in this way.

The importance of continued discussions on the decolonisation of heritage culminated in the summer of 2020 when the *Decolonise* and Black Lives Matter movements challenged our understanding of what it means to decolonise, and what decolonising public spaces and museums from colonial remnants must entail. Now we also understand that decolonisation is not just about returning ancient objects taken from one place and held in another. We now know that to decolonise means to abolish all visible and invisible ties to colonisation, and to refrain from practices and societal, legal or political structures that in any way or form exploit or oppress people because of their race, sex, ethnicity, lifestyle, belief or any other sense of identity. Understood in such a way, there might never be an end to decolonisation; it becomes an ongoing commitment to fostering diverse societies.

It might not seem like something new, but as the year of 2020 has shown, actively denouncing all types of inequalities is a process that must never end. It has been argued throughout the book that cultural heritage plays a pivotal role in the creation of inclusive and diversified societies. To keep imagining communities as coming out of and representing mono-ethnic, homogenous societies can perpetuate a different, invisible, form of colonisation. That is why law and regulation need firstly to understand the importance of transnational heritage, and then move away from authorised heritage discourses in order, secondly, to understand that all cultural heritage will always be, in some way, transnational. And that is a good thing.

Much work has been done in terms of creating alternative and counter-narratives and reframing and challenging the grand narratives inscribed in authorised heritage discourses. But it is now also time to do away with the "counter" or the "alternative" prefixes. When communities are envisioned as flexible, constellation based and diverse, and when heritage is understood as a global commons, which we all have a duty and a responsibility to protect, and when we all have an equal right to narrate our story, we will be able to save and preserve all the different iterations of transnational heritage.

What in the end transpires and what was not necessarily visible up until this point in history is that cultural heritage and its attributes have been sidestepped in community scholarship. Now, when the colonial pasts tied to heritage cannot be ignored – and with that the importance of understanding the transnational community – the community scholarship becomes a focal interest for heritage studies.

Given the suggestion that all heritage is one way or another transnational, tied to ongoing and diverse narratives, this means that we have arrived at the conclusion that an inclusive heritage is able to drive the creation of multicultural societies, where many formations of identity, memory and belonging are allowed to co-exist. Transnational heritage will always be a constitutive element in diverse, inclusive, societies. As such, it directly affects matters that concern self-determination *as well as self-definition*[34] and *self-creation*,[35] citizenship *as well as belonging*, human rights *as well as community*, sovereignty *as well as the acknowledgement of all people*. To fully and satisfactorily safeguard transnational heritage, diverse and ever changing in nature as it may be, new and additional regulation is called for in no uncertain terms.

This book has attempted to show that our common, shared memories, narratives, pasts, presents and futures through which we move, which we embody and which constitute us and our communities, shine through heritage. And this understanding, finally, must matter to law. How we are allowed to imagine and to narrate our heritage will always affect how we imagine ourselves. This means that heritage is inherently something not external but something within us, internal, and community is always something shared,

34 Glissant, 1997:14.
35 Nedelsky, 2011.

common, global, international, yes *transnational.* It is like the words of Corneille: *Rome is no longer in Rome, it is wherever I am.* To conclude, the regulation of transnational heritage will always have to be considered as Rome in this sense, as part of who we are, and where we are. In other words, transnational heritage has to be regulated with this insight in mind: that heritage is a constitutive part of the human being, of me, of you, of us, and finally, it must be regulated as a core human right.

Epilogue

On 4 August 2020, at six in the afternoon, a strong explosion shook the Beirut harbour. The explosion was heard and seen all over the city and its surroundings. It devastated the port area in central Beirut, killing more than a hundred people and injuring thousands, as well as making around 300,000 people homeless. This happened in the midst of an ongoing global pandemic that was already gripping the city and during the continuous protests against political corruption and democratic deficiency. The blast gravely damaged the iconic Sursock Museum and its holdings. The museum was, and still is, one of the key cultural institutions in Beirut, of utmost importance for Lebanon, the Middle East and, by extension, the world. A number of other large and small galleries, including the famous Sfeir-Semler gallery, and other cultural spaces located in the same part of town, were also damaged in the explosion. The cultural losses were immense.

Beirut, historically a truly diverse and multicultural city, is a place that is used to surviving factional violence between religious groups, external paramilitary forces and even terrorists. This time the explosion that shook the city, and that dealt such a blow to its cultural institutions, did not come from any of those forces, but from bureaucratic failings connected to insufficient regulation of portside warehouses. A perfect storm caused by the simultaneity of the pandemic, political unrest, corruption and inequality all came together and contributed to the disaster. That this event affected cultural heritage is obvious.

The international community, with UNESCO in the lead, has come together to assist with emergency funding and skills towards rebuilding and reconstructing the damaged sites that are considered to be important for humanity as a whole. Global solidarity with Beirut and its people emerged, and the losses suffered were felt locally and globally. Still, some of the losses that the area has suffered might be irreversible.

This devastating accident showed us, once again, the fragility of heritage, its direct connectedness to people and their daily lives, as well as the global importance of coming together to ensure the preservation and safekeeping of the common cultural heritage of the whole of humankind.

DOI: 10.4324/9781003212683-7

Bibliography

Al-Badri, N., and J. N. Nelles. 2018. Press release for *The Other Nefertiti.*

Agamben, G. 1993. *The Coming Community*. Trans. M. Hardt. Minneapolis: University of Minnesota Press.

Ahmed, S. 2012. *On Being Included*. Durham, NC: Duke Press.

Alexander, E. P., and M. Alexander. 2008. *Museums in Motion: An Introduction to the History and Function of Museums*. 2nd edition. Plymouth: AltaMira Press.

Anaya, J. S. 1991. Indigenous Rights Norms in Customary International Law, *Arizona Journal of International & Comparative Law*, 8, no. 2: 1–39.

Anaya, J. S. 2004. *Indigenous Peoples in International Law*. 2nd edition. Oxford: Oxford University Press.

Anderson, B. 2016. *Imagined Communities: Reflections on the Origin and Spread of Nationalism.* London: Verso Books.

Anghie, A. 1992. Human Rights and Cultural Identity: New Hope for Ethnic Peace? *Harvard International Law Journal*, 33, no. 2: 341–352.

Ansong, A. 2016. The Concept of Sovereign Equality of States in International Law, *GIMPA Law Review*, 2, no. 1: 14–34.

Arvidsson, A. 2005. Brands: A Critical Perspective, *Journal of Consumer Culture* 5, no. 2: 235–258.

Assembly of First Nations and Canadian Museums Association. 1994. *Turning the Page: Forging New Partnerships between Museums and First Peoples*. 3rd edition. Ottawa: Task Force on Museums and First Peoples.

Balibar, E. 1994. *Masses, Classes, Ideas*. Trans. J. Swenson. New York and London: Routledge.

Bandyopadhyay, R. 2016. Who Owns the Past? The Politics of Religious Heritage in Contemporary India, *Tourism Review*, 71, no. 3: 234–243.

Baslar, K. 1998. *The Concept of the Common Heritage of Mankind in International Law*. The Hague: Brill.

Bauwens, M., et. al.2019. *Peer to Peer: The Commons Manifesto*. London: University of Westminster Press.

Beaumont, J. 2009. Contested Trans-national Heritage: The Demolition of Changi Prison, Singapore, *International Journal of Heritage Studies*, 15, no. 4: 298–316.

Beschea-Fache, C. 2012. Transnational Heritage in Boualem Sansal's The German Mujahid, *Culture, Theory and Critique*, 53, no. 2: 163–179.

Bhabha, H. K. 1994. *The Location of Culture*. Abingdon: Routledge.

Bhambra, G. K. 2014. Postcolonial and Decolonial Dialogues, *Postcolonial Studies*, 17, no. 2: 115–121.

Blake, J. 2000. On Defining the Cultural Heritage, *International & Comparative Law Quarterly*, 49, no. 1: 61–85.

Blake, J. 2015. *International Cultural Heritage Law.* Oxford: Oxford University Press.

Blakeney, M. 2009. *The Protection of Traditional Cultural Expressions.* Report for EC-ASEAN Intellectual Property Rights Co-operation Programme.

Blakeney, M. 2013. Protecting the Spiritual Beliefs of Indigenous Peoples – Australian Case Studies, *Pacific Rim Law and Policy Journal*, 22, no. 2: 391–427.

Blanchot, M. 2000. *The Unavowable Community.* Trans. P. Joris. Barrytown: Station Hill Press.

Bollier, D., and S. Helfrich. 2019. *Free, Fair and Alive. The Insurgent Power of the Commons.* Gabriola Island: New Society Publishers.

Borch, C., and M. Kornberger. 2015. *Urban Commons, Rethinking the City.* Abingdon: Routledge.

Borden, I. 2019. *Skateboarding and the City: A Complete History.* London: Bloomsbury.

Börütecene, A., et. al. 2016. Informing Design Decisions for Advice Mediating Handheld Devices by Studying Coffee Cup Reading. In *NordiCHI'16: Proceedings of the 9th Nordic Conference on Human–Computer Interaction*, Article No. 7, 1–10. New York: ACM.

Börütecene, A., et. al. 2017. Coffee Cup Reading as an Inspiration for Looking into Augmented Mugs in Social Interaction. In *Design, User Experience, and Usability: Understanding Users and Contexts*, ed. A. Marcus and W. Wang, 199–218. DUXU 2017. Lecture Notes in Computer Science, vol. 10290. Springer: Cham.

Börütecene, A., et. al. 2018. Through the Glance Mug: A Familiar Artefact to Support Opportunistic Search in Meetings. In *TEI'18: Proceedings of the Twelfth International Conference on Tangible, Embedded, and Embodied Interaction*, 674–683. New York: ACM.

Bradshaw, A. 2018. From the Beatles to Colin Kaepernick: A Brief History of Nike's 'Wokewashing', *Frieze*, 12 September.

Braun, E. 2020. Removal of Voltaire Statue in Paris Only Temporary, *Politico*, 17 August.

Brown, M. F. 2004. *Who Owns Native Culture?* Cambridge, MA: Harvard University Press.

Bruncevic, M. 2011. The Lost Mural of Bruno Schulz: A Critical Legal Perspective on Control, Access to and Ownership of Art, *Law Critique*, 22: 79–96.

Bruncevic, M. 2014. *Fixing the Shadows: Access to Art and the Legal Concept of Cultural Commons.* Juridiska Institutionens Skriftserie, University of Gothenburg.

Bruncevic, M. 2015. We Need to Talk About the Cultural Commons: Some Musings on Rhizomatic Jurisprudence and Access to Art, *Journal of Law and Social Research*, Special issue: Law and Art, 2, no. 6: 115–131.

Bruncevic, M. 2018. *Law, Art and the Commons.* Abingdon: Routledge.

Bruncevic, M., and P. Almenstrand Linné. 2018. A Taste of Law and Coffee – From Tastescape to Lawscape. In *TASTE: Law and the Senses*, ed. A. Pavoni, et al., 201–232. London: University of Westminster Press.

Brush Perkins, E. 2001 [1921]. *The White Heart of Mojave.* Baltimore: Johns Hopkins University Press.

Bryson Taylor, D. 2019. San Francisco School Will Cover Controversial George Washington Murals, *The New York Times*, 28 June.

Bugliosi, V., and C. Gentry. 2018 [1974]. *Helter Skelter: The True Story of the Manson Murders.* London: Cornerstone.

Cameron, D. F. 1971. The Museum, a Temple or the Forum, *Curator*, 14, no. 1: 11–24.

Carpenter B., and G. Sandford. 2003. Who Owns the Past? *US News and World Report*, 135, no. 21:58–60.

Claridge, L., and A. Xanthaki. 2016. Protecting the Rights to Culture for Minorities and Indigenous Peoples: An Overview of International Case Law. In *State of the World's Minorities and Indigenous Peoples*, ed. P. Grant, 58–69. London: Minority Rights Group International.

Coombe, R. J. 1993. The Properties of Culture and the Politics of Possessing Identity: Native Claims in the Cultural Appropriation Controversy, *Canadian Journal of Law & Jurisprudence*, 6, no. 02: 249–285.

Coombe, R. J. 1998. *The Cultural Life of Intellectual Properties*. Durham, NC: Duke University Press.

Crawford, J. 2001. The Right of Self-Determination in International Law: Its Development and Future. In *Peoples' Rights*, ed. P. Alston, 7–68. Oxford: Oxford University Press.

Crewdson, R. 1984. Cultural Property – A Fourth Estate? *Law Society Gazette* 18: 126–129.

Cronan, W. 1992. A Place for Stories: Nature, History and Narrative, *The Journal of American History*, 78, no. 4: 1347–1376.

Dalley, J. 2018. Why Artwashing is a Dirty Word, *Financial Times*, 17 August.

Delanty, G. 2017a. Entangled Memories: How to Study Europe's Cultural Heritage, *The European Legacy*, 22, no. 2: 129–145.

Delanty, G. 2017b. *The European Heritage: A Critical Re-Interpretation*. Abingdon: Routledge.

Deleuze, G., and F. Guattari. 2004 [1972]. *Anti-Oedipus: Capitalism and Schizophrenia*. Trans. R. Hurley, M. Seem and H. R. Lane, foreword by M. Foucault. London: Continuum.

Deleuze, G., and F. Guattari. 2011 [1988]. *A Thousand Plateaus: Capitalism and Schizophrenia*. Trans. and foreword by B. Massumi. London: Athlone.

Donaldson, E. C. 2018. Place Destabilized: Ambivalent Heritage, Community and Colonialism in the Marquesas Islands, *Oceania*, 88, no. 1: 69–89.

Edwards, R., and J. Stewart, eds. 1980. *Preserving Indigenous Cultures: A New Role for Museums*. Canberra: Australian Govt. Pub. Service.

Esposito, R. 2010. *Communitas: The Origin and Destiny of Community*. Redwood, CA: Stanford University Press.

Fitz Gibbon, K. 2005. *Who Owns the Past: Cultural Policy, Cultural Property, and the Law*. American Council for Cultural Policy. New Brunswick, NJ: Rutgers University Press.

Fletcher, J. 2004. *The Search for Nefertiti: The True Story of an Amazing Discovery*. London: Hodder & Stoughton.

Flessas, T. 2003. Cultural Property Defined and Redefined as Nietzschean Aphorism, *Cardozo Law Review*, 24, no. 3: 1067–1098.

Floridi, L. 2014. *The Fourth Revolution: How the Infosphere is Reshaping Human Reality*. Oxford: Oxford University Press.

Foner, E. 2003. *Who Owns History? Rethinking the Past in a Changing World*. New York City: Hill & Wang.

Forrest, C. 2010. *International Law and the Protection of Cultural Heritage*. Abingdon: Routledge.

Fox, C. 1993. The Unidroit Convention on Stolen or Illegally Exported Cultural Objects: An Answer to the World Problem of Illicit Trade in Cultural Property, *American University International Law Review*, 9, no. 1: 225–267.

Francioni, F. 2013. Plurality and Interaction of Legal Orders in the Enforcement of Cultural Heritage Law. In *Enforcing International Cultural Heritage Law*, ed. F. Francioni and J. Gordley, 9–21. Oxford: Oxford University Press.

Freud, S. 2010 [1939]. *Moses and Monotheism*. New York: Random House.

Frowe, H., and D. Matravers. 2019. *Conflict and Cultural Heritage: A Moral Analysis of the Challenges of Heritage Protection*. J. Paul Getty Trust Occasional Papers on Cultural Heritage Policy, No. 3.

Ganapathy, S. 2013. Imagining Alaska: Local and Translocal Engagements with Place, *American Anthropologist*, 115, no. 1: 96–111.

Gangjee, D. S. 2013. Property Concepts in Intellectual Property Law. In *Concepts of Property in Intellectual Property Law*, ed. H. R. Howe and J. Griffiths, 29–59. Cambridge: Cambridge University Press.

Gardner, H. 2006. *Art Through the Ages: The Western Perspective*. Boston: Cengage Learning.

Geismar, H. *Museum Object: Lesson for a Digital Age*. London: UCL Press.

Glissant, E. 1997. *Poetics of Relation*. Trans. B. Wing. Ann Arbor: University of Michigan Press.

Gordon, J. 1971. The UNESCO Convention on the Illicit Movement of Art Treasures, *Harvard International Law Journal*, 12: 537–556.

Graber, C. 2006. The New UNESCO Convention on Cultural Diversity: A Counterbalance to the WTO? *Journal of International and Economic Law*, 9: 553–574.

Grasmuck, S., and A. M. Hinze. 2016. Transnational Heritage Migrants in Istanbul: Second-Generation Turk-American and Turk-German 'Returnees' in Their Parents' Homeland, *Journal of Ethnic and Migration Studies*, 42, no. 12: 1959–1976.

Greenfield, J. 2007. *The Return of Cultural Treasures*. 3rd edition. Cambridge: Cambridge University Press.

Gulliford, A. 2002. Who Owns the Past? *Public Historian*, 24, no. 2: 138–140.

Hahn, M. 2006. A Clash of Cultures? The UNESCO Diversity Convention and International Trade Law, *Journal of International Economic Law*, 9, no. 3: 515–552.

Hanania, L. R. ed. 2014. *Cultural Diversity in International Law: The Effectiveness of the UNESCO Convention on the Protection and Promotion of the Diversity of Cultural Expressions*. Abingdon: Routledge.

Hardin, G. 2009 [1968]. The Tragedy of the Commons, *Journal of Natural Resources Policy Research*, 1, no. 3: 243–253.

Hardt, M., and A. Negri. 2017. *Assembly*. Oxford: Oxford University Press.

Herscher, E. 1998. Many Happy Returns? New Contributions to the Repatriation Debate, *American Journal of Archaeology*, 102, no. 4: 809–813.

Hicks, D. 2020. *The Brutish Museums: The Benin Bronzes, Colonial Violence and Cultural Restitution*. London: Pluto Press.

Hilty, R. M. 2009. Rationales for the Legal Protection of Intangible Goods and Cultural Heritage, *International Review of Intellectual Property and Competition Law*, 8: 883–911.

Jakubowski, A. ed. 2016. *Cultural Rights as Collective Rights*. Leiden: Brill.

Janes, R. R., and R. Sandel. eds. 2019. *Museum Activism*. Abingdon: Routledge.

Janke, T. 2003. *Case Studies on Intellectual Property and Traditional Cultural Expressions*. World Intellectual Property Organization, Study No 1.

Janke, T. 2005. *Submission to Stopping the Rip-Offs Inquiry*. National Indigenous Arts Advocacy Association.

Johnson, S. 2019. Art Institute Will Sell 300 Ancient Chinese Artworks via Auction, *Chicago Tribune*, 24 May.

Jones, J. 2016. Artwashing: The New Watchword for Anti-Gentrification Protesters, *The Guardian*, 18 July.

Kapchan, D. ed. 2014. *Cultural Heritage in Transit: Intangible Rights as Human Rights*. Philadelphia: University of Pennsylvania Press.

Katyal, S. K. 2017. Technoheritage, *California Law Review*, 105, no. 4: 1111–1172.

Katyal, S. K., and A. R. Riley. 2009. In Defense of Property, *Yale Law Journal*, 118: 1022–1048.

Kenety, W. H. 1990. Who Owns the Past – The Need for Legal Reform and Reciprocity in the International Art Trade, *Cornell International Law Journal*, 23, no. 1: 1–46.

Kinsella, E. 2019. Eight Artists Withdraw Their Work from the Whitney Biennial as Protest of Warren Kanders Spreads to the Museum's Marquee Show, *Artnet*, 19 July.

Klein, N. 2010. *No Logo*. 2nd edition. New York: Harper Collins.

Korkman, Z. 2015. Fortunes for Sale: Cultural Politics and Commodification of Culture in Millennial Turkey, *European Journal of Cultural Studies*, 18, no. 3: 319–338.

Lai, J. C. 2014. *Indigenous Cultural Heritage and Intellectual Property Rights: Learning from the New Zealand Experience?* Heidelberg: Springer.

Lange, B. 2013. *Nefertiti*. New York: Chelsea House.

Lange, J., and M. Henderson. eds. 2017. *Entangled Memories: Remembering the Holocaust in a Global Age*. Heidelberg: Winter.

Latour, B. 2017. *Facing Gaia: Eight Lectures on the New Climatic Regime*. Cambridge: Polity.

Lefebvre, A. 2005. A New Image of Law: Deleuze and Jurisprudence, *Telos*, 130: 103–126.

Lefebvre, A. 2006a. Habermas and Deleuze on Law and Adjudication, *Law & Critique*, 17: 389–414.

Lefebvre, A. 2006b. We Do Not Yet Know What the Law Can Do, *Contemporary Political Theory*, 5: 52–67.

Lefebvre, A. 2007. Critique of Teleology in Kant and Dworkin: The Law Without Organs (LwO), *Philosophy Social Criticism*, 33: 85–104.

Lefebvre, A. 2008. *The Image of Law: Deleuze, Bergson, Spinoza*. Redwood, CA: Stanford University Press.

Lefebvre, H. 1991. *The Production of Space*. Trans. D. Nicholson-Smith. Oxford: Blackwell Lewinski, S. 2008. *Indigenous Heritage and Intellectual Property: Genetic Resources, Traditional Knowledge and Folklore*. Alphen aan den Rijn: Wolters Kluwer.

Liderman, M. 2019. The Witness Blanket, an installation of residential school artifacts, makes Canadian legal history, *The Globe and Mail*, 21 October.

Lindahl, H. 2019. *Legal Governance in Times of Crisis*. Lecture given at the Department of Law, University of Gothenburg, 25 October.

Lixinski, L. 2013. *Intangible Cultural Heritage in International Law*. Oxford: Oxford University Press.

Lixinski, L. 2015. Cultural Heritage Law and Transitional Justice: Lessons from South Africa. *International Journal of Transitional Justice*, 9, no. 2: 278–296.

Lixinski, L. 2019. *International Heritage Law for Communities: Exclusion and Re-Imagination*. Oxford: Oxford University Press.

Lixinski L. 2021. *Legalized Identities Cultural Heritage Law and the Shaping of Transitional Justice*, Cambridge: Cambridge University Press.

Macmillan, F. 2008. The UNESCO Convention as a New Incentive to Protect Cultural Diversity. In *Protection of Cultural Diversity from a European and International Perspective*, ed. H. Schneiderand, P van den Bossche, 163–192. Mortsel: Intersentia.

Macmillan, F. 2012. Finding Space in the Margins? Recognising the Rights of Indigenous Peoples in the WTO. In *International Trade in Indigenous Cultural Heritage: Legal and Policy Issues*, ed. C. B. Graber, J. Lai and K. Kuprecht, 88–117. Cheltenham: Edward Elgar.

Macmillan, F. 2013. The Protection of Cultural Heritage: Common Heritage of Humankind, National Cultural "Patrimony" or Private Property? *Northern Ireland Legal Quarterly* 64: 351–364.

Macmillan, F. 2015. Cultural Property and Community Rights to Cultural Heritage. In *Property and Human Rights in a Global Context*, ed. T. Xu and J. Allain, 41–63. Oxford: Bloomsbury.

Macmillan, F. 2021. *Intellectual and Cultural Property: Between Market and Community*. Abingdon: Routledge.

Malraux, A. 1967. *Museum Without Walls*. Trans. S. Gilbert and F. Price. New York City: Doubleday & Co.

Massey, D. 2005. *For Space*. London: Sage.

Massey, D. 2007. *World City*. Cambridge: Polity.

Mastalir, R. W. 1992. A Proposal for Protecting the 'Cultural' and 'Property' Aspects of Cultural Property under International Law, *Fordham International Law Journal*, 16, no. 4: 1037–1093.

Mbembe, A. 2003. Necropolitics. Trans. L. Meintjes. *Public Culture*, 15, no. 1: 11–40.

McDonagh, L. 2015. From Brand Performance to Consumer Performativity – European Trade Mark Law after the Rise of Anthropological Marketing, *Journal of Law and Society*, 42, no. 4: 611–636.

Merryman, J. H. 1986. Two Ways of Thinking about Cultural Property, *The American Journal of International Law*, 80, no. 4: 831–853.

Merryman, J. H. ed. 1999. *Thinking About the Elgin Marbles: Critical Essays on Cultural Property, Art and Law*. 2nd edition. The Hague: Kluwer Law International.

Merryman, J. H. ed. 2006. *Imperialism, Art and Restitution*. Cambridge: Cambridge University Press.

Merryman, J. H., A. E. Elsen and S. K. Ulrice. 2007. *Law, Ethics, and the Visual Arts*. 5th edition. Alphen aan den Rijn: Kluwer International.

Mihai, M. 2014. Theorizing Agonistic Emotions, *Parallax*, 20, no. 2: 31–48.

Miller, T. 2017. *Greenwashing Culture*. Abingdon: Routledge.

Miller, Z. 2020. Transitional Justice, Race, and the United States, *Just Security*, 30 June.

Moore, N. 2000. A Distant Hand Fell from His Shoulder, *Law & Critique*, 11: 185–200.

Moore, N. 2004. So You Love Me, *Law & Critique*, 15: 45–64.

Moore, N. 2007. Icons of Control: Deleuze, Signs, Law, *International Journal for the Semiotics of Law*, 20: 33–54.

Morton, T. 2013. *Hyperobjects: Philosophy and Ecology After the End of the World*. Minneapolis: University of Minnesota Press.

Mouffe, C. 2014. By Way of a Postscript, *Parallax*, 20, no. 2: 149–157.

Murray, J. 2007. Deleuze and Guattari's Intensive and Pragmatic Semiotic of Emergent Law, *International Journal for the Semiotics of Law*, 20: 7–32.

Murray, J. 2013. *Deleuze and Guattari: Emergent Law*. Abingdon: Routledge.

Mussawir, E. 2011a. *Jurisdiction in Deleuze: The Expression and Representation of Law*. Abingdon: Routledge.

Mussawir, E. 2011b. The Activity of Judgment: Deleuze, Jurisdiction and the Procedural Genre of Jurisprudence, *Law, Culture & the Humanities*, 7: 463–483.

Nafzinger, J. ed. 2012. *Cultural Heritage Law*. Cheltenham: Edward Elgar.

Nancy, J.-L. 1991. *The Inoperative Community*, ed. C. Fynsk. Trans. P. Connor. Minneapolis: University of Minnesota Press.

Nancy, J.-L. 2000. *Being Singular Plural*, ed. W. Hamacher and D. E. Wellbery. Trans. R. D. Richardson and A. E. O'Byrne. Redwood, CA: Stanford University Press.

Nancy, J.-L. 2009. The Confronted Community. In *The Obsessions of Georges Bataille: Community and Communication*, ed. A. J. Mitchell and J. Kemp Winfree, 19–30. New York: State University of New York Press.

Nedelsky, J. 2011. *Law's Relations: A Relational Theory of Self, Autonomy, and Law*. New York: Oxford University Press.

Newitz, A. 2016. One of the Greatest Art Heists of Our Time Was Actually a Data Hack, *ArsTechnica*, 3 November.

Nora, P. 1992. *Les Lieux de mémoire*. Vol. I. Paris: Editions Gallimard.

Novic, E. 2016. *The Concept of Cultural Genocide: An International Law Perspective*. Oxford: Oxford University Press.

Nykolaishen, S. 2012. Customary International Law and the Declaration on the Rights of Indigenous Peoples, *Appeal: Rev. Current L. & L. Reform*, 17: 111–128.

O'Keefe, P. 2007. *Commentary on the 1970 UNESCO Convention*. 2nd edition. Builth Wells: The Institute of Art & Law.

O'Keefe, P. 2008. The 'Right to Take Part in Cultural Life' under Article 15 of the ICESCR, *International and Comparative Law Quarterly*, 47: 904–923.

Ostrom, E. 2011 [1990]. *Governing the Commons: The Evolution of Institutions for Collective Action*. Cambridge: Cambridge University Press.

Ostrom, E., and C. Hess. eds. 2007. *Understanding Knowledge as a Commons: From Theory to Practice*. Cambridge, MA: MIT Press.

Packer, M. J., and J. Goicoechea. 2000. Sociocultural and Constructivist Theories of Learning: Ontology, Not Just Epistemology, *Educational Psychologist*, 35, no. 4: 227–241.

Pakulniewicz, A. 2017. Lidl Replaces the Police, *Eurobuild*, 28 March.

Pallasmaa, J. 2012. *The Eyes of the Skin: Architecture and the Senses*. 3rd edition. Chichester: Wiley & Sons.

Palmer, N. ed. 1998. *The Recovery of Stolen Art: A Collection of Essays*. London: Kluwer Law International.

Papadimitropoulos, V. 2020. *The Commons: Economic Alternatives in the Digital Age*. London: University of Westminster Press.

Parfitt, R. S. 2018. Fascism, Imperialism and International Law: An Arch Met a Motorway and the Rest is History… *Leiden Journal of International Law*, 31, no. 3: 509–538.

Pariser, E. 2020. To Mend a Broken Internet, Create Online Parks, *Wired*, 13 October.

Petersen, J. B. 2001. Who Owns the Past? *American Anthropologist*, 103, no. 1: 193–194.

Prott, L. V. 1996. UNESCO and Unidroit: A Partnership Against Trafficking in Cultural Objects, *Uniform Law Review*, 1, no. 1: 59–71.

Prott, L. V. 2012. *Strengths and Weaknesses of the 1970 Convention: An Evaluation 40 Years after its Adoption*. Background paper, second edition for participants in the Second Meeting of States Parties to the 1970 Convention Paris, UNESCO Headquarters, 20–21 June 2012.

Prott, L. V., and P. J. O'Keefe. 2007. 'Cultural Heritage' or 'Cultural Property'? *International Journal of Cultural Property*, 1, no. 2: 307–320.

Purdy, J. 2015. *After Nature: A Politics for the Anthropocene*. Cambridge, MA: Harvard University Press.

Rahmatian, A. 2007. Universalist Norms for a Globalised Diversity: On the Protection of Traditional Cultural Expressions. In *New Directions in Copyright Law, Vol. 6*, ed. F. Macmillan, 199–231. Cheltenham: Edward Elgar.

Reilly, M. 2018. *Curatorial Activism: Towards an Ethics of Curating*. London: Thames & Hudson.

Represa, M. 2020. Sensual Collages Made from Surf Magazines and Gay Erotica, *AnOther Magazine*, 9 October.

Ross, A. 2016a. Death Valley is Alive, *New Yorker*, 7 November.

Ross, A. 2016b. The Timbisha Shoshone of Death Valley and the Shadow of Trump, *The New York Times*, 15 November.

Said, E. 2014. *Orientalism*. New York: Random House.

Sandahl, J. 2019. The Museum Definition as the Backbone of ICOM, *Museum International*, 71, nos. 1–2: iv–9.

Sax, J. L. 1990. Heritage Preservation as a Public Duty: The Abbé Grégoire and the Origins of an Idea, *Michigan Law Review*, 88: 1142–1169.

Selkirk, A. 1997. *Who Owns the Past? A Grass Roots Critique of Heritage Policy*. London: Adam Smith Institute.

Shyllon, F. 2000. The Recovery of Cultural Objects by African Status through the UNESCO and UNIDROIT Conventions and the Role of Arbitration, *Uniform Law Review*, 5, no. 2: 219–240.

Silverman, H., and D. Fairchild Ruggles. 2007. *Cultural Heritage and Human Rights*. New York: Springer.

Simon, N. 2010. *The Participatory Museum*. Santa Cruz: Museum 2.0.

Simpson, T. 1997. *Indigenous Heritage and Self-Determination: The Cultural and Intellectual Property Rights of Indigenous Peoples*. Copenhagen: IWGIA.

Slater, C. 1995. Amazonia as Edenic Narrative. In *Uncommon Ground: Rethinking Human Place in Nature*, ed. W. Cronon, 114–131. New York: W. W. Norton.

Smith, L. J. 2006. *Uses of Heritage*. Abingdon: Routledge.

Sorkin, M. 2018. *What Goes Up: The Right and Wrongs to the City*. London: Verso.

Spivak, G. C. 1988. Can the Subaltern Speak? In *Marxism and the Interpretation of Culture*, ed. C. Nelson, et. al., 271–313. Basingstoke: Macmillan.

Stamatoudi, I. 2011. *Cultural Property and Restitution*. Cheltenham: Edward Elgar.

Strati, A. 1991. Deep Seabed Cultural Property and the Common Heritage of Mankind, *The International and Comparative Law Quarterly*, 40, no. 4: 859–894.

Sutter, de, L., and McGee, K. eds. 2012. *Deleuze and Law*. Edinburgh: Edinburgh University Press.

Thornberry, P. 2002. *Indigenous Peoples and Human Rights*. Manchester: Manchester University Press.

Tyldesley, J. 2018. *Nefertiti's Face: The Creation of an Icon*. London: Profile Books.

Vertovec, S. 2009. *Transnationalism*. Abingdon: Routledge.

Voon, C. 2016. Artists Covertly Scan Bust of Nefertiti and Release the Data for Free Online, *Hyperallergic*, 19 February.

Vrdoljak, A. F. 2008. *International Law, Museums and the Return of Cultural Objects*. Cambridge: Cambridge University Press.

Vrdoljak, A. F. 2014. Human Rights and Cultural Heritage in International Law. In *International Law for Common Goods: Normative Perspectives on Human Rights, Culture and Nature*, ed. F. Lenzerini and A. F. Vrdoljak, 139–175. Oxford: Hart Publishing.

Vulliamy, E. 2016. Artists 'Steal' Queen Nefertiti Bust by Secretly Scanning and Releasing 3D Printing Data Online, *The Independent*, 25 February.

Wakefield, S. 2021. *Cultural Heritage, Transnational Narratives and Museum Franchising in Abu Dhabi*. Abingdon: Routledge.

de Wall, E. 2011. *The Hare with Amber Eyes: A Hidden Inheritance*. New York: Picador.

Wallinder-Pierini, L. 2018. The Buddhist Dharma for Sale: Who Owns the Past? The Internet and Objects of Worship, *Journal of Global Buddhism*, 19: 95–111.

Warne, K. 2019. Why Australia is Banning Climbers from This Iconic Natural Landmark, *National Geographic Traveler*, April/May.

Warshaw, M. 2010. *The History of Surfing*. San Francisco: Chronicle Books. Kindle Edition.

Waxman, S. 2010. *Loot: Tomb Robbers, Treasure and The Great Museum Debate*.
London: Old Street Publishing.

Wilder, C. 2016. Swiping a Priceless Antiquity… With a Scanner and a 3-D Printer, *The New York Times*, 2 March.

Willems, W. J. H. 2014. The Future of World Heritage and the Emergence of Transnational Heritage Regimes, *Heritage & Society*, 7, no. 2: 105–120.

Zumbansen, P. C. 2012. Transnational Law, Evolving. In *Encyclopedia of Comparative Law*, ed. J. Smits, 899–925. 2nd edition. Cheltenham: Edward Elgar.

Conventions

European

European Convention of Human Rights (1953)

Convention for the Protection of the Architectural Heritage of Europe (1985)

The Framework Convention on National Minorities (1995)

The Faro Convention on the Value of Cultural Heritage for Society (2015)

ILO

The International Labour Organization Convention on Indigenous and Tribal Peoples, Convention No. 169 of 1989

United Nations

Convention on the Prevention and Punishment of the Crime of Genocide and various other military conventions (1951)

United Nations International Covenant on Civil and Political Rights (1976)

United Nations International Covenant on Economic, Social and Cultural Rights (1976)

UNESCO

Hague Convention for the Protection of Cultural Property in the Event of Armed Conflict and its two Protocols (1954)

Convention on the Means of Prohibiting and Preventing the Illicit Import, Export and Transfer of Ownership of Cultural Property (1970)

Convention Concerning the Protection of the World Cultural and Natural Heritage (1972)

Convention on the Protection of the Underwater Cultural Heritage (2001)

Convention for the Safeguarding of the Intangible Cultural Heritage (2003)

Convention on the Protection and Promotion of the Diversity of Cultural Expressions (2005)

Charters, Codes, Declarations & Recommendations

France

The French commitment to returning cultural heritage to Africa, 18 December 2020. https://www.elysee.fr/emmanuel-macron/2020/12/18/restitution-des-biens-culturels-une-promesse-tenue-pour-une-nouvelle-page-des-relations-entre-lafrique-et-la-france (accessed 28 December 2020)

ICOM

ICOM Code of Ethics for Museums (2004)

ICOM Guidelines on Deaccessioning (2019)

United Nations

Universal Declaration of Human Rights (1948)

Declaration on the Granting of Independence to Colonial Countries and Peoples (1960)

Declaration on the Rights of Indigenous Peoples (2007)

UN Committee on the Elimination of Racial Discrimination (CERD), General Recommendation no. 32, The meaning and scope of special measures in the International Convention on the Elimination of All Forms [of] Racial Discrimination, 24 September 2009, CERD/C/GC/32

UNESCO

UNESCO Charter on the Preservation of the Digital Heritage (2003)

Recommendation concerning the Protection and Promotion of Museums and Collections (2015)

USA

American Alliance of Museums Code of Ethics for Museums (1994)

American Alliance of Museums Direct Care of Collections: Ethics, Guidelines and Recommendations (2016)

Comments & documents

UN Human Rights Committee (HRC), CCPR General Comment No. 23: Article 27 (Rights of Minorities), 8 April 1994, CCPR/C/21/Rev.1/Add.5

Washington Conference Principles on Nazi-Confiscated Art (1998)

UNIDROIT

Convention on Stolen or Illegally Exported Cultural Objects (1995)

National law

Swedish Museum Act, Museilag (2017:563)

EU law

Directives

EU directive 93/7/EEC from 15 March 1993 on the return of cultural objects unlawfully removed from the territory of a Member State

Regulations

Regulation (EC) no 116/2009 from 18 December 2008 on the export of cultural goods

Case law

Australia

Neowarra v. State of Western Australia, [2003] FCA 1402 (Austl.)

European Court of Justice

Sieckmann v. German Patent and Trademark Office (C-273/00)

European Court of Human Rights (ECtHR)

Podkolzina vs. Latvia (2002)
Debelianovi vs. Bulgaria (2008)
Khurshid Mustafa and Tarzibachi vs. Sweden (2011)

Inter-American Court of Human Rights

Mayagna (Sumo) Awas Tingni Community vs. Nicaragua (2001)

USA

Supremev.McSweeney, Chapter 4 Corp. D/B/A Supreme v. Leah C. Mc Sweeney and LCM Productions Inc, United States District Court, Southern District of New York, 13 Civ. 1588 (KMW), 2019

Digital resources

Archmap. The Twists and Turns of the Traffic Police Building. n.d. http://archmap.lt/en/articles/lietuviu-keliu-policijos-pastato-virazai/ (accessed 27 December 2020)

Archmuziejus. About Architectural Communication and the Case of the Police Building at Giraitės Street 3. 4 April 2017. http://archmuziejus.lt/en/about-architectural-communication-and-the-case-of-the-police-building-at-giraites-street-3/ (accessed 27 December 2020)

Art Law Blog. 2019. Architect of Washington Principles Takes Stock. 8 January 2019. https://www.artatlaw.com/blogpost/architect-washington-principles-takes-stock (accessed 27 December 2020)

Baltic Course Online. Lithuania's Heritage Chief Sees Attempts to Stop Lidl Investments Unacceptable. 17 October 2016. http://www.baltic-course.com/eng/real_estate/?doc=124818 (accessed 27 December 2020)

British Museum. Edmund de Waal: Library of Exile. https://www.britishmuseum.org/exhibitions/edmund-de-waal-library-exile (accessed 27 December 2020)

Cosmo Wenman. Thingiverse – Nefertiti. 13 November 2019. https://www.thingiverse.com/thing:3974391 (accessed 27 December 2020)

Cosmo Wenman (b). The Nefertiti 3D Scan Heist is a Hoax. 8 March 2016. https://cosmowenman.com/2016/03/08/the-nefertiti-3d-scan-heist-is-a-hoax/ (accessed 18 February 2021)

Decolonise UKC. https://decoloniseukc.org/ (accessed 28 December 2020)

Decolonise UKC Twitter. https://twitter.com/DecoloniseUKC (accessed 27 December 2020)

ICOM. ICOM Announces the Alternative Museum Definition That Will Be Subject to a Vote. 25 July 2019. https://icom.museum/en/news/icom-announces-the-alternative-museum-definition-that-will-be-subject-to-a-vote/ (accessed 27 December 2020)

ICOM. Museum Definition. 2020. https://icom.museum/en/resources/standards-guidelines/museum-definition/ (accessed 27 December 2020)

Library of Exile. https://libraryofexile.infoteca.it/start (accessed 27 December 2020)

Open Glam. https://openglam.org (accessed 28 December 2020)

UNESCO. 2019. Female Military Trained by UNESCO in Protecting Cultural Property. 8 October 2019. https://en.unesco.org/news/female-military-trained-unesco-protecting-cultural-property (accessed 27 December 2020)

UNESCO. List of Intangible Heritage. n.d. http://www.unesco.org/culture/ich/en/lists (accessed 27 December 2020)

Verso. Kanders Must Go. 29 April 2019. https://www.versobooks.com/blogs/4295-kanders-must-go-an-open-letter-from-theorists-critics-and-scholars-updated-list-of-signatories (accessed 28 December 2020)

Podcasts

Art Newspaper Podcast. The Week in Art: Should Museums Sell Works of Art? 17 May 2019. https://www.theartnewspaper.com/podcast/should-museums-sell-works-of-art-plus-activism-at-the-whitney-biennial

Hyperallergic Podcast. Michael Rakowitz Discusses Withdrawing from the 2019 Whitney Biennial, and His Leonard Cohen Problem. 17 May 2019. https://hyperallergic.com/500947/michael-rakowitz-whitney-biennial-leonard-cohen/

Monument Lab Podcast. https://monumentlab.com/podcast (accessed 28 December 2020)

Index